The Viking legacy of North East England

Arthur Dinsdale

GW00602778

All rights reserved.

No part of this publication may be reproduced or transmitted, in any form or by any means, without prior permission from the publisher or copyright holder.

Copyright Arthur Dinsdale 2009

ISBN No. 978-1-907257-00-1

First Published in 2009 by
Quoin Publishing Ltd.,
17 North Street, Middlesbrough
TS2 1JP

Back cover picture: A painting of *Sondra* by the author.

Acknowledgements

I thank Gilbert Fraser for permission to reproduce the excerpt *'John Leask'* from the book *'Shetland Whalers Remember'* (ISBN No. 0 - 9541564 - 0 - 4). John was the only survivor of the whale-catcher Simbra in 1947. This book portrays unimaginable stories of Shetland's finest men frustrating the war-time enemy to provide whale oil and other by-products important to make glycerine for explosives during the Second World War.

Thanks also to the Francis Frith Collection, for permission to use the photograph, Middlegate Street, Hartlepool 1955 – where I spent the first six happy years of my life in my Granny's eighteenth century property.

Thanks to Ian Macdonald, photographer of Whitby, for printing and enhancing my whaling negatives developed at sea with two soup plates and my cabin washbasin.

Thanks to all the good people who contributed to my healthy and steadfast upbringing and to the teachers who kept my attention deficiency to zero with a few swipes of the cane! I was a bit of a dreamer. We kids soon got the hang of it, it's called self-discipline – it keeps you out of trouble and can save your life!

Thanks to the operative men who taught me to work steel to a thousandth part of an inch, yet manage great chunks of steel and iron weighing a few tons and assist in bringing rude matter into due form. Resulting in a beautiful ship.

Finally, many thanks to the district nurses, doctors and nurses in James Cook Hospital Oncology Deptartment and later Teesside Hospice who cared so well for my dear wife, Dorothy, for many months 2006 - 2007. Dorothy never complained and the nurses loved her. She was so easy to live with for fifty-nine good years.

It's very simple, if you want to be happy, make someone else happy, it works! Be kind to each other!

I hope this book will make some profit to be used to support Teesside Hospice and local charities.

Arthur Dinsdale

Contents

Introduction

The rivers of North-East England have spawned a breed of men who altered the lives of millions of people all over the world.

The River Tyne produced the early railway. The first passenger train ran from Darlington to Stockton-on-Tees. Over many years, great industries evolved as the banks of the river enabled ships to be built. Coal was mined nearby in Durham and transported by the early railway to both rivers. It was exported by ships to London and Europe. Alum was extracted along the Yorkshire coast. It was needed for dyeing cloth. The North-East was like Aladdin's cave to men who could exploit it.

In 1927, at Stockton-on-Tees, a Chemist called John Walker found by accident that a chemical paste hardened on a stick and struck against a hard surface flared into flame. He applied this knowledge to produce the friction match. The tinder box was made obsolete!

Later developments on the Tyne included the steam turbine, invented by Charles Parsons. This high-speed engine was superior to the reciprocating steam engine for generating electricity and propelling warships.

Another man from the Tyneside area, Joseph Swan, was one of many men demonstrating an electric light bulb with a carbon filament.

This practical production of the North-East's wealth was not wholly an accident.

The North-East's climate provided the cold, wet days that gave men the urge to do practical things to improve the life of their families and themselves.

Captain James Cook born, a few miles from the River Tees, was of the same breed but a different type of man with a desire to know what existed over the horizon. With his skill of mathematics and navigation he altered the map of the known world.

I suspect something in the genes was at work in the people of this area.

In 850AD a few men from Denmark and Norway arrived in long-boats. The Danes landed on beaches along the Yorkshire coast. The Norwegian Vikings landed further north in Northumbria. They were sailors, second sons of farmers who would inherit no land in the small country of Denmark. They brought other skills with them including working in metals.

In 1932 these skills eventually resulted in the fabrication of the Sydney Harbour Bridge by the Dorman Long Company Ltd., Middlesbrough. It was shipped to Australia and erected to connect the south to the north shore of the Harbour.

In 1947, at twenty-three years of age, I had the good fortune to sail with the descendents of those early Norwegian sailors on a ship built on the River Tees. I got on well with them. They nicknamed me 'Danskegutt'. In Norwegian this means 'Danish boy'. When I was told my nickname, I asked them why they chose to call me 'Danish'. The answer surprised me: 'You speak Norwegian with a Danish accent and your name "Dinsdale" is derived from "danesdahl" meaning, "place of the Danes".'

I was an engineer on the ship and all the commands were in Norwegian, the syntax was the same as English, so I picked up a working knowledge of the language.

There is a village called Dinsdale near Darlington near the River Tees, it is about as far up-river as it would be possible to row a longboat. A few early Vikings must have made camp there.

My Norwegian Danish accent is possibly due to my Yorkshire–Teesside accent. The Danes have a more guttural voice. I'm not an expert in such matters but it seemed to me that the Norwegian voice is noticeably thinner.

After a formal dinner at a Yorkshire hotel near the coastal town of Whitby, I was asked to respond to the toast to the visitors. I made the formal thanks then told this apocryphal story of our first early ancestors.

Eric Bloodaxe and the lads were going from their very sedate village in Denmark for a night out in Sweden.

They set sail in their long-boat, heading north-east, but after a few knots – that's how they measured distance – a heavy fog came down. They pressed on, trusting their bit of string and piece of lodestone compass.

After a few hours, they suspected they were lost. The fog persisted. Eric decided to turn back. There was no wind, so they rowed for hours. Eventually they heard the sea breaking on the shore. Wherever they were, they were weary and would make camp until the fog lifted. They pulled the boat up on the beach. Eric and a couple of the lads went inland to kill a couple of wild boar that roamed all over Europe. That's the reason for his name; he was the butcher.

The other lads gathered timber and made a great camp-fire. Eric returned, and the wild pigs were prepared and roasted. The young sailors lay around the sand dunes, feasting and drinking. They carried a spirit on the ship called *aquavit* ('water of life'), just for emergencies, you understand. They had a few drinks to loosen up the voice. A couple of the boys told a saga or two. They sang a few homely songs that sailors have always sang about Barnacle Bill and Maggie May and other well-known sea shanties and ditties. Only one thing was missing. It was soon put right.

Introduction

On the top of the high cliff, out of sight in the fog, was a monastery. The nuns heard the merriment going on down there. The smell of roast pork wafted up to entice them. St. Hilda wouldn't have approved but the young nuns made their way down to the beach. They were immediately invited to join in the feast. There was no impropriety – that the girls complained of – a bit of slap and tickle perhaps. When morning came the fog lifted. The lads prepared to sail back home East towards the rising sun. Eric promised the girls they would return again as all sailors do. In a way, I suppose it was the start of a European Union.

The monks in the monastery had seen what had been going on and were jealous. Unbeknown to the Vikings they wrote in their chronicles that these Vikings were coming over in their long-boats with swords, raping and pillaging all over the countryside.

The moral of this story is, never believe all you read in the newspapers!

Historic accounts are written by the victors. For a few hundred years the monasteries prospered as the Viking settlers came to these shores from the ninth century as farmers and traders. There probably were disputes at times, as there are in most businesses, but the monks were strong men who built with stone, well able to defend themselves in most cases. It was always the victor who wrote the history, they had the last word in their chronicles.

The good life for the monasteries ended when King Henry VIII in the sixteenth century was short of cash. His men chased the monks off their estates, probably molested the nuns, and knocked the monasteries about a bit.

They were rough old days, some people who were friends of King Henry inherited the Monks' estates and called it progress.

CHAPTER ONE

The early years – my idyllic childhood

The first six years of my life were spent at my maternal grandmother's house in the ancient borough of Hartlepool because of my prosperous father's foolish ways. My mother left him – with me a few weeks old. She returned to her family home taking me with her. I came from a broken home – I was lucky!

Hartlepool headland, going back to Anglo-Saxon times, is built for the most part on an outcrop of magnesium limestone. It rises out from the North Sea, forming a peninsular with the only beach facing south on the east coast, locally known as the 'Fish Sands'. This beach was a delightful suntrap, sheltered behind the twenty-five-foot, fourteenth century, old town wall. My Granny's cobblers' shop, where the family lived, was only a couple of hundred yards from this fantastic playground.

It is alleged by mischievous neighbouring towns that during the Napoleonic War the fishermen, having captured a ship-wrecked monkey, washed ashore on ships' timbers and unable to understand its chattering, decided it was a French spy and executed it by hanging it on this very beach. This story cannot be true, since Hartlepool fishermen would surely have known what a Frenchman looked like!

Several Whitby fishermen died of wounds received in the battle of Trafalgar, as testified by tombstones in the church grounds high above the town. The fishermen of Hartlepool would be very familiar with Whitby and many would have fought with their countrymen.

A battery of cannon was set up on Hartlepool's Heugh, a high cliff facing the sea, to repulse an expected French invasion in 1805, but the invasion didn't happen, the Heugh battery was maintained with two six-inch guns and another six-inch gun mounted at the lighthouse battery for 109 years.

They first came into action during the German fleet's bombardment on 16th January, 1914 at seven minutes past eight in the morning.

At the time, my mother, nineteen years old in January 1914 (her birthday was the 29th), was on her way to work going along the old town wall walkway to the harbour crossing ferry. These boats were large flat-bottomed rowing boats manned by old fishermen. In those days when shipyards at Middleton were working at peak times these ferries carried about forty men across at a time.

The route to West Hartlepool then was to go through Middleton – a village now demolished that has been an industrial estate since 2006 – then walk the three miles or so to the 1850-built town of West Hartlepool. The Anglo Saxon 'Ancient Borough of Hartlepool' (circa 650AD) is now amalgamated with West Hartlepool and sadly called 'The Headland'.

With shells exploding in the town, my Mum ran back home to find people evacuating their homes expecting a German invasion. She didn't say but I expect they joined the evacuation. What a dreadful experience. Being near Christmas, most families carried their Christmas cakes with them.

My wife Dorothy (nee Fell) told me her mother, living at No. 1 Rowell Street which looked on to the breakwater, tore up bed sheets to bandage the injured. Her mum, Sally, swears a priest who she tended to was a German spy. In a town like Hartlepool everybody knew everybody else and he was a stranger.

One hundred and nineteen people were killed and many wounded in the thirty-five-minute bombardment.

The Hartlepool gun batteries did serious damage to one of the three German battleships and the raid was not repeated. The batteries were finally dismounted about 1960. They are now being established as an historic site.

The Ancient Borough has a rich history, with an early Christian monastery, the eleventh-century St Hilda's Abbey, holding relics from the past thousand years.

The fourteenth-century sandstone town wall remains in part along the south-facing beach with what was called 'Pilot's Pier', creating a harbour that, until the Second World War, sheltered the few remaining fishing cobles of the fishermen, at one time numbering fifty or more.

A cut in the pier opened up to float fishing cobles into a slipway at high tide, where the boats were pulled into a repair shed. It's still there today unused.

The beach, only a couple of hundred yards from my granny's house, was my playground from the time that I could walk, going with the older kids during the long school holidays and learning to play shops whilst using seaweed and stones from the seashore as goods.

Going to Fish Sands I would go from Granny's kitchen through the passage that went from the kitchen past the side of the 'best room' – for the want of a better word for it. This room contained a nicely veneered upright piano with two brass candle holders each side of the music stand. It was never used in my time.

I have been told by a ninety-five-year-old relation that Aunt Jennie played very well and the family, of three brothers and three girls, stood round the piano and sang the sweet ballads of those days. At the time I had often wondered if it was ever played. It was only as an old man of eighty-four that I was told by my mother's old cousin, Marjorie Lumsden (nee Wardell), of these sing songs.

Then passing the stairway that went to a landing to the two front bedrooms of the house was the cellar door, never used. I only saw it open once and the cellar had rough wooden stairs and was half-full of rubble.

This ended the passage and I went down two steps into the shop, past the shop counter with repaired shoes waiting to be collected. The front doors opened into Middlegate Street. One door was left open on fine days, it had a highly-polished brass sneck, which was well worn by a couple of hundred years of thumbs opening and closing it.

Returning home from my adventure on the beach, I passed through the cobbler's shop, where Uncle Arthur stood at his bench, on which would be laid the tools of his trade. Working away with a sharp knife, he used to cut the leather, then, with a mouthful of nails, he would pick one from his mouth to lightly hammer it in round the new sole. Thin slivers of leather and dust laid all over the place.

The walls were built from limestone rocks worn rounded from the beach, held together with limestone mortar and plaster.

There was no bathroom in the house. The family used the kitchen, bathing in a galvenised tin bath put in front of the fire, with hot water from the copper kettle.

The back bedroom, my room, was accessed from a staircase behind a door in the kitchen. The first three stairs turned through ninety degrees, then up a narrow stairwell to a small square landing and the bedroom door.

In the old kitchen, a square table covered with a dark green chenille cloth stood in front of a long window of small, square panes, which opened with a sliding frame. This was never opened because, probably being the original window when put there in the early 1700s, it was secured with many coats of paint.

Granny sat for hours on an upright kitchen chair by the window next to the table, with the kitchen range on her left. On the other side of the fire by the curtained-off set pot was a black bentwood rocking chair, with well-used cushions and a crocheted woollen shawl thrown over it. She never sat in this rocker; I suppose it was Grandad Alex Wright's chair, although Aunt Jennie used to sit in it sometimes. I often had a good rock in it, or sat gazing into the fire as puffs of gas emitted from a piece of coal and caught fire, and glowing ashes dropped twelve inches through the bottom grate behind the brass fender. These ashes were taken out on a shovel in the morning and put on the small garden at the back of the house. Fresh coal would be dragged onto the fire as required from a store on a stone shelf, above and behind the fire.

Another table of similar dimensions to the dining table (about four foot six inches square) stood at the other side of the kitchen in front of a kitchen dresser. A rough set of six pine shelves about nine inches wide stood against the whitewashed roughly plastered wall. Willow pattern plates stood at the back of one of these shelves with jugs, bowls and other kitchen items.

This property was demolished in about 1956 as part of the Council's slum clearance.

A local lady magistrate and historian, Miss Sivright, having her shoes repaired one day, had asked Aunt Jennie if she could look the property over and told her that from the design of the windows, the through-passage and so on that the property had been built in the early 1700s.

I didn't see much of my mother, Jessie. She would be working until nine or ten o'clock at night across the street in the shoe shop she had created. This shop had been empty but Uncle Arthur and his wife lived above the empty shop.

My mum rented the shop and paid a joiner to put shelves on the walls and build a counter with a cash drawer in it. She then went to Lengs, a shoe wholesaler in Stockton, and ordered shoes to stock the shop. Women didn't have the vote until 1928. This was 1924/5 so mum put the business into her brother's name because my father could have claimed it in law. My mother did get a court settlement from my father in 1926, a good allowance of one pound and ten shillings plus a further ten shillings a week for me, total: two pounds a week. As manager of the shoe shop she would do very well!

Aunt Jennie would put me to bed. It's only now I realise how much she did for me. The Wrights worked well together. I never heard a raised voice in that house.

At four years old, I didn't have a teddy or anything to go to bed with, but going to bed with a candle was comforting. Later, I had a night light, a short dumpy candle in a cardboard ring placed on a saucer. These burned for several hours and gave a warm glow in the big whitewashed bedroom. I lay listening to the burble of family voices in the kitchen below my bedroom until I drifted off to sleep.

My mattress was filled with feathers and often felt a bit damp. Aunt Jenny put a hot water bottle in my bed, it was only left in with me when I was older. There was a washstand in the room with a big bowl and jug. I never saw it used.

The large copper kettle on the hob (a shelf next to the open fire in the kitchen) was kept filled to supply constant hot water. There was no kitchen sink or drain. Piped water had been introduced sometime in the nineteenth century and the brass tap was positioned about eighteen inches from the floor in a corner of the kitchen with a galvanised bucket under it to catch any drops. Aunt Jennie would wash my face and hands with a flannel from a bowl in the kitchen. In the summer I washed myself from a bowl on a big wooden box in the hard-standing part of the rough garden. The only useful thing grown

1955 – Middlegate Street, Hartlepool. Granny Wright's cobbler's shop is on the right , this side of the man on the ladder.

1908 – The ancient water gate, Sandwell Chare, Hartlepool.

there was mint, used in the kitchen to make mint sauce for lamb.

Leaving my granny's shop, I would say hello to my Uncle Arthur, who was generally working at his 'last' – a metal post on which a metal foot was held by a rope over the instep in a loop, with Uncle Arthur's foot in it to hold the customer's shoe firm so that it could be repaired. Other times he might be stitching a sole onto a shoe. He didn't stitch many. It seemed difficult to do with the pedal-operated machine. He was a father figure to me and showed me how to sharpen and use a knife and then how to cut leather by pulling the leather at an angle past the blade.

To get to the street, I stepped through the green front door. Only one side of the door was kept open unless the weather was very bad. I then stepped down onto the flagstone pavement and turned right outside the shop to run up Middlegate Street as far as the post office, then turn right again into Pinder's Chare (it was really called Vollum Chare, after a former mayor or worthy resident), which got the name 'Pinder' from the draper's shop on the corner.

This chare led past the rounded end of the post office through to the High Street which was demolished in the late 1950s. The ancient High Street had existed for centuries and was obliterated, leaving only a narrow road to the magnificent Parish Pump.

I would then run across the wide cobbled way, past the row of shops on the south side of the High Street (now 1938 semi-detached houses with back gardens) to a narrow street laid with sets (blocks of stone) called Sandwell Chare.

This chare, a local name for a wide passageway, gave access to the beach through the town wall's gothic arch, protected by v-shaped battlements on the seaward side designed to repulse fourteenth-century Scottish raiders invading from the sea.

In the Spring high tides, the sea came through this arch in the wall and at times threatened the nearby houses. This arch is still there but the ground level has been raised about six feet and steps made to go through the arch.

A wide breach in the wall had been made many years previously to allow horse and carts to transport the fish landed on the beach. This part of the wall was restored when the demolition of the fishermen's croft took place in the late 1950s. The demolition of the fishermen's croft enabled the builders to level the land, raising it along the wall in the area of the arch with steps, thus eliminating the flooding.

This idyllic childhood existence ended when, at the age of six, I was dragged screaming by my mum to the little Prissick Church School. Over eighty years later, I still remember that very well – it was the best yelling performance of my life!

The school occupied a plot of land east of St. Hilda's Church cemetery. This plot is now a small grassed island surrounded by road.

On the way up Middlegate Street, the local baker 'Geordie Markum', whose bakery was opposite the Borough hall, tried to console me but, heartbroken, I only wanted to go on the sands, what else was there in life for a six-year-old?

My first lesson in this small two-roomed school (also now demolished) was to sit at a table and to unpick a piece of coarse cloth. This may have been to stuff a toy with. I don't remember the teacher saying why, and at the time didn't care. I was probably – nay, I was definitely – uncooperative. Come to think of it, I was probably being punished. I didn't misbehave but I wasn't used to being restricted.

School wasn't much of a challenge after my beach education and a lot less fun!

Miss Walker, a tall, formidable woman, was the headmistress but it was Miss Hunter who took the class I was in, a pretty woman who wore rimless Pincenez spectacles perched precariously on her nose. She was obviously going to tame this wild little individual.

We were given a slate and stylus but I lost some item of issue. I can't remember what it was – it's still a mystery. It has only occurred to me now that another kid must have nicked it!

I do remember I got a rap over the knuckles with a ruler for losing it. I yelled and was very confused; I'd never been smacked before! This was the first of many injustices in my life that I still find confusing. Why do people want to control me?

In winter, a great coal fire threw heat into the classroom. It was surrounded by an enormous metal fire guard with a brass rail along the top. Small bottles of malted milk, each with a cardboard lid and a press-out middle to put in a drinking straw, was warmed by this fire for our break.

I distinctly remember Betty Cox, the coalman's pretty daughter. She wore bright red knickers and short skirts which must have excited me even at that age because I was dared to run into the girls' toilet, which I boldly did, and make Betty bend over and display the pretty red knickers to the lads crowded round the toilet door.

Betty seemed to think it was fun, too. I didn't get a smack for that. Today I would probably be put on the sexual offender's list!

Granny Wright (nee Scott), had married Alexander Wright who had, with his cousins (including James Barrie, later Sir James, author of *Peter Pan*), been left a legacy of sixty pounds each by an uncle on the Barrie side of the family; this may have assisted them to set up their business in Hartlepool.

I don't think I have any of James Barrie's talent for children's stories, but my granny's father, Thomas Lawson Scott, was a wood carver, an artist! I do have the ability to draw and paint a picture.

Alex and his brother Peter had opened two shoe shops with Peter in charge, while Alex operated a cobbler's shop and lived with Margaret Ann, my granny, behind the shop.

When No. 14 Middlegate Street was demolished in the late 1950s, the site was covered by a bus station. In 2006, the bus station was replaced by gardens and a town square with trees and a toilet block.

About thirty yards west of the cobbler's shop, beyond Northgate, a square led off to cottages in Sunnyside. Another street led further west to the inner-harbour fish quay. An entrance to the north side of the harbour was on the left, along Northgate. It may still be there.

The trolley buses with solid tyres came down the bank of Middlegate Street from Durham Street and stopped outside Granny's shop before turning into Northgate. It was a busy corner with people passing from the shops waiting to catch the trolley bus and others dismounting from the buses to return home.

Mum told an amusing story of Granny when they were young. Grandad Alex and Granny went to the theatre every Monday night. This particular night at an interval in the live performance, a white screen was lowered to the stage and the first silent movie was shown. It must have been an extravaganza with a cast of 'thousands'.

When the parents returned home, the family asked: 'What was the show like?' In her broad Geordie dialect, their mother replied: 'It was arll reet, but where are arll those folks ganna stay the neet in Hartlepool?' She evidently thought the action was taking place outside the cinema and reflected onto the screen inside. Not such a daft idea because a camera obscura could do just that.

On Saturday evenings the Salvation Army bandsmen and some of their ladies, all in uniform, would assemble at the junction of Middlegate, Northgate and Sunnyside (the adjoining square with a narrow road leading to the fish quay). They formed a circle and held an open-air service. The mellow tone of the brass instruments playing gentle hymns created an air of peace and tranquility over a wide area.

At the end of the service, pennies were thrown onto the cobbled surface in the middle of their circle, to be picked up before the leader mounted the flag in his holster. They then formed fours and, generally playing a triumphant 'Onward Christian Soldiers', with the leader carrying the flag flying aloft, they marched up the bank of Middlegate Street to the Salvation Army headquarters beyond.

Two of their ladies would make a collection of coins from passers-by with little dark blue cloth pouches mounted on wooden handles as they returned to their headquarters in Lumley Street.

A friend of Granny lived in a cottage down Sunnyside and I would be asked to visit her and take the kitchen's waste greens for her hens, It was probably a social thing. These old girls had no family and liked to see the kids. Mrs Barker's husband was killed in the Boer War and his photograph in full dress uniform stood on the mantlepiece in a silver frame. A china dog kept guard at each end of the long mantlepiece with its brass rail and tasselled drape.

Another friend of Granny's, Dorothy (Dossie) Lilly, also kept hens at the back of her house and I was sent occasionally to take stuff for her hens. I thought it was a good idea to keep hens and Dossie would give me a few grains of corn to feed them. Food was plentiful in this way. Fish was cheap and generally plentiful, except in bad weather when the boats couldn't get out. There were no private freezers, of course, but an ice house was built in the harbour. I was taken in it once. It had a few frozen sides of beef hanging there. Mainly it provided the fishing boats and fish quay with ice to preserve the fish for a few days.

Years later, during the war, Uncle Arthur kept a dozen or so hens in his cellar at No. 11 Middlegate, which had a window. This was behind the shoe shop Mum had created.

I don't know why my Mum didn't do that during the war but there was probably a shortage of chicks by then. We knew nothing about keeping livestock either.

On Sunday mornings, about eleven o'clock, I was given a jug and a shilling and sent over the corner of Northgate to the Golden Lion pub to ask Mrs Ibbetson, the Landlady, for a pint of beer for Mrs Wright's dinner table please.

The pub, never very busy in the depression of the 1930s, was always empty at that time of the morning. As I walked in to the bar, the smell of the hops fascinated me. I gazed in wonder at the spittoons on the floor freshly filled with sawdust. It seemed a tranquil place where men could sit and relax after a hard day's work. There wasn't much of that, though. The shipyards in the depression had no orders, few men were employed and would have been glad of any work.

They couldn't afford to buy beer but congregated at street corners in their dishevelled clothes, cloth caps and white silk mufflers (scarves). These mufflers replaced ties, since shirts in those days had loose collars held with a stud at the back of the shirt neck. The working man wore a shirt without the starched collar, which required regular costly laundry.

If a foreman required a few men for a casual job, he would know where to find them.

There was a 'market' for men who would present themselves at the shipyard gate on the off chance that they would be selected for a few days' work. This situation existed up to 1939, when I started my apprenticeship. It ended when the shipyard geared up for war and, thankfully, did not return after.

Some of these unemployed men, if they could get hold of an old bike, would go a few miles north of Hartlepool to gather sea coal from the beaches. Seams of coal were exposed under the sea bed. This coal broke away and was washed up as fine black gravel on the beach at every tide. In places, it was two or more inches thick. The coal was easy to rake up and put into sacks. A couple of hundredweight bags were slung across the bike and trundled home by the man straddled across the back wheel when the road permitted the load to freewheel. A couple of bags would provide warmth and fuel to cook for their families. Any extra that could be gathered was sold cheap to help other unfortunate people.

When a storm broke away an abundance of sea coal, better-off people took advantage of the opportunity to buy it. This black-market-income got the unemployed through the hard times. Sea coal burnt very hot and bright. Being fine it was useful to help bank-up a fire for the night along with tea leaves saved from the teapot during the day.

Other men would go fishing. They didn't have fancy fishing rods, just a hand line with two or three hooks fastened on it above a sinker made of lead, if it could be found from an old bit of lead pipe, but a stone with a hole in it would do! The sinker was twirled round the head with about three feet of line in the hand and let fly over the sea. It required experience to catch fish, knowing when the fish would be inshore.

August was a time of plenty when the sprats came in. Sprats were similar to a long sardine and came in thick shoals close up to the beach. Mackerel chased them and they too could be seen jumping out of the water close to the beach. So close, in fact, that young lads could wade in and throw mackerel on to the beach to be taken home for tea! At this time of year in the twenties and thirties, the sea was thick with fish as they migrated annually slowly down the coast.

Later I put this glut of fish down to the decimation of arctic whales up to the beginning of the twentieth century, after which, whaling became uneconomical.

On Sundays in the summer, people paraded en famille along the extensive promenade in their best costumes. Aunt Jennie used to take me to the Abbey Church of Saint Hilda. I was too young to find it interesting but did it to please her. We then would have a bit of a promenade saying 'Nice day' to the mums and dads with their offspring. I did have a feeling that I was different not having a dad. I had mixed feelings about it; I would have resented a strict or bad parent so I accepted my situation.

Everybody needed to have shoes repaired in those days. We paraded proudly. Wright's the Cobbler had a monopoly!

When I was five years old, Aunt Jen took me to St Mark's Methodist Church's bazaar. A pretty little girl with golden curls presented the Lady Opener with a bouquet. She was four years old and her name was Dorothy Fell. Her father was chief draughtsman and design engineer at the Richardson, Westgarth's shipyard.

I was captivated by Dorothy Fell and would look out for her on the Sunday parade. Through the years I caught glimpses of her but our eyes never met. When I was nineteen years old at the Saturday-night dance in the borough hall. I was standing chatting with my friends. We generally chose to dance with the girls in our group but I noticed Dorothy was standing at the far side of the floor.

It was the first time I had seen her at the dance. She was standing with a friend. I'm sure I wouldn't even have thought of going over to ask her for a dance. She was out of my league. The mystery of life was at work. More of that later.

Going back to my younger days, across the road opposite Granny's cobbler's shop, Granny's half-sister, Lily Wardell, lived behind a fresh fish shop for a few years before they moved to a big house on the sea-front, No. 1 Albion Terrace. They still had the shop, but now lived in style.

Granny Wright's father, Thomas Lawson Scott, died, the mother married again, a man called Johnson. Lily was born a Johnson, a half-sister to Granny. These things were never discussed then, but Marjorie, ninety-five years old and the last of the Wardell (nee Johnson) family, told me that when Lily was seven years old, both her mother and father had died and she came to live with her half-sister my Granny Margaret Ann, now married to Alexander Wright. This was how families cared for each other in the days when there was no social services.

My Great-Grandad, Thomas Lawson Scott, was a wood carver, an artist. I wish I knew more about him, where he worked and so on.

Lily had married George Wardell and they had five daughters and three sons: Norah, Lily, Elsie, Margery and Winnie. Harry worked on the fish quay, Arthur became a sea captain and Lawson, my age, was called up early in the war. He was in the army and fought in Italy. After the war he worked in a grocery business in the South Bank area of Middlesbrough. His wife had a post office in Thornaby for some years. They retired to Great Ayton but with my own work and family problems I lost touch with them altogether.

Uncle George and Aunt Lily Wardell had a lovely little cottage for a few years in the charming village of Elwick, a few miles north of Hartlepool. This led to my first ride in a motor car when I was five years old.

I was returning from my daily sortie on the fish sands and as I approached Granny's shop, Aunt Lily was getting into their recently purchased car. She called me over: 'Come on, son, we're going to Elwick Get in.' Aunt Jennie heard and came to the shop door she took me inside to clean me up before I was allowed to climb up on to the running board and plonk myself down alongside Harry Wardell, who was driving. This new mode of transport was fascinating. As gears were changed by Harry, the car jerked forward and we were off along Northgate the five miles or so to Elwick.

I can't remember more about it. I don't think we stayed long but the car ride was memorable.

Uncle George was a good businessman and well up in the fish business. He was a buyer with an office on the fish quay and a herring curing house (kippers) on the edge of the town, one of many. It was a pongy, fishy area but not too near the town.

Hartlepool then was a big fishing port and July and August were the busiest months of the year in the 1930s. Up to a hundred boats (herring fishing drifters) arrived. They were mainly Scottish, some Dutch, some local and some from other ports like Lowestoft arrived.

Uncle Arthur did a bit of business, selling white rubber thigh boots and yellow waterproof smocks to the fishermen. He had them hanging outside above the shop window.

When I was thirteen he arranged for me to have a trip to sea with the skipper of the herring drifter *Fisher Queen*. I had a couple of trips and Uncle Arthur always gave me a bass (a shopping bag made of woven strips of palm leaves, which were common in those days). This was to bring back a few pounds of herring. Uncle Arthur at No. 11 Middlegate Street then fried them in oatmeal in a big black iron pan on the fire for our breakfast.

The *Fisher Queen* was a wooden boat with a small two-cylinder steam engine about three feet high and a simple coal-fired boiler. We left the fish quay, then went to the coaling quay. A wooden chute cascaded about a ton of coal amidships between the scuppers and the coaming, the engine man lifted a round iron manhole and shovelled the coal into the bunker hold. That done, we sailed out of the Victoria Dock into the channel past the Middleton Ferry, Fish Sands and Pilot Pier, to the sea.

I soon accepted the primitive conditions on these fishing boats. The toilet was a small wooden barrel with a rope handle. You'd catch a bit of sea water in the barrel over the ship's side, then sit on it at the stern with trousers round the ankles hanging on to the gun'nel (top of the bulwark) as the deck rose and fell with the swell. You'd do it and chuck it.'

The whole vessel stank of dried old fish. It seemed to permeate the ship's timbers, but after a time the smell became almost addictive, inhaling it in deep draughts.

We sailed for about nine hours at about eight knots as far as I could judge, then stop. *Fisher Queen* now drifting, wallowed in the swell, then set up a steady roll. I felt a bit queasy for a while. Action on deck took my mind off the rolling.

The lads cast the net. The net, ten feet deep with green glass floats attached to the top and lead weights at the bottom, was flung over a long wooden roller fastened to the bulwark. It ran out for what seemed to me hundreds of yards with yellow buoys at intervals to show other boats the position of the net.

A small gaff sail at the stern now kept *Fisher Queen* head up to the wind. This reduced the rolling a bit, but not much. I much preferred the steaming motion.

The net was hauled in by hand, one man at each side of the wooden roller and the herrings shaken from the net on to the deck. With wooden shovels, they were then put down the hold. This operation was repeated until the catch was suitable to return to the fish quay in good time to satisfy the buyers.

After watching this operation, I became very tired. It was long past my bedtime and I slept on the floor of the wheelhouse. I awoke to find we were approaching the coast and with the sea air I felt reasonably refreshed. I watched as the coast appeared, then was able to pick out landmarks: the lighthouse and piers. We steamed between the port and starboard buoys that indicated the dredged channel into the harbour. I was looking forward to my breakfast with Uncle Arthur.

Fisher Queen came bow up to the fish quay and made fast. It was about nine in the morning. To arrive late meant a poor price if other boats had arrived with good catches. The buyers didn't want more for retail. In this case, the fish would be sold at a low price to be salted down in barrels for export to Russia and other parts of the world.

Wooden boxes were on the quay. Two men in the hold shovelled the herrings into a willow basket. This was hauled up with a rope round the winch drum over a pulley on the ship's derrick until it was level with the quay. Another rope swung it over to the quay as the winch lowered it near a box, the contents were then poured from basket to box. Each box when full held a measure known as a krann. Give or take a few fish, I suppose.

When there was a glut of herrings, one or two boats had to go to sea to dump their catch. It didn't happen often – most went for curing as kippers or bloaters – but in the thirties tons of fish were salted down into big barrels. Salting the herrings was done by Scottish fisher lassies. They came down from Scotland as the herring fleet moved slowly down the coast following the shoals of herring.

The lassies lodged with local families. If the catch of fish did not require salting, there was no work. They didn't waste their valuable time and had to earn a living, so they knitted fancy cable Scottish pullovers for sale. Even as they walked around the town in small groups, they knitted as they walked along, generally in twos and threes. They carried the wool in a linen bag slung over their shoulder. They were happy girls, laughing and chatting in their Scottish brogue, and were well liked by the townsfolk. They lodged with the same families year after year.

When there was a glut of herrings, the fish were tipped into long wooden troughs about ten feet long and four or five girls worked at each side with green waterproof aprons, taking their knives from the apron front pocket to gut the fish, working at great speed, then – fish scales everywhere – packing them tightly into the barrels with a shovel of salt on each layer until the barrel was full.

Uncle George, cigar in mouth, in brown suit and trilby, gold chain across his waistcoat, although a busy man always had time for me and was very kind. His youngest son was Lawson; he and I were some kind of cousins, I suppose. As I have said, his mother and my Granny were half-sisters. In our infancy we were brought up together. With busy parents, a girl was paid to take us out in a double pushchair. Later we were both put into sailor suits, but Mum never could persuade me to wear the sailor hat. A few times only, under protest!

In winter I had to wear soft leather gaitors from just above the knee to the ankle, with lots of round buttons down the side. A button hook was required to fasten them round the leg from ankle to thigh. I hated them! They took ages to put on and made my legs sore, the short trousers were still draughty and the tops of my legs were cold in winter.

The Wardell family prospered with the abundance of fish and had moved from living above the shop premises into a big three-storey house on the sea front.

No.1 Albion Terrace over-looked the Tees Bay. This house had two big basement rooms, not really cellars. The front room had a window half above ground level. This was the kitchen with a large fire and range, the other a dark laundry.

Lawson and I played in the big attic rooms, where originally servants would have lived. He had many expensive toys: guardsmen soldiers four or five inches high and an old rocking horse, probably second-hand that was well worn and had served some family well.

He also had a toy lantern slide, a more modern toy, a cinematograph that used a few feet of celluloid film wrapped round a spool to show moving pictures by cranking a handle for a few seconds of action.

Cinema was just coming to town in 1929, at the Palladium Cinema in Northgate we saw Tom Mix silent cowboy films on Saturday mornings. The noise of the kids shouting things like 'Look out! He's behind you' was deafening!

The manager would walk down the aisle shouting 'quiet!', which was futile and only added to the noise.

Tom nearly always ended up unconscious locked in a barn that the baddies had set on fire. We had to go next week. And there was Tom, always with a white Stetsun hat, up and at 'em again. We never knew how he escaped. The baddies always wore black stetsun hats.

Uncle George's business included a Bedford lorry and I was allowed to go with the driver Richard Thomas (married to George's daughter Norah) to take a load of herrings in boxes to the fish merchants in Whitby, on the cliff under the Abbey. This was early in the season, when the herring boats were not going into Whitby.

In 1937 it was a long journey, over the Transporter Bridge through Guisborough on to the moor road. We had to stop after climbing up Burke Brow a long climb of about a hundred feet with sharp bends top and bottom. At a parking area at the top we pulled in to let the engne cool down. Dickie would take the plugs out and clean them. The next hazard was negotiating Jolly Sailors, a steep bank that had an 'S' bend at that time (so called because of the pub there – now the bank is much reduced), then down bank nearly all the way to Whitby. The five mile pull back up didn't bother the Bedford Lorry now we were offloaded. We delivered herrings to Nobles & Fortunes fish merchants. They had kipper houses where they smoked the herrings under oak chipping fires. They are still there today in 2009, sending kippers all over the world.

We were given a ham tea with salad and cherry tomatoes, bread and butter and big mugs of tea. Nice friendly people. I was a lucky lad to associate with so many nice people.

I didn't know it at the time but my father had a forty-eight-ton yacht, *Penn Donna*, in Whitby harbour about this time. I was told by a captain who went with him. They motored over to France with his friends aboard.

Hartlepool had its own pilot boat, known by the locals as *The Cutter*. Probably derived from a previous pilot sailing cutter. It was run as an association by the pilots. The boat was quite a substantial craft, with a funnel painted light brown and a black band at the top, a coal-fired boiler and steam engine of course. It was designed to go out into the bay for long periods to meet ships arriving at the port. At high tide *The Cutter* would go alongside the ship and a pilot would climb up a rope ladder to guide 'her' into the harbour. The channel being rather narrow, it was under the almost permanent attention of a bucket dredger, which clanked like a broken church bell all day every day in the harbour. Well, nearly every day!

Mum had a school-friend, Marjory Raine, who had married a pilot and a day out was arranged on the pilot boat. We walked along the old pier, where she was always berthed when not at sea. We climbed down the side of the pier onto the vessel and, sitting round the stern, we were soon out in the bay to wait for the cargo ships coming up the coast.

There was a party atmosphere, with the families of other pilots aboard. Fish were caught and taken to the galley to be cooked. Coming alongside a Frenchman – it could have been any nationality – as the pilot clambered up the ladder. Mum called up in her schoolgirl French for some bread, A crewman appeared and threw a loaf down, which, together with mugs of strong hot tea, refreshed the company nicely. The business of the day over, we returned to the pier in good spirits. A happy day!

We often went by bus to Middlesbrough to visit Mum's younger sister, Lily, who married Richard Metcalf. They had moved into a new house, built in about 1928, in Devonshire Road, Linthorpe. Sometimes we went by bus to the Transporter Bridge. This bridge was built in 1911 and is still running today. It is not a conventional bridge with a roadway. A tower of steel girders at each side of the river carry a track from which a trolley is pulled back and forth across the river by a steel rope round a giant electric-driven drum. Suspended from the trolley by wire ropes is a platform capable of taking several vehicles, depending on their size.

I enjoyed this route but at other times we went round the road via Billingham. Don't ask me why. These were the early days of long-distance buses put on the road in Teesside by an ex-army sapper after the Great War called Mr Blumer. Hence 'Blumer's Buses'. Previous to this, extensive road travel was not available.

The route was quite an adventure. When we reached Billingham Bottoms, which flooded regularly, going up the bank into the village the passengers all had to get out to enable the bus to reach the top. The engine generally boiled and steam erupted from the radiator. The bus would stop and wait until the engine had cooled, and once water had been added to the radiator, off we went again.

Mum had told us previously that ferry boats plied between Stockton and Middlesbrough along the River Tees and went to Hartlepool. Mr William Lillie in his *History of Middlesbrough* gives a good account of the early days.

In August in Hartlepool the Wild Beast Show, as it was called, came to town and set up in the High Street. Murphy's roundabouts came to town every year, with 'roll a penny' stalls, a boxing booth and four-wheeled trailer cages with lions and other poor beasts.

I was fascinated by the 'roll a penny' stalls. I was given a few pence at a time to play with and soon learnt the odds were against me and I later taught my son the same lesson on gambling on a visit to Blackpool.

Giant swing boats, holding about twenty people, were operated by steam.

Electricity from generators on top of giant-wheeled traction engines driven by leather belts from the steam engine shaft supplied rows of lights round the jumping horses and other gaily painted roundabouts. At this time, most houses were lit by gas, oil lamps or candles.

Imagine the excitement, seeing all these coloured lights! An organ played, with mobile figures pirouetting to the music, highly polished brasses on everything.

I was very fascinated by these steaming, fancy monsters, Traction engines with wheels twice my height, snorting steam, huffing and puffing as the flywheel spun round, the leather drive belt to the generator slapping in rhythm to the crank of the engine. So much so that when the show left town passing granny's shop, at three years old I followed it for about a mile to the railway station and was caught up there by my caring, breathless Aunt Jennie. I was well satisfied with myself. I'd seen them safely out of town. After the High Street had been demolished in the name of slum clearance in 1938, the show's venue was moved to the town moor, which being grassland soon became a quagmire in rain.

On the last Saturday of Carnival, a parade took place. The parade assembled at the old barracks near Marine Drive and came along Durham Street and down Middlegate.

It made a circular tour of the Ancient Borough, to disperse where it had started, at the well-constructed barracks, probably built, like the gun batteries, to repel Napoleon.

We waited a long time, to a youngster, on the pavement for the procession to appear. First we heard the brass band in the distance and as the music got louder kiddies' faces would appear from between the adults' legs, looking anxiously up the road, then Councillor Tommy Hopper the organiser, came into view, stepping proudly out, alone in the middle of the road followed at a respectful distance usually by the Blackhall Colliery Brass Band. I would watch agog the chap with the big bass drum. Boom! Boom! Boom!

Then arrived the King and Queen of Carnival, theatrical crowns sat jauntily on their majestic white wigs, faces made up with powder, lipstick and wimples. In appropriate royal dress, they sat on elaborate line paint-decorated plywood thrones on an equally polished and decorated flat four-wheeled cart drawn by two magnificent shire horses, their hooves waxed and well groomed, their harnesses with brasses polished to perfection. In later years, this flat cart was replaced by a motor lorry, equally polished up but the horses were sadly missed.

On the float, the Court Jester and female attendants in medieval dress lounged about, throwing coloured streamers into the crowd. Some streamers trailed along the road for yards, adding colour to the scene.

21

The townsfolk entered into the spirit of things, everyone cheering and waving.

Then came the floats entered by local business people, some by individual street parties, interspersed with other folks in fancy dress. Bicycles decorated with coloured paper were pushed proudly along by their owners.

Individual costumes, some quite scary to a doubtful youngster, ran from side to side of the road, half naked bodies with seaweed or straw skirts painted as mermen or native savages waving wooden spears. Old ladies were screaming and laughing enjoying the attention given to them.

Being a small town, it created a wonderfully pleasant atmosphere among the locals and encouraged friendship where there may have once been doubt and suspicion.

This era was renowned for kids' jazz bands. The kids in bright-coloured taffeta uniforms played kazoos, a small trumpet with a paper disc that vibrated to create a trumpet noise when blown, the tune given with a throaty buzz. The bands were led by young high-stepping majorettes in short flared skirts, each step exposing firm white thighs and tight rounded knickers. At thirteen years of age, the sight of these girls awakened my hormones. It puzzled me but I ignored it. They were showing off and looked very playful with their fancy parading.

These majorettes twirled their silver maces overhead and occasionally flung them high in the air. They never failed to catch them in the twirling rhythm established by the marching tunes of the kazoos.

Following the older majorette was a minor majorette, imitating the steps of her senior. Next would come two well-built juniors, carrying the banner poles in a socket on a leather belt, the banner elaborately decorated with a gold fringe and the name of the band spelt out often in gold letters on the banner, with the street or area denoting the band's origin. The banner poles were supported fore and aft with silk-like ropes held at the shoulder by four outriders, self-conscious, high-stepping youngsters.

.The jazz bands were very popular with the public. The kids enjoyed the discipline and were obviously very proud as they strutted their stuff, smartly obeying the orders to mark time or advance as the procession was held up for one reason or another. Signals were given by whistle from one of the proud ex-army dads who had trained them.

They came from pit villages and towns far and wide, their banners proudly displayed names such as Wood Street (a Hartlepool band) and pit villages like Horden and Easington despatched a bus load of jazz bands with their competitive banners.

As many as four or five bands would arrive by coach to swell the parade. Each band had one or two anxious mothers who would walk alongside an embarrassed daughter. Mum carried a shopping bag of first aid: a bottle of water; a flannel to cool a fevered brow; a hand towel; and such like. One or two dads discreetly encouraged young sons to 'chin up' as they marched along. It was a fairly long route round the town. It could be quite an ordeal for a young chap.

One float that was entered for many years by the Collins family had the wives heavily made-up, pantomime-style, dressed in their summer finery, lounging in deck chairs with potted plants and drinks on tables, while the men in pinnies (kitchen aprons) were doing the washing, possing at the tub, and ironing. This in Hartlepool, the home of Andy Capp and his wife Florrie, created roars of laughter and banter from the crowds lining the street. This was the 1930s, when reality was very bleak with the depression and so many men unemployed.

Uncle Alex, my mother's brother, was unemployed for three years and the means-test committee decided that, as his mother had a business, he was not eligible for dole, she had to keep him. So the business had to keep Uncle Arthur the cobbler, Granny, Uncle Alex, Aunt Jennie and me! Five of us! Jessie, my mum, made a useful contribution with the shoe shop though. We lived a lot on fish, as it was cheap during July and August when the herrings were in.

Uncle Alex took me over the ferry to the Richardson, Westgarth shipyard in Middleton. The remains of the ferry can still be seen at the west end of the town wall. From the Middleton landing stage we walked to see what was probably the last ship launched at Richardson, Westgarth shipyard.

I was about five years old then, in 1929. Uncle Alex had been a skilled turner, machining engine parts to thousandth-of-an-inch, using callipers that required a delicate touch in the work of the shipyard. Later, about 1934, he got work at Reyrolles electrical factory at Hebburn on Tyne.

Only then was he able to marry, at fifty, a very sweet lady. They got a council house in Hebburn and as a skilled machinist they became mildly prosperous.

She was another Aunt Jennie for me and very kind. She made us presents of her home-made wonderful toffee. When Uncle Alex died, she gave me a sum of money he had left for me. I think it was about one hundred and fifty pounds. Alexander Wright was a kind and upright gentleman who died at eighty years old. His wife, Jennie, died a few years later.

Uncle Arthur the cobbler, had been in Harry Tate's Navy during the Great War. This was coastal defence, armed trawlers, mine sweepers and anti-submarine defence.

They were in constant active service. He rarely spoke of it . He was a doer and had a set of roof ladders with three sections that extended by pulleys and ropes to reach the roof of his property. He knocked a hole in a brick wall to put in a window and another for a door. For our pleasure, he created a holiday living hut. There were no caravans in those days. It was very substantially built of half-inch tongue and groove boards with framed windows. The whole thing mounted on four twelve-inch iron wheels, which kept it off the ground even if it was not very portable. When this was on site, he built two small bedrooms on to the hut, which made it very comfortable for the family.

This holiday bungalow was situated at Crimdon Dene, a deep well-wooded cleft where a narrow river – generally dried up in summer – ran through to the beach. This dene is about five miles north of Hartlepool. We could go there by bus but it was just as quick to walk the five miles along the beach from the north side of the headland, carrying our food supplies.

There were only a few huts in the early days, with oil lamps for light, a primus stove to cook with, but a 'pot-belly' stove on cold days, which then took the place of the primus.

The wooded dene was wild so we tidied it up for fuel. There was plenty of dead wood, which we carried to the hut to feed the pot belly of the stove. Water was carried from a spring on the south side of the dene in white enamel buckets, with lids. The water bubbled out of the side of a grassy bank. We had made a chute from a tin can to enable the water to run into the buckets. It tasted beautiful, brilliantly clear, soft and sweet.

The river was dried up unless heavy rain had fallen, then most of it ran into the sand when it reached the beach. It was ideal territory for safe adventure expeditions and, with my cousin Arthur, Uncle Arthur's adopted boy four years younger than me, and Martin, a nephew of Aunt Lily, we had many happy days.

Hartlepool had a thriving croft of fishermen's cottages. The Cambridge Building was a three-storey tenement building facing the harbour. Most of these properties were occupied by families of fishermen conveniently near their boats, the cobles.

These boats were double-ended (sharp at both ends), unlike the Whitby cobles, which had a transom stern.

Double-ended boats are better for a beach landing, and an oncoming wave cannot easily push the boat broadside on to the beach where it might be swamped. They were at this time, in the 1930s, being motorised.

When the older kids were at school, I was a loner on Fish Sands. Poking my nose into what was going on, I would watch the men drill a hole through the stern post of a coble to pass the propellor shaft through. The engines were generally second-hand lorry engines complete with gear box. They were mounted on wooden blocks near the stern. These vessels had been sailed with a square sail hanging from a spar suspended from the mast up to this time, almost in the same way as an ancient Viking ship.

The square sail was pulled up the mast on the spar with the clew (a bottom corner) fastened at the bow, the other held at the tiller. They sailed well. The spar could be pulled across the beam to sail not too close to the wind but they were easy to manage by one man and tack upwind. They were not without long heavy oars to manoeuvre in harbour. These oars were fitted with a pin and thole (a metal ring) to keep them secure if it was necessary to let go of the oar to handle a line. They were well balanced so that manpower was not wasted pulling the boat when lack of wind left the coble becalmed.

I saw how the fishermen moved their boats from the beach to the water on wooden pit props, of which there was a plentiful supply in those days. Hartlepool imported shiploads of pit props for the Durham coal mines. Often ships would come into port listing after passing through a storm on their way over from Norway. The deck cargo of props sagged over the side of the vessel, leaving a trail of props astern in the sea. The props were about eight feet long and four to six inches in diameter. They would wash ashore for days after the ships arrival.

The cobles were got in and out of the water by being pushed to slide over the line of props, laid a couple of feet apart on the soft sand. If this was done at high tide, there would be ample time to repair or repaint the coble's hull before the tide returned. To the kids on the beach, it was a bit of fun and everyone was happy to lend a hand.

Later, when living in Middlesbrough, every school holiday I stayed at Granny's. With my friends, we would hire a boat for a few pence from Mr Bond, who had six boats for hire moored along the town wall, near to where the ferry crossed over by the lifeboat station.

With the hard economic times of the thirties, Mr Bond had little business hiring his boats. We kids were probably his only customers and if we could put together threepence or so we could have a boat as long as we cared to use it.

We would row for hours to Landscar Rocks near Seaton Carew. These rocks were only visible at low tide and we were warned to keep a weather eye out.

We learned to handle a boat here from the age of eleven, at times sculling from the stern, which was easier than rowing and done standing facing aft, pushing the oar with the body and twisting the blade left and right to act on the keel as a lever.

As a child there was a lot to interest me around Granny's shop. Often, if the trolley bus driver coming down Middlegate Street was careless in turning the corner, one or sometimes both trolleys would come off the overhead wires.

The conductor, often a bit annoyed, would pull a long bamboo pole from under the bus. This pole had a hook on the end. With this he hooked it on to the trolley and set the little wheel on to the wire. It wasn't always so easy, since, having come off the wire in the first place it wouldn't stay on in that same place.

The conductor would then have to keep the trolley on the wire with his pole until the driver was able to move the bus a few feet furthur along to a section of wire in easy reach of the trolly.

Photographs of Granny as a young woman, 'a Scott' show her with a strong face, a firm mouth, high cheekbones, dark hair and brown eyes, slim with a straight back, in a skirt down to the floor.

My memory of her when I was five was of a grey-haired old lady, slightly stooped, still with the long black skirt and the face strong but well wrinkled. The chin square, the mouth firm, aged sixty-five. She was born in 1863, christened Margaret Ann Scott the daughter of Thomas Lawson Scott, a wood carver. She died, aged eighty-seven, in 1950.

Meggie, as her contemporaries called her, was an ardent snuff addict and had a black oblong snuff box. It was probably made of bone. From a very early age I was invited to have a pinch and was shown the art of taking a pinch by putting a little between finger and thumb, placing it on the knuckle of the other hand, sniffing to both sides of the nose with the resulting explosion of a sneeze. She suffered from bronchitis badly in the winter; maybe taking the snuff helped to relieve her condition. I don't remember her ever sneezng or having a cold but her chesty cough in winter seemed never to end.

The house was very damp, the walls being built with pieces of limestone from the beach, worn round by the sea and held together with lime mortar to a thickness of eighteen inches. A heavy sustained downfall of rain, wind-driven against a wall, would see the rain soak through and run down the wall in the room in droplets.

Granny said the property had been a tavern called the White Hart, the name being visible under the repainted shop front when they had first occupied the property. After some research by my friend Cliff Thornton, it appeared the property had extended through to the Main Hotel in the High Street, the Middlegate Street property being for the carriages, horses and staff.

There was a carriageway next to the property, which had led to the back of Granny's property. Her property had been separated from the carriageway by a six foot-high brick wall at the back of No. 14. The yard area was paved with building bricks round a drain where rain and kitchen waste water ran away.

Across the yard at the back of Granny's property was a brick-built flush toilet next to a coal house to hold a few bags of coal. Adjacent property had signs of gable ends of once-connected roofing, indicating that smaller dwellings, maybe stables and cottages, had existed round the yard.

The house had not had running water originally. The town pump in the High Street was not too far away. The obsolete town pump still stands there today. A magnificent tower of cast-iron tracery, painted dark green minus the handle, topped with a ball pinnacle. It stands in the centre of what was once a wide, part-cobbled historic high street, below the Abbey Church of St Hilda.

Now after centuries, thanks to social-engineering vandalism, all that remains is a minor road, gardens and a car park. This is now to be further modified to create a town square. Not another improvement! It has been planted with mature trees and shrubs, will require expensive maintenance and do little to bring money into the town.

Granny's kitchen had an earth floor with a few concrete flags, later filled around the once-open hearth with concrete. Linoleum covered most of the floor and hookey mats, made from cast-off clothes cut into strips and prodded through sheets of sacking stretched on a wooden frame, gave some insulation to the feet .

The original open hearth was about six feet wide A thin steel rail was still there in the ceiling where cooking was done hanging from chains above the hearth fire.

It had been brought into the nineteenth century with a cast-iron kitchen range on the left side and a cast-iron oven next to the fire basket, which was about a foot wide and with the oven raised on brickwork. The two-foot-square chimney allowed most of the heat to escape, if not all of it.

On the right of the small fire, which was enclosed with fire brick, a shelf level with the fire coals often carried a black enamel pan of stew but at all other times it carried the ubiquitous copper kettle, which maintained an unlimited stream of boiling water.

At the back of the fire was a deep shelf where a shovel or two of coal was kept, this to be dragged forward as required. When it was available, sea coal was supplemented here. To the right of the kettle was the brick housing of the set pot. This was a metal dome dropped into the brick box hanging by its flanged top. It could heat five gallons of water filled with buckets from the tap and heated with hot coals from the fire, previously built up for the extra need, thrown into an opening under the pot.

There was no drain tap; the hot water had to be bailed out with a ladle. A wooden lid normally covered the set pot and firewood was stored there when not in use.

Except on Mondays, washday, the set pot and things stored above it were covered by a curtain hanging from a brass rail fastened under the mantle shelf.

On washday, Aunt Jennie and Grandma started early. Hot coals were shovelled under the set pot already filled with water. A small wooden table put out in the yard to scrub the collars and other soiled things.

The poss tub in earlier times, was a wooden barrel, but an improved model in galvanised steel with small corrugations, to assist in the agitation, was purchased. Soap flakes (yellow bar soap sliced thin with a knife) was added to the hot water then the soiled clothes were 'possed' with a wooden 'dolly' (an agitator of round wooden post with slots and holes drilled into the bottom), which had a handle bar at the top, waist height, to lift, turn and thrust up and down on to the clothes in the tub thus agitating the water and sloshing the clothes in the lather. Handkerchiefs were boiled and a 'blue bag' was put in with white clothes. Don't ask why! Supposed to make them whiter, I believe.

Uncle Alex disappeared after breakfast most days, but very early on Mondays. Being unemployed and 'kept' for three years, sadly, he must have been humiliated.

He had an allotment three miles away with a hut to keep his garden tools in. I went with him once or twice. He grew the usual veg and a few flowers. Uncle Alex was a gentle man in every sense of the word.

He shaved with a cut-throat razor generally humming to himself music from *The Merry Widow*, 'Deliah, O Deliah'. He was a member of a working men's club, a misnomer since they were nearly all unemployed.

On Christmas morning he would take me to the club, not far from Middlegate, when the children of members were given a 'treat'. This was a brown paper bag with an apple, some monkey nuts (peanuts in the shells), a few boiled sweets and an orange. Maybe a penny bar of chocolate, too.

By early Monday afternoon, wash day was over and all dried. Dinner was a stew: the left-over Sunday roast meat with added vegetables. I was glad to see order restored and the kitchen put straight. I was often given dripping, spread on bread with a good sprinkle of salt. This was the fat which 'dripped' from the beef. It was delicious!

The high mantle shelf, over the fireplace, about six inches wide, ran the full width of the six-foot hearth and was covered with a six-inch drape of green velvet like cloth, with small tassels along the overhanging edge.

A hexagonal mahogany-framed mirror hung above the middle of the shelf, to the right of which sat the tea caddie, a tin box of black enamel with Chinese figures in medallions on each side. A vase held wooden spills used to light the single gas mantle from the fire. This was the only source of light except for the fire.

Granny would read the newspaper laid open on the square table with its chenille cloth, her mouth moving as she quietly read each word. She told me her parents paid sixpence a week for her schooling. Her father was the wood carver, Thomas Lawson Scott, a good craftsman and artist, I think.

Also on the mantle shelf was a little brown teapot, never used for making tea. Aunt Jennie would take a few pence from it on a Saturday night when the cobbler's shop closed, usually about nine o'clock, to take me across the road to Billy Robinsons' fruit and sweet shop. We would gaze at the abundant display of sweets and decide what to buy this week.

Next door to Granny's shop and joined to the property by a room over the ancient carriageway was a bit of a pretentious, ornamental-timbered building. It had been the public library. This library was moved to a much bigger purpose-built building far along Northgate, paid for from a bequest by a wealthy Scottish man, Mr Carnegie, who made his money in steel in America and left it to provide libraries to many British towns.

The old library was of later vintage to No. 14 and adjacent to the general post office and sorting office separated by a chare (a passage about six feet wide leading to the High Street). The library was taken over by Mr Pinder for a draper's shop and later by Mr Robson as a chemist shop. That too was demolished by a crazy council who seemed determined to destroy the ancient borough of Hartlepool.

Just fancy, in 1938 they destroyed the ancient High Street to put gardens in its place. Why gardens, when there were the wonderful promenade and the beaches with a view over the glorious Tees bay? This destroyed the old town. The folk of the demolished properties were all re-housed miles away, which then destroyed the small shops and pubs and so on. The town needed houses and people. Planning gone mad!

CHAPTER TWO

My later childhood and first job

Aunt Jennie was one of six children, which was not unusual in those days. Three boys (Willie, Arthur and Alexander) and three girls (Jennie, Jessie and Lily).

Jessie, my mother, married Fred, who during the Great War was in the Royal Navy as a marine engineer. How he managed that, I don't know.

Mum said he had worked in a hatter's and hosiery shop. However, he was very capable mechanically and obviously intelligent, being able to print his own photographs and maintain his motorcycles, which was not easy in those days.

Many years later in his last years, after we were reconciled, he told me that he was on duty aboard ship (I think he said it was the battleship HMS *Orion*) when a boiler furnace crown came down! This very dangerous damage happens if the water in the boiler becomes lower than the circular furnace that goes through the boiler. The heat then softens the steel furnace and the pressure of steam inside the boiler forces the top of the furnace to buckle down onto the fire. 'They blamed me!' he said in his tired old voice. It suggests that the duty engineer failed to check the boiler water sight glasses, a routine on each watch. The gauge can give a false reading. I suspect he took the blame for one of his stokers, as it was not like him to neglect his duty at that time.

Jessie and Fred had a happy courtship. They used to go to the countryside on Fred's motorbike (not many about in those days). Mum told me he played the cello whilst she played the piano. He told me in his last years: 'She didn't play very well', he was still annoyed with her! She must have had other good points because Jessie fell pregnant and that wasn't unusual in those days either!

They married when she was twenty-one years old, shortly after Fred was called up to the Royal Navy and Jessie visited him in Chatham. He was on battleships and some of his photographs of the fleet were taken at Scapa Floe.

His father George Simon (he didn't like the Simon!) was in Australia when the war started, and left his wife to look after their general shop in West Hartlepool. They were pretty well off, because young Fred had expensive things like a plate camera and an Indian motorcycle, which were wealthy toys in those days.

Things didn't go well for Granddad in Australia. He had bought cattle to put on the land and, as the story goes, flash floods came and he lost everything.

He took to the bush. He once told me he used to light his pipe with a magnifying glass and the sun. Can't have smoked at night, then – unless he had a camp fire!

Doing odd jobs with no hope of getting back to the U.K. At the outbreak of the First World War he joined the 10th Australian Light Horse regiment, who fought at Gallipoli in 1915. He was wounded on night patrol by a Turkish shell splinter. When taken back to Australia and recovered from his wound, although discharged, he joined up again and fought on the western front in France until the end of the war. He then asked to be discharged in the UK. That was one way to get a passage home!

I have a letter he wrote to my mum in March 1918. In copying ink pencil, he describes the lack of sleep in the trenches when the guns were firing. His letter shows great affection for Jessie, his daughter-in-law. How difficult it must have been to communicate with his wife Ada when he was in Australia. It took a ship six weeks to steam to the UK and ships didn't leave every day. It may have been possible to send a telegram by then, but, it would have been costly.

This was my grandfather, George Simon Dinsdale. I saw him regularly when I was old enough to go alone to visit the family on a Saturday. I pedalled on my fairy bike from our house on Granville Road to Yarm Lane Stockton, about eight miles.

George was a good man with horses and had started work in a livery stable at the age of ten – when he decided he'd had enough of school. He must have been a good scholar because by the age of seventeen, he was put in charge of the 'entire' (the name given to a stallion) and his duties were to take the stallion round to the various big houses and other stables to serve the mares. This would entail keeping a book, entering the dates of the serve and collecting the fee, a responsible job for a young man.

After the war he got a job with Ashmore Benson, Pease and Company, a famous firm in Stockton in those days. His work was to look after the carriage horses for the director's stables.

Granny Dinsdale had sold the shop in Derwent Street, West Hartlepool, after the bombardment by German battleships. 500 houses were damaged by the shells. She bought a nice house, No. 11, Austin Avenue, Hartburn, a suburb of Stockton.

In 1916 George was with the Aussies in France, where communication was easier. He may have had leave to visit her, as there are photographs of the family with the men in uniform. Jessie lived with her mother-in-law at Austin Avenue. Eric, my eldest brother, is shown in a photograph of the four generations, about two years old with his great-grandfather and namesake, Francis Eric (a coach driver), Grandfather George, and Fred.

After the 1914 – 1918 war, motor vehicles were becoming more popular, so the directors of Ashmores decided to invest in one, as it was probably more economic than the horse. They asked Grandad if he knew anyone who could help them and Grandad said: 'Yes, my son knows about motors'. Fred had had motorbikes since he was about seventeen and was now returned home from the Royal Navy.

The directors asked Fred to go down to the Midlands to the factory, purchase the car and drive it back on roads that had not changed much since the stagecoach days.

Since no one knew how to start the thing, or drive it, Fred (my father) was offered the job of chauffeur. He taught Granddad to drive, and this was the beginning of the garage business. It included a taxi service for a while, then car repairs and eventually the distributorship for Rover cars in the South Durham and North Yorkshire areas.

This business was developed from houses in Stockton. They were big houses and the family moved from Austin Avenue to live there when one became vacant. The house next door was eventually used for the business, selling Rudge-Whitworth motorcycles as well as cars.

In the early days, before petrol pumps, Fred had a shed, to store two gallon cans of Pratts petrol. The shed was put by a beck in what is now the West End Bowling Club car park at Hartburn. The council objected to it and said it was obstructing the path or something like that, so my mum said that Fred put timbers into the beck and moved the shed back to comply with the order.

My mother told me people would sometimes call at the house late at night to buy petrol. I assume this was when they lived near in Austin Avenue not far away from the shed; they most likely had a few cans at the house for just such an occasion.

Fred and Jessie had lived en famille with his mother and father until I was born, then Jessie left and returned to live at Hartlepool at the Wright family home. There was a legal separation.

It wasn't long before Jessie, who had an eye for business, found the means to help her family, as indeed she had helped Fred before the kids arrived.

Alexander Wright had died tragically by his own hand as a result of his brother, Peter, embezzling the accounts of their two shoe shops, leaving his wife and running off to Australia with a woman.

The shame of this probably accounted for Granny very rarely leaving the house. Uncle Arthur, who had been in the Royal Navy until 1918, now worked in the shop repairing shoes and supported his mother, my granny. He was married and lived across the road in Middlegate Street above an empty shop.

Jessie now rented the empty shop and had a local joiner fit it out with shelves and a counter.

She then went to Leng's, a wholesaler in Stockton, and ordered a stock of good quality Portland shoes. The business thrived.

Problems eventually arose when I was about six years old, Arthur's wife, Lily, a good person, who was very kind to me but not well versed in business, got into the habit of taking money from Jessie's till, 'just to buy a few things'.

This would upset Jessie's bookkeeping, I imagine she would have had an arrangement with Arthur for her to take a wage for running the business, but the business was in Arthur's name.

It was time for Jessie to move on and her younger sister, Lilly (another Lilly), who lived in Middlesbrough was the answer. We stayed with her and her husband Richard Metcalfe over Christmas in 1930. I remember it as a rather depressing time. I didn't know why we were moving from Hartlepool. I wasn't told and I didn't ask.

Uncle Richard was training to be an architect but at nineteen, during the First World War, he was called up to the army. He was badly wounded in France and had his right arm amputated (and other wounds) but slowly recovered. His mother and father were taken over to France to see him in hospital, it was that bad. Eventually he was able to work and finally became head of pensions in Newcastle.

He had a peculiar problem with meals, and would only use his own personal knife, fork and spoons, to the extent that my aunt had to take them out with her if they were to visit friends or relations. He didn't mind me watching him shave and he showed me how he was able to fix things to the washbasin to overcome his disability.

It wasn't desirable for us to stay too long with Aunt Lilly and Uncle Richard 'Tricky Dickie' as you might say! I think he didn't like little boys, probably due to his wartime injuries. It must have been difficult to adjust.

Somehow Mum found a married couple who wanted to let two rooms in Granville Road and we lived there until able to rent a house nearby.

The houses in Granville Road were in the form of a long terrace with a small front garden, each about fifteen feet by twenty.

A panelled front door with a second door, half panelled with a top half of decorated glass, opened on to a short passage, with stairs at the end.

Downstairs there were two rooms and the staircase leading up to the back bedroom, which passed through to a bathroom. From this small landing, three stairs led up to the other two bedrooms, the front bedroom having two flat windows above the downstairs bay window.

They were warm houses, but the outside toilet was down a narrow yard some twenty feet from the back door. We had many hard frosts in the thirties and the toilet froze up every winter despite Mum's efforts with a small oil lamp and attempts at insulation.

Mum used to swill and scrub the yard with copious buckets of water and a stiff broom regularly until her later years: she was a hard worker. Windows were cleaned with hot water and a splash of vinegar. The windows were of the sash type whereas the top frame could be pulled down and the bottom frame could be pulled up. Counter-weights in the outer frames with ropes attached to the window frames were intended to make this easy but several of the ropes were rotted. The agent was loath to have them repaired and the many coats of paint over the years caused them to jam but it was home and Mum was fairly content.

A couple of years after living in the two rooms, Mrs Wade at No. 68 said to my mum that they were buying a house and if she took the key for No. 68 to the house agent, he would let her rent this house!

Mum was able to afford it at one pound per week and a married school friend and her husband Jim Pilcher, who lived in Middlesbrough, helped her to move, carrying our bits and bobs the short distance from No. 58 to No. 68.

Mum now had her own place, and with money she had earned as wages from the shoe shop, she set about furnishing it. I shared her pleasure with each piece. We bought a little sideboard, a three-piece suite and a wind-up gramophone. We went to Woolworths and bought records at sixpence each by Gracie Fields, a favourite. The most important item was, of course, the piano, which was second-hand, as were most of the things, but it was a happy home for me until I was twenty-three and went to sea.

When she had to give her home up at sixty-seven years of age, the whole effects raised only twelve pounds ten shillings!

A whole house with three bedrooms was a vast improvement to the two rooms we rented from the Johnston family, where Mum would ask me to play quietly so as not to disturb Mr Johnston. He was a recruiting sergeant in the Army. He had fair hair and a rosy complexion with a ginger moustache and plump, round face, a pleasant man but rather intimidating.

We had the front room and the back bedroom; Mum would have had to share the kitchen stove with Mrs Johnston. What a crime to have to live like that, after having five children to a man who wouldn't provide her with a home of her own.

One night in the early hours of the morning, when I was about seven years old, there was a slight earthquake! I woke to feel the room vibrating and things rattling on the chest of drawers. It was quite scary for a few seconds.

During this time, my mum hadn't been feeling too well. The doctor had been and called it the result of the 'change of life' and collected his fee (one guinea. That was half my mum's weekly income. No National Health Service in those days!

One day Mum collapsed heavily from a dining chair to the floor while we were having a meal. I screamed and Mrs Johnston came running in. She was a very nice person with two daughters, Eileen and four-year-old Dorothy.

Mum became good friends with their eldest daughter and later, when we were living at No. 68, Eileen (then nineteen) would bring her boyfriend along and Mum would play the piano and amuse them for an hour or so. It was very sad when Eileen died shortly after. I don't know what of – in those days a lot of young people died of mysterious diseases.

As there was no telephone in any of the houses, someone must have gone out to call an ambulance. This took Mum first to the Carter Bequest Hospital, where they discovered she had typhoid fever, a contagious disease contracted from open drains. Mum said later she had passed a smelly drain. This put the medical top brass in a tizzy as Carter Bequest Hospital had to be fumigated.

It was the first local case of typhoid for fourteen years and Mum was moved to West Lane Hospital which was then a fever hospital.

Aunt Jennie was told of my predicament. I don't know how, maybe by telegraph. She came over and took me to stay again at Hartlepool. I'm glad they didn't take me to Aunt Lilly's house. Uncle Richard was a bit highly strung. He once lifted me up by the hair when I misbehaved at the table. I can't remember what I had done but my Uncle Alex wouldn't have done that – he would have teased me and made me laugh.

I don't remember going to school at Hartlepool on this occasion – it would have been near the summer holiday. After some weeks, when my mum had recovered and was convalescing, Aunt Jennie took me by bus to visit her but I was only allowed to see her through a closed window, standing in the hospital grounds. It was, I remember, a very high window but Mum looked very happy now she was recovered and later told me how good the nurses had been to her. In fact, one nurse became a close friend and visited us when we had moved into No. 68.

Mum liked people and people liked her. A school friend of hers, Jim Pilcher, had flown in the pre-RAF Royal Flying Corps. I think he was a pilot. He certainly flew! He worked in the unemployment office and in his spare time had got a few of the unemployed chaps who could play a musical instrument together and formed a band. They played at small dances in church halls.

Jessie (that's what they affectionately called her) would have them round to our house and they would have a musical evening.

Jim could play any instrument, it seemed. He played the guitar, and then he got the latest thing, the slide guitar, when Hawaiian music was all the rage. He had a go with the banjo and played the piano accordion. They were good friends for many years. Jim's wife, Rose, went blind in later life and Jessie would take her out for the day. This gave Jim a bit of support until Jim's job moved them to Northallerton. We did go to see them once or twice but gradually lost touch.

CHAPTER TWO – *My later childhood and first job*

Mum eventually spent her last three years in Nunthorpe Hall, a council-run old people's home. She accepted it with dignity and, in fact, enjoyed the company of the old men in there.

She got the bus into town and went to see her friends at Mrs Scraftens Temple of Light Spiritual Church in Southfield Lane, just off Linthorpe Road. She usually called at our house for her tea and after supper I would take her back to the hall.

Up to the age of fourteen, I occasionally went with Mum to the little spiritual church. I used to give the hymn books out. The service consisted of a couple of the old hymns, then a lesson from the New Testament.

Mrs Scraften (a plump, motherly type) would give an uplifting address then pray for a few minutes, then just standing quietly, eyes closed, hands clasped she meditated and then give three or four 'messages'. It was uncanny – there was nothing funny going on, the room was fully lit, she just spoke quietly in her own voice.

I was sat next to Mum and Mrs Scraften said: 'That young man sitting next to you, I can see his name in gold letters, I don't know what it means but it's there' (that's all she said!). When I was sixty-four and installed in the Chair at my lodge, wishing my Mum could know of the honour bestowed on me, I was marched into the dining room and sat in the big chair at the top table I turned to the honours board where all the names of the past masters were inscribed, there in gold letters was 'Arthur Dinsdale, Master 1988'.

Fifty years later Mum's spirit was there. I like to think so, anyway!

My wife, Dorothy, also had a similar experience. While I was whaling in the Antarctic and communication was practically nil, she stayed a couple of weekends with my mum. Dorothy was living with her mother and her recently-married step-father. Dorothy's mum was a kindly, trusting woman and had made a big mistake in this marriage. Dorothy's father had died six years earlier and this 'gentleman', who had worked with her husband and was considered a friend, had said: 'You sell your house, Sally, and we'll buy a new car. I'll sell my house and buy a more modern house'. But the car was driven by him and the more modern house was in his name only. Now his personality changed. His wife had died three years ago, now he had his twenty-four/seven housekeeper

Dorothy often worked late in the office and subsequently could take afternoons off early. She took the bus from Hartlepool to Middlesbrough on Friday to stay with my mum. I think she would confide her anxiety to my mum, with no word from me to either of them. Mum took her to Mrs Scrafton's little spiritual church. After her meditation, Mrs Scraften, with her eyes closed, said: 'I've got a gentleman here and he's doing this,' raising her left hand and passing her right hand, with the fingers pointing down towards the forearm, 'and I don't know what it means. Does anyone know a gentleman who did this?' Dorothy raised her hand in acknowledgement.

Dorothy's father was the design engineer in the shipyard, when he came home from work he would take his jacket off and put an old smoking jacket on. He was a heavy smoker of Gold Flake cigarettes. He removed his handkerchief from his left sleeve and stuffed it with his fingers in the sleeve of the other jacket.

Mrs Scrafton passed his message to Dorothy: 'He just wants to say: "You mustn't worry, everything will be all right".' Dorothy's father had a very good obituary in the local paper stating what a well respected man he had been in the community and Parish Church.

Dorothy and I were married on 16th of June 1948 after, in late May, I returned from whaling in South Georgia. It had been all right for fifty-nine years up to 2007, when Dorothy joined her father once again. I sense that I had been selected to take care of her by his spirit. I fell in love with her when I was only five years old and she was four but our eventual meeting had been more than a coincidence.

Living in Middlesbrough from the age of seven I mixed with the kids near Granville Road and attended the Parish Church with them. We did the Stations of the Cross with the young vicar. I joined the cub scouts at St Aiden's Church, where we met in the church hall. It wasn't very inspiring after my days with the fishermen on the sands at Hartlepool but it was all that was going.

The scout camp came along, but it was to cost seven shillings and sixpence. I knew Mum was short of money and had other priorities so I dropped out; Hartlepool was a better venue for adventure.

I wasn't academic at school, although good at art, but there was no route from a secondary school to a job in art. I may have found the way with parents who were able to guide my education, but it didn't seem to be so important in those days. I always had a feeling that I didn't belong in this environment.

Kids would ask: 'What does your father do'. Most of their dads were on the dole. It was always a source of embarrassment – I had a father but I didn't have one! They wouldn't believe me if I told them what he did – driving around in posh cars and riding to the hunt – they would think I was crazy! I didn't feel deprived but something was lacking. However, it was better than living in a household of rows and violence.

I attended Victoria Road School, built in 1862 as Middlesbrough expanded. Mr Johnston was the headmaster. I was only average, perhaps a bit below average. The teachers were all characters, strict but kind, and at Christmas were able to hand out many freebies gleaned from food companies. We all went home with a bag full: a model glider, made from balsa wood which was propelled into the air with an elastic band; model houses to cut out and stick together; things like that with the advertising logos printed on them. I remember 'Shredded Wheat' was one.

I got the stick a few times from the teachers – it really hurt! Fingers black and blue across the palm of the hand. I was mainly punished for not concentrating, I was a bit of a dreamer, I think. Selective in what I wanted to learn, I would say!

Mr Makereth, the maths teacher, didn't need to use the stick. He walked with a bit of a limp (war wound we suspected), had a sergeant major's moustache and voice. This induced immediate attention and respect, no day-dreaming here, though he might have had a kindly twinkle in his eye, but we wouldn't dare chance it!

The English teacher, 'Pop' Hornsby, was plump with a pink bald head and a ring of snow-white fluffy hair from ear to ear. Cigarette ash dusted his grey three-piece suit, which reeked of tobacco smoke. He was the one who gave me the stick, for nothing. I was in the wrong place at the wrong time. I had to have it because my pals were up for it. Or Pop was having a bad day at the races.

Pop took us through *The merchant of Venice*, the boys taking turns to read out the lines, and poetry, too! I can still remember the odd line: 'I will arise and go now, and go to Innisfree, and a small cabin build there, of clay and wattles made'. Another favourite was: 'My name is Ozymandias, king of kings, look on my works, ye Mighty and despair!' We were expected to remember the lines, and we did! In our last weeks at school at the age of fourteen, Pop decided to prepare us for the real world and he said: 'No more English, boys, I'm going to teach you about engines'.

We learned about steam engines with eccentric sheaves that operated the valves and moving parts; then the internal combustion engines, two-stroke and four-stroke; then diesel, the suction, induction, compression and exhaust – that was interesting! Reciprocating engines.

It took six months before I found a job. It was decided I should stay at school in the meantime, I had a temporary job as a telegraph boy for a couple of weeks, before Christmas 1938. It was beginning to dawn on me that there was no such thing as a level playing field and I was looking up hill!

Permanent boys, with their uniforms and pillbox hats held on with a chin strap, got the best telegrams to take out to the posh areas where they would be sure of a small tip, and in easy reach of the office, with a well-maintained bike. The poor temps? No uniform, just a broad leather belt with the pouch for the telegrams and a bike that seemed to have a mind of its own. They were very heavy machines with a plate below the crossbar bearing the GPO number and were hard work to pedal. They'd be good for going to the beach to collect sea coal.

This temporary job could have resulted in my being kept on as a regular boy but I think what scuppered me was the night I was given telegrams for three different places around Middlesbrough. The last house was in an unfinished road that no one had heard of.

In my determination to succeed ,I eventually found this address. It never dawned on me to take the telegram back. It was raining and dark, I was soaking wet and to make matters worse, to my horror, the house was only half built.

When eventually I got back to the office, the boss was waiting to go home. 'Where've you been,' he grumbled, not impressed with my story. I have never learnt the lesson – all through my life I was taught to persevere and do my best. Mum used to say: 'Keep your nose to the grindstone and you'll get on.' It only seems to give you a sore nose to try too hard. It may pay if you work for yourself. I found out the hard way that any credit made is generally usurped by others but I could never change, I was always keen to please.

I think my wage for that two weeks was eight shillings and a few pence which was good to have because inflation was reducing the value of my allowance from my father.

I went back to school for a while and then got a proper job, as a lab boy at the borough analysts Pattinson and Stead in Queen's Square, Middlesbrough. The job entailed setting up equipment for different analysis procedures, taking instruction from a well-worn little red note book.

It was well within my capability, but as they used all glass equipment, there was the terror of breakage when the analysis was over and we had to dismantle and clean it.

The boss, Alfred Scholes, had a habit of coming down the lab in his three-piece suit with a pipe in his mouth, a test tube in one hand and a beaker in the other, shouting round his pipe: 'Water, boy!' At this, whichever one of us was in the lab (there were two lab boys) had to run to the hundred-and-fifty-gallon distilled water barrel and open the tap for him to put some water into the test tube. With a bit of common sense, he could have carried the vessels in a wooden rack and disposed of our services.

He was a fierce-looking character in an expensive brown tweed suit with a heavy gold chain across his waistcoat, a Victorian-type of man with a strong head of tweed-looking hair, a big moustache to match and a Roman nose.

I found later he had been a distinguished Freemason, whose name is in gold letters on the same Erimus honours board as mine.

There wasn't much future in this job, as lab boys grew up to take samples from iron ore boats in the docks. I'd been to the docks and seen the job. There was iron ore dust everywhere and the ships were unloaded at all hours. I didn't fancy it one bit!

At the age of thirteen, my mother had put my name down for an apprenticeship at Smith's Dock shipyard at South Bank. I didn't have much expectation of being selected, as jobs were usually handed down from father to son. This is natural in a way but hard on the youngest son of a playboy father.

The First Sea Lord of the Admiralty came to the rescue! The shipyards were going to be busy. I got a letter from Smith's Dock asking if Arthur would come and help us build ships for the war effort. It was dated 13th September 1939, ten days after war was declared. I was flattered!

I put my notice in at the analysts – they didn't want me to leave. This was a first! However, their war work was no match for building ships. I think it was a Wednesday when I presented myself at Smith's Dock, along with about ten other young hopefuls. By this time not having a father didn't bother me.

He must have tried to be a father to me in my early years but not very successfully. For my fifth birthday he had a model speedboat made for me, a copy of Seagrave's world speed-breaking vessel. Made in wood, with an electric motor, it was about eighteen inches long, but he didn't present it to me and sadly he never saw me sail it. It consoles me now to think that he must have designed it and thought of me.

When I was four years old, Mum and I went by bus to Stockton to a jetty down Boathouse Lane to the riverside near the Victoria Bridge. They had obviously arranged for him to take me out in one of his outboard speedboats.

He entered races in these speedboats and had a carpenter build them on the business premises. He won thirteen silver cups that were proudly on display in his office. What a price my family paid for those silver cups.

It is odd that my parents could arrange things like this ride in a speedboat of all things, yet were unable to get together again. I'm sure Jessie always hoped they would be together again, especially in her last years.

She always said he would send for her at the end. He had done so once when he was arrested by the police, drunk and disorderly in Thornaby, and Mum had gone to the police station and got him out.

I was plonked in the side of this funny little boat with no seat. With a roar of the outboard motor, he set off up and down the river at full speed, about thirty mile per hour. I was scared stiff, hanging on to the side of the boat as it bounced about, yelling my head off, which he didn't seem to notice, perhaps because of the roar of the outboard engine and the slapping of the hull on the water. There were a lot of people lining the bridge watching this demonstration, he was showing off (I don't think he was trying to encourage me to go to sea). It didn't put me off going to sea later in life anyway.

I think I must have disappointed him. Maybe that's why he lost interest in me. He didn't have much idea about getting along with youngsters.

Years later, my mother had tried to get her allowance from my father raised. The maximum was the same as in 1926, so she paid a chap to take her to Glaisdale where father had a house. I went with Mum in the car because I'd never been further than Saltburn and a car ride was a novelty. When we got there, we were about three hundred yards from the terrace of houses, if indeed it was his house. I took a snap with an old box brownie camera I had been given by a sympathetic cousin of my mother, it was a Wednesday.

On the Saturday I cycled over to the business to see my granddad. As I walked in, my brother, who had been brought up by their granny with my brother and sister, saw me and without speaking went smartly into the office, where the great Fred surveyed his pile.

I don't think I'd taken my cycle clips off my trousers when the great man strode out and in his domineering voice asked me what the hell I was doing at Glaisdale. Before I could reply – as if it was any of his business – he told me to bugger off, which says a lot about the man and his character. What a bully! He must have had binoculars to see me, as I was nowhere near his property! I was on a moor road three hundred yards away or more.

I got on my bike and returned home, very depressed. It appeared so final! I didn't see my grandad for a few years after that. I missed the shilling pocket money he gave me every week when I cycled over to see him but more than that, I'd lost my only grandad. Once during the war he had taken me in a car to a paddock where he kept big white goats for milk and, I suppose meat, but I wasn't given any to take home; the war rations were very hard for two people without means to supplement their food supply. Some people caught rabbits, I suppose, but we couldn't even grow a carrot.

I became totally isolated from my father's side of my family. I enjoyed Dorothy's family. In 1954, married and living at No. 34 Newstead Road, I was never told that my granddad was in a nursing home, only a couple of hundred yards from my house.

Sadly, he died there at eighty-four and I never got to see him. My older brother Jack told me he had died and I took my elder brother, Eric, to the funeral, Eric, the eldest, had learning difficulties. Mum said he was too long in the birth and had lacked oxygen. He could read and write and go messages. He was gentle and generally well behaved.

Eric had been taken to live with my mum, with a gratuity of one pound and ten shillings per week.

Eric appears to have been a nuisance in Fred's household after his grandparents died, there was no one to look after him. Fred was perhaps realising what a stable marriage was worth – housekeepers are no substitute. It may have been cheaper to have provided his wife with a home for his family in the first place!

In any case, Eric was company for Mum and it was good for both of them until she couldn't manage the house because of past operations for cancer. This eventually took her strength and with the help of the social services I was able to place Eric at a Roman Catholic home in Chorley, Lancashire, run by the Brothers of Charity, to whom I am very grateful. It was arranged with my father's secretary for the one pound and ten shillings to be sent to them.

When Mum went into a council home in Nunthorpe, we paid the rent on No. 68 Granville Road for a year until she settled in. It took the best part of two weeks to empty the house.

The old piano I gave to the family next door. They had two girls who wanted to learn, so I gave them all Mum's music, too. It was a watershed to me, but I still cherish the memories and often one of Mum's old songs comes into my mind and the words of Nelson Eddy and Jeanette MacDonald singing 'Sweethearts' bring Mum close to me.

When I was sixteen, my ten-shilling-a-week allowance from my father was cut off. Now I had to support myself, earning only twelve and sixpence a week at the shipyard. An apprentice did not get the wage of an errand lad in those days – you were supposed to be imposing on the firm by learning a trade, but they made sure you earned your coppers.

I was sixteen when we got our first wireless set. When I was fourteen, Mum said we could afford to buy a wireless set or an electric Hoover. It was becoming difficult for her to take the hooky mats out in the yard to beat them over the line to clean them. Hooky mats were made on a frame with strips of old clothes pushed through the hessian sacking stretched onto a frame. Later 'up-market' mats were made using different coloured balls of wool, pushed through the sacking into loops in patterns drawn on the hessian (sacking). The loops were then fixed with glue on the back of the mat and the loops cut to make a pile.

Coal fires made a lot of dust and dirt. With the old adage 'What you never have you, never miss' in mind, I decided Mum was more important than a wireless set. Two years later Lily Redman (nee Wardell) a half-cousin to my mum, and her husband Fred, called at our house one afternoon and gave us their old wireless set (there was nothing wrong with it) as they had bought themselves a new one.

It was a nice way to disguise their charity. This Fred was a freemason, as was my father, but he had no charity for his own family, poor rich man!

I was told by a chap I once met: 'What a grand chap your father was: I've seen him put a five pound note on the bar and say "Drinks all round".' This was when five pound notes were white and more than a week's wage for a working man. I thought to myself, tell me about this chap, I don't seem to recognize him.

An antenna led into the house from the previous tenant, when I plugged it in to the wireless and switched on, Churchill was making his famous 1940 speech: 'We will fight them on the beaches'. We certainly lived in interesting times. The Chinese wish 'interesting' times on their enemies. I had my full share!

That old wireless served us for many years, but it never replaced Mum's music on the piano. Without prejudice, I thought she played very well, obviously she had plenty of practice by then. Fred should have given her more time. He missed the best years of her life.

I was in Albert Park, when the sirens sounded at eleven o'clock that first day of the war. Sunday 3rd September 1939. A group of us, all about the same age, had made friends and met regularly in the park on the big green opposite the tennis courts.

We were from all areas of Middlesbrough. Three came from the West Lane area. Others came from Grove Hill. There were about seven of us, sometimes more, boys and girls. We had passed many happy hours that summer doing nothing in particular, chatting, gossiping, larking about. None of us had money. I was given nine pence to go to the cheapest seats in the cinema, up in the 'gods', where the seating was in steep rows high above the rear stalls.

That morning the wail of the siren at eleven o'clock stopped us in our tracks. We stood like rabbits in front of a stoat, expecting bombs to drop any minute as we had seen in Poland on the news reels at the cinema.

'What shall we do?' was voiced by one of the boys. There was no sound of aeroplanes. It was such a beautiful sunny day, it seemed unreal. Someone said quietly: 'We'd better go home.' There was no panic, we all agreed we had better go home, as our parents would be worried for us.

Casually, as we had done many times before we wandered away in the direction of our homes, saying 'Bye!' to one, turning, to repeat it to another, until our voices faded in the distance. I have never seen any of those fleeting friends again since that day. Nothing happened for weeks, but I never ventured into the park again.

I lost my Middlesbrough friends but I still managed to maintain my Hartlepool friends of long standing. A very good friend was Alan Martin, we were friends from the age of five, until he was called up into the army at eighteen. His mother was a lovely person and the family were very kind to me. I was impressed with their family life. It was something I recognised as missing in my life, in my brothers and my sister, too, I suppose.

His father Joe was a rugby football referee. He would take Alan and I to a rugby match he was to referee at, at the Friarage field, near the site of the now-dismantled gun battery. I was very upset to hear by word of mouth from a third party when we were fifteen years old that his father had died. When I eventually called at Alan's they made my condolences easy for me.

With my friendship with the Martin family, I was privileged to see Cliff Harrison, a famous international, play a few games of rugby.

When Hartlepool Rovers won the Cup I was only about five. I witnessed their homecoming with a brass band playing 'We are the Rovers' to a well known hymn tune, leading the team waving from the open top of a bus coming down Middlegate Street to the people lining the pavement.

Alan's older brother became a teacher and later a headmaster. He had two sisters: Margaret, who married well; and Mary, who caused a bit of gossip by her innocent flirting with a handsome church curate.

Only Aunt Jenny could say: 'They are only good friends.' But then again, she would say that about the most torrid affair. She was a gentle kindly person who never raised her voice.

Another perk from my friend was a little job we once did for a relation of the Martins. These relations, the Proud family, had a bakery business and they did the catering for the Floral Ball.

Alan asked me if I wanted to give him a hand to take the cakes from the shop in Northgate to the Borough Hall, where the dance was to take place. We were only kids of fourteen or so. I would do anything legal with Alan.

We went along to the shop early in the evening. The cakes were on heavy wooden trays on a custom-built tricycle. The tricycle had three wheels, two at the front with a wooden box between them about a cubic square yard. The machine was too heavy for us to pedal the thing. So, one either side we pushed it about the half mile upbank to the hall. I remember when we got inside, pausing for breath, the place was beautifully decorated. Hartlepool is very proud of its Borough Hall. It has a wide balcony round three sides of the arena, with coloured lights along the bottom edge. People not dancing could sit there and watch with refreshments from the bar at the rear of the balcony. The reward for this little job was a sixpence, I think, but we didn't get a cake.

Later, at seventeen, we were together one weekend. I had no money, so Alan gave me a ten-shilling note. He did it so naturally it left me without embarrassment. I didn't offer to pay it back, I doubt if I could at the time – but I have repeated his generosity myself since, with other young people in the same fix as I was, which eases my conscience.

Alan eventually married and settled in Hong Kong as a teacher. He played the piano well and in their front room in Rowell Street introduced me to classical music when he played Chopin and pieces by other composers.

Sadly I lost touch with Alan and his family. The difficulty of communication, my living in Middlesbrough, having no telephone in the house and our going different ways led to a gradual parting. I owe him and his happy family a great deal of thanks for showing me the value of a cultured family lifestyle. They will know somehow, they did a good job on me.

CHAPTER TWO – *My later childhood and first job*

I saw Alan only once, many years later, in 1946 after the war, as I walked along the promenade to Dorothy's house near the 'new' pier. He was with an ex-girlfriend and we spoke with difficulty of our current affairs.

He was out of the army and then about to go to university. He did a BSc and moved above my level. He looked older: the smile with the eyes, mouth and dimples was no longer there. Our lives had changed but the childhood we shared would be remembered by us both. It was the only thing we had in common now.

He would remember the summer of 1939, just before the war. Sid Wall made a threesome of us. We met at the Martin's house, changed into our swimming trunks and went down Rowell Street a hundred yards to the beach.

What made this so memorable was that it was high tide at six o'clock in the morning and that was the time we chose to swim. We were in the sea for about five minutes came out, dropped our wet trunks and ran up and down the beach in the buff to get our circulation going. I thought my willy was ruined, it had shrunk so much.

We used the towels we had taken with us to dry our cold stiff bodies, put on coats lent us for the event by Alan's mother and dashed about up the cast-iron stairs from the lower promenade, sixty feet up to street level, then to Alan's home (No.16 Rowell Street) feeling fit and ready for anything.

In Middlesbrough, from about eight or nine years old, I used to go to the nearby Gaumont Cinema on the corner of Southfield Road and Linthorpe road. This had been a rather grand opera house. It was where my father had picked up a barmaid who became his mistress until she died of a brain tumour at forty years of age.

I went to the side door and paid my eight pence for a seat in the upper circle. There were three circles and this was the top one. 'The Gods', we called it.

I went there nearly every week alone and saw many great films. My favourite actor was Spencer Tracy. He was a father figure to me, and always took the part of a kind man who's philosophy set a good example to the young guys.

When I got older, I ventured further afield and went to other cinemas in town, always alone except when there was a film my mum wanted to see. She liked musicals with Gracie Fields or Nelson Eddy and Jeanette MacDonald. Then she bought the music and played it on the piano and we would sing the songs.

I made other friends who, like me, were in reserved occupations, war work. We got together and we enjoyed a restricted social life. Cinemas were closed for a time, then allowed to open when the bombing was re-evaluated. Dance halls had to close at ten p.m. This was relaxed later when the enemy was finding he'd bitten off more than he could chew.

The blackout was a problem. Mum had to buy blackout material to line the curtains. Sticky brown paper tape was stuck across the glass of the windows, supposedly to prevent injury from splinters. To go out at night when there was no moon it was possible to bump into a low kerb or other obstacle, but people became accustomed to the conditions.

Barrage balloons protected important industrial sites. When we got geared up for enemy planes, a field near Brambles Farm was planted with about fifty rocket guns. They were all coordinated to fire at once and make a 'box' of anti-aircraft explosion, covering a large area of the sky. It was a very hostile environment for any aircraft.

I rode home on my bike one night from work during a raid and wondered what the red flashes and tinkling noises were, then I realised it was shrapnel from far-away guns that I couldn't hear. I was wearing my steel helmet but I pedalled to a shop doorway and took cover for a few minutes until the shower was over.

It cheered me greatly to see one of our night fighters chasing a German bomber low over our house along Granville Road, their engine exhausts spitting flames. Before they disappeared over the rooftops, I saw the fighter send a stream of tracer bullets into the bomber. Then I thought of the young German lads so very far from home. I doubted they would see home again, and I felt rather sad for them.

Chapter Three

The apprentice marine engineer

During my first day at the shipyard we were taken by a personnel manager, Captain Tee (ex-army, I suspect), in groups to the various departments: boilermakers, joiners, shipwrights, plumbers, electricians and the engine fitters. That was my goal, to build ships' engines. These were steam engines, which our English teacher Pop Hornsby had taught us the workings of.

The indentures, listing the contract between Smith's Dock Ltd. and the apprentice, had been signed and a big red seal attached, I was given a clock card number, 168.

Now I had a five-year commitment with three nights' evening classes at Constantine College, Middlesbrough, during the winter months. This was made more difficult with the air raids that seemed to take place regularly at dusk.

Captain Tee handed some of us over to the engine shop chargehand, Tommy Urwin, a dapper little chap in a light brown boilersuit and the ubiquitous cap. He had a slight Geordie accent spoken through a full set of white false teeth and big, kindly brown eyes. When he took his cap off he was as bald as a billiard ball and his head was just as white. I'd made a faux pas by at first calling him 'sir'. I think he maybe thought I was being facetious, but looking at my innocent face he, father-like, told me confidentially it was ok just to call him Tommy.

Tommy took us round the machine shop, which was open to the erection shop where the engines were assembled Scores of machines, big and small, were busy turning out parts of engines: connecting rods, piston rods, bits and pieces. We paused at a lathe turning what I thought looked like things familiar to that mentioned by our good old English teacher, Pop Hornsby.

The lathe was about fifteen feet long, with a round piece of steel about two feet six inches in diameter revolving in the jaws of the machine. Long shiny steel curls streamed out four or five feet from the hard tool, biting into the front edge of the material being turned.

The operator said: 'I bet you don't know what these are!' pointing with a grease-stained hand to a couple of finished items lying there waiting to be taken away.

'Well, they look like eccentric sheaves to me,' I said, fifteen years old, full of confidence with the knowledge Pop Hornsby had given me.

Triple expansion steam engines under construction in the engine works at Smith's Dock.

1940 – The HMS Halcyon *left dry dock for active service, returned next morning like this.*

The turner's mouth opened in surprise, the greasy belly of his boilersuit heaving as he laughed and said jokingly to Tommy: 'He's a clever young bugger!' It was very much later I learnt not to be so clever, as it upsets dull people.

I went home full of speculation. My mother had a happy home, but money was tight. I was conscious of my trousers, repaired with patches, sometimes darned, and I kept away from kids who might make fun of me. I would have been in the fashion today.

I enjoyed hearing my mum play the piano and we'd sing all the old songs of the music hall: 'Nellie Dene', 'Just a song at twilight', and so on.

My Mum had loads of music in books and in sheets, they'd be worth a fortune today. I was always happy to be home.

As a youngster I had been in the Cub Scouts at St. Aiden's Church. I went to the church occasionally with a friend of mine, the Stations of the Cross at Easter and such like. Mum wouldn't go – she went to a spiritualist church and I enjoyed going there with her. It had a friendly atmosphere and lovely hymns (I gave the books out). But I wasn't very happy with the Cubs, mainly because I hadn't a dad like the other kids and when it came to going to camp, it cost seven and sixpence and I didn't think Mum could afford it so I dropped out of the Cubs.

I was happier at Hartlepool, anyway! Every holiday, Easter, Whitsuntide, August – weeks galore. But now I was working it was very much curtailed. We worked fifty-six hours a week. Saturday from half past seven until noon. The shipyards gave us one week's holiday – without pay. Half a crown (two shillings and sixpence) was stopped from our wages every week and paid out to us for the holiday week.

A big problem for me was getting out of bed in a morning for work, or even not for work! We had an old alarm clock that was not very accurate. It was out by twenty minutes or so daily, fast or slow! I had taken the back off it a few times, to clean it with a drop of paraffin on a kiddy's paintbrush and adjust the regulator, but the old clock seemed to have a mind of its own. I had relied on the works buzzers for a time check, but now I had a wireless to give me a check, the horror of being late for work still remained with me for six days a week, when I had to be up at six o'clock.

No street houses had central heating in the thirties. The winters were very cold but No. 68 Granville Road was a warm terrace house. We were never cold in that house. Mum had a small gas fire that she burned all night in the kitchen, and with a bit of banking up we sometimes managed to keep the coal fire going until early morning. It could be quickly restored with newspaper and a few sticks of wood. The shovel propped up in front of the fire with a newspaper blocking the air going up the chimney increased the draft through the fire grate. This made the fire glow and increase rapidly. The newspaper became scorched, and if not handled with prompt care, it burst into flames. Some unfortunate folks set the soot in the chimney on fire, often resulting in the fire brigade being called. We had the chimney sweep to put his brush up the chimney regularly so thankfully never had that misfortune.

I returned to the shipyard to start work on a Monday morning at half past seven, to start my apprenticeship. It was about eight miles east of Middlesbrough, on the river bank near the small town of South Bank. I could get there on my bike but in winter I often took the trolley bus. I had a fifteen-minute walk from home to North Ormesby to catch the trolley bus, then arriving at South Bank it was a mile-and-a-half walk to the shipyard gates. The main gate was only opened for motor traffic early in the morning. Men walked through narrow alleyways to where their clock cards were in racks.

The gateman was a nasty piece of work. In a cheap suit, he thought he was a cut above the men clocking on. If the trolly bus was a bit late it was often a race against the clock to get in before the starting time of half past seven.

There stood the important gateman, checking the final minute with his cheap pocket watch in one hand and the narrow entrance gate in the other. Looking at his watch through bottle-bottomed spectacles, when the second hand touched twelve he slammed the gate shut. Even if a chap was only a few feet away after running the last hundred yards, slammed shut! The man was locked out, humiliated to wait outside until eight o'clock to be admitted. His pay would be docked for the half-hour anyway with the time stamped on his clock card. It happened to me a few times, otherwise I enjoyed working there.

On my first day as an apprentice, I walked into the engine erecting shop, it was big enough to house an airship. There were four of us lads, I think: Sid Simpson was one; cheery Harry Almond another.

Tommy quickly went round, setting the lads to work. My first job was to polish engine handrails that were fitted between the cast-iron columns of the open engine. These handrails were forged in the blacksmith's shop from an inch steel bar, covered with thin black scale, a 'lug' forged at each end to fasten them to the engine columns.

We were given an old fourteen-inch flat file and, putting the handrail in a six-inch bench vice, pushed the file back and forth with both hands in a swinging action to cover the roundness of the inch bar of the rail.

It could take all day to do one. Doing this all day, I went home very tired, especially so because we were given old files which were not sharp in the hundreds of small teeth that cut away the hard scale caused by the forging, so we learnt 'stickabillity', slogging on until the final handrail, polished with emery paper, was fitted gleaming to the engine standing in the workshop. Pride in the work was reward enough.

It wasn't long before we realised that some of our handiwork was being sent to the bottom of the sea by the U boats!

We had to go to the blacksmith's shop to collect the handrails. This shop was a big, dark corrugated steel shed was about a hundred feet long, and maybe forty feet wide. Down each side of this black coal-dust floor area were ten hearths with glowing red fires, each reflecting the shadows of the blacksmith and his 'striker' in their leather aprons working at the anvil. Round each hearth was a host of the smithy's tools with a tank of water to quench the work as required.

Some smiths were making handrails for the deck, others chains of different dimensions, steel rings to reeve a rope through, steel wedges, drifts for the platers to drive into a hole in the steel plate to line it up for a bolt – these men could fabricate anything.

In the centre of the building stood six heavy mechanical hammers, which were operated by compressed air. Often we passed a team of men, blacksmiths and strikers reducing a big red hot ingot of steel into some part of a ship.

It was difficult to tear oneself away from the ancient technology that went back to the bronze age: glowing steel, sparks, heat, noise and dust forging something useful from a red-hot lump of metal.

Finding the handrails for our job, we had to tear ourselves away from the interesting spectacle to take them back to the fitting shop, making sure we got the right ones.

Part of the equipment used in drilling metals with a pneumatic drill was called a stand. They came in various lengths. This led to a trick played on a new starter. The young apprentice was asked to go to the store and ask for a long stand. The storeman would know the score and say: 'Okay, son, wait there', then turn and get on with checking his paperwork. After some minutes the lad would tumble to the joke if he was bright enough. Returning to the squad, taking it in good part, he later enjoyed playing the joke on another new boy.

The holiday week was always the third week in July. This was so that maintenance of the services could take place. Cranes were overhauled, air compressors serviced. It generally rained that week.

The two foremen, with black bowler hats and navy blue three-piece suits, were Billie Dixon (related to a past shipyard owner of the River Tees, Railton Dixon) and Tommy Brand.

These were authoritarian figures, with the power to sack a man on the spot, I suppose their job was to co ordinate the materials and so forth. Tommy Brand seemed to be always walking around with a sheaf of papers in his hands, looking worried to death, whereas Billie stalked about to keep people busy. He was 'retired' early because his ideas of constructing the engines caused problems of interchangeability of spare parts, which was not good for His Majesty's ships at sea.

Tommy Brand's brother, Stan, replaced Billie. Stan was a gentleman, easy to talk to and very kind. He broke the dress code of a foreman by wearing a trilby hat instead of the black bowler.

When I had a wheel spindle break with metal fatigue in my Douglas motorbike and unable to find spares, I took the pieces to Stan and within a few hours he had arranged a lathe to make me another one. I don't think he had any children but I would have liked a dad like him.

Now a time-served engineer, working overtime in 1946 on a whale catcher with a Norwegian-designed two-stroke steam engine that Smiths had built, the Fredrikstad Damp Motor, on last-minute jobs, the engine stop-valve was found to be siezed with only hours to go before the ship was to sail on sea trials. Stan asked me to go to the South Bank on my bike and call out a turner to make a replacement part. It was nearly midnight when I called at the turner's house and found lights still on. I knocked at the door, the chap answered and I told him the problem, he was taken aback and said: 'But I'm decorating the living room'.

He considered for a few seconds, and finally said: 'I'll be there in twenty minutes'. I peddled back, relieved to tell Stan the good news. I like to think it wasn't because of the war effort the chap was willing to come in but because it was for Stan.

Sadly, Stan died at the age of fifty-two from a heart attack while cutting his garden hedge. By this time I had 'swallowed the anchor'. Avoiding the shipyard and river to subdue the urge to ship out again, I started work at ICI chemical complex at Wilton.

Stan's funeral coincided with the end of my six-to-two shift. I got to the church in Eston early and sat in a back pew, while the church became full.

The service over, I came out of the church to a vast crowd lining the path three deep on each side to the grave at the back of the church. The whole of Smith's Dock must have been there and probable most of the South Bank community.

Stan Brand was very highly respected and sadly missed. What a pity my father was unable to receive the affection I had for the men who influenced me most. I couldn't hate my father but it was difficult to understand why he at that time obviously hated me.

As time passed, my work as an apprentice had become more skilful. With specially-shaped chisels, forged by our tool smith Billie Atkinson, we cut oilways in the soft white metal bearings, scraping the metal to give clearance for the oil to reach the crown of the bearing. The crown was then bedded in on to the shaft using a thin blue oil to show the high spots. These were scraped carefully away until a satisfactory surface on the bottom third of the bearing was obtained leaving the sides clear to allow oil to get to the bearing surface.

Using short lengths of one-millimetre thin soft lead wire laid on top of the shaft, the bearing was bolting up.

Opening it up again, the thickness of the wire was now squeezed by the top half of the bearing. A micrometer was used to measure the thickness of the lead wire now, to determine the clearance of the bearing: a thousandth-of-an-inch for every inch diameter of the shaft. These bearings were drip fed with oil from mechanical oil boxes with small brass pipes mounted over the engine, for the few who may be interested. These 'open' engines ran at a top speed of 250 revs per minute, throwing excess oil out into the engine room so the oil had to be given with judgement. Sometimes a few drops of water would create an emulsion thus keeping the oil in the bearing longer.

When the engine had run for a few hours, the soft white metal in the bearings developed a glass like hard skin. It was only a few thousandths-of-an-inch thick but with proper lubrication the bearings would last for years. Now who was the clever chap who discovered that, I wonder.

Another of the early jobs Tommy gave me was that of fettling steel castings of big ends, the newly cast steel bearings, later to be lined with white metal. This was then machined to the diameter of the crank shaft before we bedded them in as described above.

The castings had to be ground to bright steel with an air-driven grinder, where the hot white metal was poured in round a mandrel to suit the size of the shaft.

The shipyard only used air-driven hand tools and had big compressors and air tanks that supplied the whole yard with compressed air by through two-inch steel pipes with tapping at intervals to connect various machines, such as a drill, rivet hammer or other machine tool. The grinder created lots of loamy sand dust and breathing masks were unheard of. We wrapped a length of muslin cloth round our faces, but it was expensive stuff, so any old cloth would do! A good cough would produce lots of black phlegm. I still had my tonsils, which may have helped reduce any damage. This was not an apprentice's job but I think there was an emergency of supply or some such thing, war work!

There were one or two little dictators in the shipyard. The time clerk/gateman, with his cheap pocket-watch and suit, was one.

The practice of locking men outside the gate, if a minute or two late, probably began during the serious unemployment of the thirties. In good times, proud craftsmen would not have tolerated it, but shipyards were always a case of feast or famine, subject to world trade and the demand for ships.

Times of depression allowed honest men to be subjected to humiliating treatment. This slamming the gate in a man's face had persisted until the very bad winter of 1943. The UK had some very bad winters during the forties, snow froze twelve inches deep in places on the roads. Men struggled to get to work, they had a base motive – no work, no pay. Mum needed the money, so I was pleased to get there somehow. The better motive was, of course, the war effort.

At mid-morning, men would see where the foreman was, and if all was clear, put a billycan of water onto the near red-hot coke stoves situated round the workshop to heat the place. This was to make a can of tea. There was no morning tea break, but when Stan Brand was made up he pretended not to see cans of water being boiled on the stove. It was embarrassing, because Stan was a good foreman and we didn't want to be disrespectful. But having a bowl of porridge at six thirty in the morning, it was a long time to wait until twelve o'clock for a cup of tea.

Sir Eustace Smith himself had decided that if the men were prepared to walk ten miles to work over snow and ice for the war effort they were worth a bit of consideration! He ordered the gates never to be locked again during working hours. This idea gradually permeated down through the ranks and rather late in the war a ten-minute break time was officially allowed. What a difference it made. I felt able to relax and think about the job more. I felt more comfortable all round.

The cold weather created difficulties fitting out the ships with engines and all the auxiliaries, pumps and electric generators. A frozen crane hook could fracture when loaded so the hook was lowered to the quay and a bit of fire made round it. It wasn't allowed to stand round to warm cold hands, if a foreman came along I suppose he'd think he was losing face. We were obliged to move respectfully away. The winter of 1943 was exceptionally cold with minus degrees centigrade for many days.

I witnessed a shipyard manager called Mr. Campbell, who walked around in the gaffer's bowler hat, kick over a brazier of burning scrap wood of which there was always an abundance. This was because men would warm their hands there and it had three or four tea cans being boiled on it. This attitude was slowly being eroded and eventually the fifteen-minute tea-break was established without any loss of production, it probably improved!

The 'them and us' attitude further eroded when enemy planes flew up the river. This happened a few times. Managers from the office came round the yard with megaphones shouting: 'Take cover'.

On Bank Holiday Monday 3rd August 1942, things were going badly in the war. We were working the holiday. We were working two shifts for a time: six a.m. till two p.m, and two p.m. until ten p.m. I was returning from the store to the workshop when I saw a twin-engine enemy plane come in from the sea low over the river to avoid the barrage balloons. I heard a machine gun, it was slower than I had imagined one would be, tac – tac - tac! I didn't think it would be one of ours, there wasn't any guns of ours on the river to my knowledge, which was a great pity. I dived into a cast-iron cylinder lying outside the workshop for a second or two, but as the engine's noise faded, curiosity asked me where had he gone. It was later that day I heard he'd gone up river and bombed the railway station, which wasn't very clever of the pilot. Seven people were killed, but the Station was up and running again in a couple of days, minus the ornate Victorian cast-iron and glass roof. It would have been more effective to the German war effort if the pilot had sunk a couple of our, near ready-for-sea, Royal Navy corvettes. They were tied up at the fitting-out jetty. The German lads didn't get back home on this occasion. It was recorded they were shot down over the North Yorkshire moors on that occasion.

Steam engines required a lot of water and ships could only carry a limited amount of high-quality water for the boilers. The answer to this problem was found in the early steam ships, the condenser! The steam, after doing any work in the engine or the winches, the steering engine or the cabin radiators was piped back to the engine room. The pipes carrying the used steam were connected to the condenser. It was here the steam condensed on brass tubes, through which cold sea water was pumped by a centrifugal pump. The pure condensed water then was pumped back to the boiler with a high-pressure pump to overcome the boiler pressure of two-hundred-and-fifty pounds per square inch (PSI).

The condenser was bolted directly to the back of the engine to accept the exhaust steam from the low-pressure cylinder, which actually operated on the vacuum created by the condenser.

A job to teach the apprentice teamwork was to assemble a steam condenser. This was a steel vessel about ten feet long, wider at the top where the steam from the main engine came in to condense on the seven hundred or more brass tubes. These tubes were fitted into brass end plates about an inch thick at each end of the steel vessel.

Wherever possible, steam from the boiler was condensed back into water and any leaks quickly sealed. In some parts of the world, water was more expensive than fuel oil.

The tubes were passed through the brass end plates that were drilled and threaded to form glands round the tube ends. One brass end plate was covered with a thick piece of plywood to prevent the tubes moving while the tubes at the other end were packed round with quarter-inch round lamp wick soaked in linseed oil. The apprentices had to make their own tools to stem this wick into the internal threaded glands machined into the brass tube plate. When each gland was tightly packed a brass ferrule was screwed in place to maintain a seal for the steam against the sea-water that went through the tubes. This seal was vital, if the condensed water was contaminated with any mineral impurities, such as salt from the sea water, it could cause serious damage to the boiler.

A team of four boys cleverly selected by Tommy, worked in pairs, an older boy with previous experience and a younger boy in each pair. Each pair would take turns to prepare the lamp wick, cutting it to a suitable length for each tube and soaking the bundles in a can of linseed oil. The other pair packed the glands, fitted the brass ferrules and tightened them, careful not to shear the top of the ferrule. this would make it impossible to remove or tighten if it leaked when tested.

If it did happen that a brittle brass ferrule sheared off, wails of denial arose! Help would be required from a more advanced engine fitter to pick out the broken part of ferrule embedded in the end plate, care taken not to damage the screw thread or furthur surgery would be required. Small picking chisels would be made to suit the job, but time would be wasted!

Each pair of apprentices would probably pack half a row of tubes, then change places with the other pair, until the whole end plate was complete. It took days. The plywood put there to stop the tubes sliding out now was removed and this end was now packed and ferruled up tight.

It was now necessary to test the work for leaks. This was a wet, cold business in winter. All open branches (connections) on the condenser, which in the engine room were connected to pipes carrying exhaust steam, were now blanked off. The condenser was filled with water with a hosepipe. It took a few hours to fill, then the moment of truth! A 'bucket' hand-pump took ages to pump water into the condenser up to about forty-five PSI. The condenser would normally operate at about twenty-five inches of vacuum. Under test it was filled with about five tons of water. Anxious lads waited for the leaks, it could take some time for the leak of water to creep past the badly compressed oil-soaked wick.

The first leak appeared 'It's one of yours,' the innocent party would shout. 'We didn't do that row', would be the reply. A few more would be found so denials were put aside and co-operation was in order to avoid the horror of having to empty the condenser to repack the offending glands, then fill it again and pump it up.

A bit of gentle tightening would generally do the trick, minding that we didn't shear off the ferrule. Discretion and a bit of useful competition to improve one's ability and pride in a good job, well done. Thus working with others was introduced, it was like a great big family. As such, liable to a few rows, but generally happy. I thought so anyway!

Smith's Dock had a work's canteen. I had gone there for a dinner to suppliment our rations at home. The beef was sliced razor-thin, but it included a bit of Yorkshire pudding and mashed potatoes. The gravy was thin too. This helped Mum to feed me, but I wondered what she would have for dinner.

The authorities, aware of the situation, opened British Restaurants in most towns, where a meal was available at a subsidised price. In the summer, during the dinner hour on a fine day, some of us walked from the shipyard the couple of miles to Bennet's corner in South Bank and had a dinner at the British Restaurant there.

I sat with a friend from the workshop and his wife. She was a tracer in the drawing office at Smith's Dock, they came to the British Restaurant to be together, I suppose. His wife could have gone to the Smith's Dock's staff canteen but he would not be considered staff and would have to use the workers' canteen.

Quite a lot of chaps had amusing nick names. An apprentice in my year was called 'Blossom'. His name was Harry Almond, hence almond blossom. He was a lovely lad with rosy cheeks, always a happy face and temperament to match. A machinist nicknamed 'Chocolate' was not so happy. An innocent apprentice who used the name to him would arouse his anger. His name was Huntley, and Huntley and Palmer's made chocolate biscuits. I never knew his first name but had no cause to contact him, thank goodness. I wonder what my nickname might have been.

As if I didn't have enough to do what with building marine engines for the Royal Navy, going to night school to prepare myself for a sea-going engineer's job, now at eighteen years of age, Winston Churchill wanted me to join the Home Guard!

At eighteen I was not only asked to work overtime but every Sunday morning now saw me in khaki uniform with a Lee Enfield .303 rifle, a fourteen-inch bayonet and five rounds of ammunition, only issued for night guard duty and at times of imminent invasion. This was the time of the D-Day landings when German paratroops may have caused a diversion in the North-East.

On two occasions a dispatch rider on a motorcycle knocked us up about one o'clock in the morning to tell me to report to HQ: Bright Street, Middlesbrough. I duly put on my uniform, picked up my rifle from the hall stand and said goodbye to Mum. It didn't occur to me at the time that I might never see her again. I clattered off in my hob-nailed army boots to the headquarters in Bright Street, a sitting duck for any german paratrooper.

We were stood to for many hours. I can't remember how long but it was taken seriously by the 8th Battalion Green Howards Home Guard Commander Captain Lillie, chief librarian of Middlesbrough.

I was in Headquarters Company, one of about a dozen signallers. We were taught Morse Code by lamp and flag up to twelve words a minute, hopefully.

A good job we had been taught by Pop to remember things. We also operated 38 wireless sets strapped to our chest in the field to a 21 set at HQ. This was by voice but we were warned not to say too much because the enemy may be listening – which was more than we could do most of the time!

I think the 38 set had a range of half a mile but according to the manual it was three miles, if the wind was in the right direction – only joking, but the signals were very weak.

I went over to Hartlepool quite often now, just for a couple of hours during the week. One night in 1938, aged 19, I was going back home rather late to get to work the next morning. It was thick fog. Never mind, I thought, it may only be local. I said goodnight to Aunt Jennie, got on the old motorbike and set off. A couple of hundred yards along Northgate, I could hardly see the curb to find my way along the road. I stopped when a policeman asked me how far I was going.

'To Middlesbrough', I replied.

He told me: 'The fog is all over the North'.

I turned back to stay another night with my gentle Aunt. I would stay overnight at Aunt Jennie's whenever I was able to get away from my duties to see Dorothy. In winter, I travelled on the bus but many times on my old push bike, with no gears. It was a shorter distance over the Transporter Bridge, in spite of having to wait for the platform to come over. Murphy's law says it will always be on the opposite side to the one you arrive at. The road from the other side of the river went through marshland salt flats and over Greatham Creek. There were a few houseboats berthed alongside the creek. These and a lonely barrage balloon unit were the only signs of humanity for the seven miles of road.

In the dark of the blackout, I often heard a far-off air raid siren, this would cause several decoy lights to appear on the marshes hoping the enemy planes would be encouraged to drop their bombs there instead of on the town. They were not deceived to the best of my knowledge, thank goodness! The headlamp of my bike had a device made from a discarded tin of fruit with slots cut to allow the light to shine forward but not above where it could be seen by enemy planes.

I was always glad to get to the Transporter. Sometimes if a headwind had delayed me and the last crossing had gone I might be lucky and call over the 'foy' (ferry) boat. The foy boatman would row over. Carrying my bike down the steps to the boat. I was taken across for sixpence, which saved me another five or six miles cycling round the road through Haverton Hill at midnight. Having to be up for work the next morning, I was glad of the service!

The next months passed quickly. The anxious days retreated, and very rarely did the German bombers keep us up at night now. Losses were more frequent for the enemy.

At Brambles Farm, on the outskirts of Midddlesbrough towards the coast, the field of rocket guns would send up a box barrage of fifty rockets at a time diverting the enemy planes. Now we also had night fighters. This was when standing at our front door I saw the night fighter streaming tracer bullets into the poor lads who had dared to annoy us. They fled easterly for the coast, back to the fatherland. Their luck was out that night!

At Smith's Dock, an enemy plane came over very low and hit the wire of a barrage balloon situated outside the shipyard. It crashed on to the railway lines a mile away. I was on two-till-ten shift that day, and it happened about eight o'clock. The sky was lit up with the flames from the plane; its ammunition was banging away for a long time. It gave me no joy. I was only thankful the ammunition and bombs were not being used against us.

The defences in the North-East seemed to be very good, the location may have had something to do with it and the RAF fighters were quickly in the area. The problem was the nights you were expecting a big raid. It was no use staying in bed if you had to get up and go to the air raid shelter.

Our house was near Albert Park. I feel sure enemy planes thought the park lakes were docks. Three or more nights (I wasn't counting) during the early days when Britain stood alone and it looked pretty hopeless, we had sticks of bombs dropped diagonally near our house.

The first time we were bombed it came as a surprise. The first six months of the war we had had a few alarms but no planes, so we ignored the alarms. We heard the plane approaching, then the bombs screaming down. Mum was sewing, I was reading a book. We were shocked, we only had time to lie on the carpeted floor. We just lay there listening to the shrieks of the bombs, four in a row, getting nearer each one, and us both bouncing on the floor with each bang! The smell of soot from the chimney and the soot and dust from the carpet made our eyes water and choked us.

Mum was more prepared for the next bombing. She put a single mattress in the cupboard under the stairs, supposedly the safest place in a house.

We didn't go there until we heard the plane approaching. There seemed to be only the one plane, they were nuisance raids, maybe two or three of them, one at a time keeping us awake all night to reduce our working effort.

I will never forget the screaming of the bombs, they were designed to do just that, then the thump and bounce with each explosion. The mattress now avoided the bouncing and the dust from the home made hooky rugs. We clung to each other desperately. In hindsight this was enlightening since Mum was not demonstrative. I never even got a peck from her many years later when I left home at twenty-three to go whaling.

I think the bombs were in sticks of four. Boom! Boom! Boom! BOOM! They seemed to get closer with each bang.

Mum and I had been weary of trailing a few streets away to the part-built Co-op Emporium on Linthorpe Road, to shelter in the basement there, and bed down on the concrete floor of the unfinished building. Mum and I carried cushions, blankets and a thermos of tea always ready for the air raid siren.

Air raid shelters were built in our road, but brick and concrete again, and not comfortable. We became bolder and when the air raid siren sounded we stayed in our beds, our confidence was rewarded very few enemy planes arrived. Brick air raid shelters were cold and damp with a six-inch concrete roof. Any improvement being we would not have to be dug out from a direct hit. We only used them a few times, by now Adolf had bitten off more than he could chew by invading Russia and couldn't spare the planes to bother us.

One night we were caught on the garden path by a bomb before we got into the shelter, it destroyed a house about 100 yards away, the dust and cordite hit our faces and hair. Mum was more upset when windows were broken and soot fell down the chimney, she was a very stoic lady without self pity. The curtains were torn just a little. Well she'd seen it all before in the first war at Hartlepool with the bombardment by German battleships.

My apprenticeship now extended to installing engines in the ships' hulls. The engine was partly dismantled in the erection shop. It was taken by rail, pulled on a wagon by the shipyard railway tank engine, to the fitting out quay. The bedplate with the crankshaft and connecting rods were lowered into the hull with a travelling tower crane. When it was near its final position, chain blocks secured it and held the floating hull steady. It was necessary to consider the tide, if it was rising it would be necessary to raise the bedplate until we had it in the correct position.

Hand signals were given from the engine room to the deck and from the deck to the driver of the crane some fifty feet up. No mobile phones in those days!

The cylinders were lowered on to the engine now. The next weeks were spent connecting up the engine and fitting out the whole ship.

The work was a bit precarious but I never felt in any danger. We were brought up to be aware of the hazards and concentrate on the job. To look out for ourselves.

On 22nd June 1940, a corvette built for the Free French Navy, La Bastiaise, steamed out on sea trials with its French crew and twelve men from Smith's Dock. Enemy planes had dropped mines near the river mouth and the corvette was sunk with a loss of many men, including the twelve from Smith's Docks and five contractors.

It was believed this was one of the first magnetic mines laid on the sea bed.

CHAPTER THREE – *The apprentice marine engineer*

The conventional mine required a heavy anchor, the magnetic mine was more suited to aircraft delivery. It would explode as the metal ship approached.

This device sank other vessels in coastal waters until a means of detonating them safely was worked out.

The apprentice who survived told me it blew the bow off the ship as she approached the mouth of the river. This older apprentice, Raymond Renwick, said he was in the tail end propellor shaft compartment when the explosion took place. He managed to get up a vertical ladder and over the side before the ship plunged to the sea bed.

Ray was in the sea with Alex Henderson, an elderly engineer, but Alex had told him he couldn't keep up and drowned before a boat came to pick up survivors. A favourite old friend of mine, Billie Pringle, didn't get out of the engine room, He was a lovely man. He told me that as a boy he remembered when it was possible at low tide to ride across the river mouth on horse back.

Many years later, I read in *The History of Middlesbrough* by William Lillie, head librarian, records of the river in 1852 and 1860. The depth of the river at low water was two-and-a-half feet and three-and-a-half feet respectivly.

By 1960, due to banking up the sides of the river with waste slag from the steel works, the depth at low tide was forty feet.

Billie Pringle was always quietly humming some hymn or other, he worked from a wooden cabin on the dock side and we apprentices loved to pop in for a gossip and hear his tales of the sea. On a cold day it was a warm oasis, he had a little pot-bellied stove in his cabin, and we would gaze at all the ships' tackle hanging around the place. There were other places like this. One was a small boiler house, who's attendant had a jack russell dog and was delighted to show off its tricks: a cigarette and match placed on a low stool and the dog taken outside, when asked to bring the cigarette the dog did so without wetting it, and then the match. All done by love and kindness!

Sadly, I learned that Ray Renwick was killed when later serving as an engineer in the Merchant Navy, his ship was sunk by enemy action.

My mother rarely cried, one such occasion was when I came home from work one Saturday.

'What's the matter, Mum?" I asked.

'That's our meat ration for the week', she sniffed.

I looked at the table, there laid on the opened wrapping paper was a piece of skin the size and shape of a small hand, one half of which had half-an-inch of beef on it.

I still had my coat on, sixteen years of age. I picked up the ration of meat and walked round to the butcher's shop. There was a couple of women in the shop, I waited until they had been served then respectfully addressed the butcher, Mr Longstaff. He was a tall, lean man with sharp features, with dark greasy hair and narrowed eyes, not a jovial type.

'This is our ration for the week', I said. 'Could you include it with a larger family's ration and give us something else.'

He looked at me with a steady gaze for a tense moment, lips pursed. I feared the worse!

'Yes son, I can,' he said, purposefully, and he wrapped up a nice bit of lean meat, perhaps a bit more than our ration. I distinctly remember he didn't weigh it!

It must be my brown eyes. I don't think he liked my mum though! The feeling was mutual!

The only other occasion I found Mum crying was when she came in from shopping, standing in queues to get what food she could, this was 1942 and the U-boats were winning.

'What's wrong, Mum?' The desperation in her voice evoked disaster.

'I haven't been able to get onions anywhere! How can I make a meal without an onion?' I must say she loved her grub!

I was relieved it was nothing more serious, but it made me realised how bad the war in the Atlantic was going. In the shipyard we all felt it! There was an air of desperation about the place, nothing but bad news.

The work was very manual. Big nuts and bolts required seven-pound hammers to tighten up the big spanners. Steel levers, heated to expand them a few thousandths-of-an-inch, had to be forced on to six-inch shafts, then hammered home with twenty-eight-pound hammers. Three of these levers were fitted to the shaft that moved the engine valve gear from ahead to astern. They hadn't to fail!

We made the ships as good as we could for the men who sailed in them.

The four dry docks were always full of ships damaged by torpedoes or mines which had managed to stay afloat, some with holes big enough to drive a double decker bus through. In some instances patched up with planks of wood and cement to get back for repair. It was very grim!

It's all on record, I suppose, but sadly a generation passes and people forget. The shipyards are no more. Oil rigs are the business now but you can't sail the seas in them to bring supplies and they cannot defend our island.

We were saved by the skin of our teeth by the United States of America.

I will never forget the help America gave us. Food, including spam, the sweetest of meats at that time, and tea with strange big tea leaves.

Not forgetting the munitions and ships, of course. An old American destroyer with four funnels arrived at Smith's Dock, one of fifty they had given us in exchange for the use of some bases.

It was refurbished and put into service. Even with this assistance it seemed a long time before the threat of defeat eventually faded.

CHAPTER THREE – *The apprentice marine engineer*

Due to the stubborn courage and words of Winston Churchhill we pulled through. People who now write of his faults cannot have experienced the times of his heroic inspiration.

When the war ended the whole of Europe and Russia were badly in need of food, millions of people had been displaced, crops and cattle destroyed.

Something had to be done to improve the situation. Whaling had gone on all over the northern hemisphere since man had created the means to capture this feast from the sea.

In the sixteenth century most European countries with a seaboard had sent ships north to this dangerous business and competition was great. Spanish ships were deployed near Newfoundland and other countries soon joined in.

The Dutch were prominent, with the British not so successful because of lack of experience. It was a long, slow learning curve. Like marriage, the whaling business was not to be entered into lightly. It was labour intensive, companies went bankrupt and ships were lost. But gradually, over the years, a steady supply of the valuable products, particularly the oil, were procured.

With the advent of the steam engine, ships could now go to the more profitable Antarctic seas. The British had a head-start with steam and territorial rights on South Georgia.

Whaling

Whaling in the North had expired in the 1850s when the 'right' whales had been so reduced in number as to make it unprofitable.

With the advent of the steam whale catcher in 1910 from bases in South Georgia, the bigger whales were caught, but by the late twenties, a world-wide depression reduced the price of whale oil from forty-eight pounds per ton to eighteen pounds per ton and the whaling companies were struggling to survive, even though whale oil was required to manufacture glycerine. Soon, with Germany re-arming, Britain would need the whale oil in large quantities to make explosives.

After the war, with Europe devastated, Britain was now bankrupt. She needed to buy food from within the Sterling area. Meat was rationed for a further eight years, until 1953.

A catch crop was the giant whales that had multiplied during the war years. The government gave license to the whaling companies to build custom-designed whale factory ships and whale catchers.

Here on the River Tees, Furnace's Shipyard built two factory ships for Salvesen Co. They were the *Southern Venturer* and *Southern Harvester*. Others were built for Norwegian owners.

Smith's Dock built the whale catcher vessels. Roughly, eight to ten were required for each factory.

Now that the need for corvettes had ceased, thousands of men who other wise may have been unemployed were employed building the whaling fleets.

Without this work, the economy would have caused serious hardship for the families of Teesside.

There was no demand for merchant ships. America had churned out Liberty ships by the dozen to send supplies to Europe.

The original whale catcher was designed by Sir William Reed (a director of Smith's Dock). They were of five-hundred tons displacement with a two-thousand-horsepower, triple-expansion steam engine, capable of sixteen knots (about twenty miles per hour). Even then, a whale could outrun a whale catcher.

A whale catcher carried a crew of sixteen men, one of whom was a teenage cabin boy. His duties were to assist the cook, as well as general duties.

The larger corvette had been designed from the whale catcher. Like the catcher, it was a good sea boat in heavy weather, but very uncomfortable!

1947 – cruising among small bergs. After dark we drifted among bergs to continue the hunt. In storms we lay on the lee side of a berg for comfort.

Approaching Leith Harbour, South Georgia, towing two whales by the tail from bollards on the deck.

Originally, it was designed for coastal command and anti-submarine service. It carried a crew of about ninety men to man the guns and anti-submarine depth charge gear.

German submarines were mainly deployed in the Atlantic. It was soon apparent that the corvettes were better used on convoy-escort duty but they lacked the range for effective long periods in Atlantic service. Later this led to the design of a bigger vessel, the twin-screw frigate, which was faster with longer range (more engines required!) This frigate was the 'river class'.

The first flower-class corvette built was called HMS *Pansy* – someone in the Admiralty had a sense of humour. I'll bet it was Churchill! The Germans were calling their U-boats aggresive names like *'Wolf'* – fancy being sunk by a boat called *Pansy*, *Hyacinth*, *Daffodil* or *Violet*!

The corvette designs were sent to other shipyards as far away as Canada and engines were even built by railway locomotive shops, there to win the war of the Atlantic.

Two of these engines were sent to Smith's Dock to supplement our output. They were okay, but we had to adjust the bearing clearances. I still remember the figure: one thousandths-of-an-inch for every inch of shaft thickness. The bearings were not pressure-fed with oil. A drip-feed system was very hit and miss!

I had been attending evening classes at Constantine College each winter for about four years. It was difficult to achieve any progress because of the war.

It did teach me something – there was a lot to know! And if I failed an examination, it didn't mean I hadn't learnt anything – it just meant that I couldn't remember it at the time! My head was full of marine engines, the Home Guard, Morse code, motorbikes, Dorothy and food, probably not in that order.

The evening class teachers were now old men with old ideas. The young men were away at the war. Engineering drawing was the main exercise and precise lines projected through all sorts of sections bored me stiff.

I wanted to be a hands-on engineer. I should have been taught about boilers and such. Draughtsmanship was a specialist subject.

Maths was another problem. I knew I had a problem with equations but didn't know what it was. The teacher knew I had a problem but didn't know how to enlighten me. I solved it in later life when my son was doing maths. He told me the secret: BODMAS (brackets off, division, multiplication, addition and subtraction). I must have missed it one night during an air raid.

I kept my books handy and knew where to look for the information. This attitude has been my modus operandi through life. The important things I remembered without difficulty. My wife wouldn't agree!

Now in 1945, with the war over, the priority was building whale catcher

1917   Commander Christiansen, the Gunner, a tense moment, an accurate shot necessary.

1928 – Smith's Dock shipyard. **Southern Empress** *whale factory alongside with five whale catchers. The large ship in dry dock No. 14 is whale factory ship* **Pelagos**.

vessels! I was employed fitting the engines in the ships. I was no longer an apprentice and keen to make some money.

I had been travelling to Hartlepool most weekends to see friends made during my early years. I had made other friends now on the regular visits. The bed I had slept my first six years in was always made up for me at my granny's. My maiden aunt Jennie ran the house and cared for Granny. My motive for these visits was the Saturday-night dance at the Borough Hall, just a few yards from the house.

I had learnt to dance at church-hall dances from the age of sixteen. The girls in the time office at Smith's Dock asked us to go to these dances and gave us lessons. In truth, to say the girls dragged us round the floor to music is a better description. The dances were excellent ways to learn the social graces, and they were well attended with a mix of ages from late thirties to us new starters of sixteen.

There was an established, unofficial, 'pecking order' from the old to the young, which was rarely invoked. There had to be no rowdiness or unbecoming behaviour, and the tendency was for the sixteen-year-olds to emulate the conduct and technique of the twenty-year-olds.

Eventually we reached a state of confidence to invite a girl we fancied to dance. As friendships with the girls advanced, they would teach us some of the 'old-fashioned' dances with fancy names such as the 'St. Bernhard waltz' and the 'Valieta. They were very happy times in very uncertain days.

The Borough Hall at Hartlepool was a major move up from church hall standards, although the same mix of dancers applied. It was here I was told by a mutual friend that Dorothy Fell would like to dance with me!

I remembered the first time I saw her was when I was five years old. My Aunt Jenny took me to a Church bazaar at St. Mark's. Dorothy, nearly four years old, presented a bouquet to the lady declaring the bazaar open. The enchantment was still there.

The thought of coming from a broken home in those days gave me problems where girls were concerned. It was with trepidation I went over to Dorothy and asked her for the dance the band was about to play. It seemed to go well. We had the 'last waltz' together and that gave me the privilege of asking her if I could walk her home.

Her answer, with a smile, was yes. That was May 1943. Everyone's favourite music at that time was 'Moonlight and Roses' and even today it evokes happy memories.

It was a pleasant walk to Dorothy's house from the Borough Hall. We made it many times over the next four years.

It was especially romantic if the moon was shining across the sea. We came out of the Borough Hall, crossed the road, then walked a few yards more through the car park to the fourteenth century town wall.

We would lean on the parapet and look over the once-busy little harbour, listening to the sea lapping on the beach. It was then a quiet stroll past the 'old' pier (the pilot pier) along the promenade as far as the 'new' pier with the lights of Seaton Carew and Redcar over the bay.

Turning left up Rowell Street, our romantic walk ended at the end house on the right, No. 1. We were together for sixty-three years and married for fifty-eight of them.

I remember the year well because it was my twentieth birthday in June and Dorothy bought me a dark red paisly tie as a present and we had only been going together for a month. I realised if I was to marry the girl I needed to do something desperate to make some money. I could see no other way to achieve it!

The work in the shipyard was hard and even with overtime left nothing much over at the end of the week.

I'd try to go whaling!

Mr Turner, a manager of Smith's Dock, had left and gone as an engineering superintendent for the Christian Salveson Whaling Company of Leith, Scotland – an Anglo Norwegian Company. I was twenty-three years of age in June 1947, when I approached the superintendent and asked if there was any vacancies for engineers on the whale catchers.

He seemed quite keen to help me and asked for my name and address and said I would hear from the company.

A few weeks later a letter arrived asking me to present myself to the Salveson Company offices, 22 Bernard Street, Leith, Edinburgh for an interview.

The end of the war had brought some improvement to our lives, but not much. The country was bankrupt, and food was still rationed because Britain couldn't afford to buy food from abroad and was having to send food over to Germany, which was a bit ironic. The rations were now just adequate; poor old Mum could get a few onions for the pot.

I had bought my first motorbike second-hand from a guy in Newcastle which a cousin of Mum's had found for me. I paid fifteen pounds for it, a Douglas with a twin-cylinder engine (fore and aft, not across the bike). It was a 1936 model, with an open flywheel and a three-speed gear change lever on the petrol tank. It had seen better days.

I went to Newcastle to collect it and the vendor showed me how to start it. After a ride up and down his street I drove it – careered more like – round to Mum's cousin's house.

I arrived at Charlie Watt's house (this cousin's husband). It was a lot different to a bicycle but I was determined to master it, as a cowboy would break in a horse. The Douglas motorbike had a long wheel-base, so it steered like a horse: very reluctantly. I had difficulty judging my direction at the speed produced by the 350cc engine, so different to my old push bike.

I had been given a pair of goggles and flying helmet – pilot, for the use of. It had a thin leather strap that fastened under my chin and, with my old raincoat buttoned up to my neck, I set off for Middlesbrough, fifty miles away.

I skated through the city streets, avoiding trams and horse-drawn carts with abandon. The front halves of my coat blown away, leaving my legs and nether regions open to the cold North-Eastern elements. I was numb down there.

A hair-raising development occurred crossing the high-level bridge over the River Tyne. I entered the box girder bridge, noting the two sets of tram lines, then unwisely proceeded to overtake the tram ahead of me. The tramlines were set in wooden blocks, which were greasy and cambered between each set of rails.

As I came alongside the tram, I saw another tram ahead of me, entering the bridge from the south side. I had to avoid being caught between two trams, which would have been a disaster since the Douglas's handlebars were wider than two trams passing each other. The oncoming tram driver sounded his horn furiously. But I had no chance of getting back behind the tram I was overtaking. There was only one option left to me: by increasing my speed, I just managed to slip in front of the tram to my left before the other tram came level. I hadn't seen it approaching because of the bend in the road, 'skating along' would be the right term for it. On the greasy wooden blocks I slipped past the tram as the bike fortunately skidded the correct way to avoid certain death. I think it was an old but intelligent machine and in my years of dealing with machines I believe that some are more intelligent than others. Either that or my spirit friends are taking care of me, most likely!

After a few weeks, I found a major problem with the Douglas. The engine rattled like a bag of hammers. The former owner had used badly fitting tools that had damaged the nuts and screw heads. The bolts holding the valve cam wheels were not properly secured and had loosened, causing irreparable damage. The chap responsible had used blunt screwdrivers as well as badly fitted spanners, which created difficulty dismantling the engine.

Spare parts were unobtainable, partly due to the war. My brother Jack, who was working at Smith's Dock at the time, came to the rescue. After a couple of days of making enquiries, he was able to tell me where there was an old Douglas engine at a garage near my home. I went round and paid two pounds and ten shillings for this but had no means of getting it round to Granville Road. It was only a couple of hundred yards so they kindly delivered it for me. I was able to strip this engine down for the parts I required.

I was back to the old push bike that Granddad had given me for my thirteenth birthday. I had removed the engine from the Douglas and stripped it down on the kitchen table. Mum was very good about it. She didn't complain about the smell of dirty engine oil. I think she enjoyed the fact that we were starting again where Fred and she had once been.

Eventually I got the best half of one engine fitted to half of the other and still had a few bits over.

I used it for a while, going back and forwards to Hartlepool, but now with a lot more knowledge, decided it was time to move upmarket. I sold it for forty-five pounds soon after making it just about roadworthy and bought a 1939 250cc BSA. I would have liked the new Matchless with teledraulic forks but it was ninety-five pounds with a long waiting list and beyond my dreams.

I had to use the bicycle some of the time because the petrol ration wasn't enough to motor every day to work, and I also wanted petrol to go to Hartlepool at weekends.

When the invitation came from Salveson Co. of Leith, Edinburgh, for an interview as a Third Engineer Whale Catcher, it was the BSA that took me there: one hundred and fifty miles of ancient Great North Road, which my great-grandfather, Francis, may have done many times as a coach driver.

The interview wouldn't take long, I hoped. I set off at five in the morning and, avoiding Princess Street by approaching from the east, arrived at Salveson's offices about eleven o'clock, a seven-hour journey.

On the way, passing through Newcastle and Morpeth at about nine o'clock, I was ready for a break. I saw an isolated pub just over the border. I wonder if I can get some breakfast there, I thought. The morning was beautiful, with blue sky and no wind. There was nothing on the road as I chugged over to the door of the pub. I dismounted and pulled the bike up on to its stand and walked stiffly to the pub door.

The landlord was sat at a barstool in his empty pub, gazing out of the door, admiring the sunny morn as I walked in. He must have wondered what I was doing walking into his pub at that time of the morning and was taken unawares when I asked if he could give me something to eat.

I told him where I had come from and where I was going. 'Ayyyye,' he said, while he considered how to satisfy a genuine traveller. He hailed his good lady in the back room: 'Can ye make this laddie a sandwich?' – 'Will that de yeh?' he said to me as an afterthought.

'Aye! Champion!' I replied in the vernacular of my native Teesside.

I sat at a small, round table on a cast-iron pedestal near the open door. The landlord's good lady brought me a thick beef sandwich. 'What will ye have tae drink?' said the landlord from his barstool as he looked on approvingly. I considered for a moment and decided that, thirsty as I was, a pint wouldn't go far wrong. This would have been illegal at nine o'clock in the morning in

74

England. But I needed to restore myself to my personal comforts.

After having eaten and feeling thus restored I paid the man, then as I was fastening my coat he put a glass of whisky in front of me. 'On the house,' he said benevolently and insisted I drink it.

It may have been a double or an unfamiliar Scottish measure! I was quite a bit tiddly for a mile or two. I kept giggling and running into the grass verge but it put some warmth into me and I soon recovered. A good job the A1 was quiet! It was just a country road in those days and I had no problem following the route as it turned west to Musselburgh then along the Firth of Forth to Leith. 22 Bernard Street. I got off the bike and pulled it up on the rear stand. My legs were numb with cold again, very stiff as I walked like a cowboy to Salvesen's office doors.

Mr Turner saw me straight away. He seemed interested in my mode of transport and kindly gave me a seat. The interview was a formality. I can't remember much about it. I did sign some papers and was then 'on the books'. The pay was twenty-eight pounds per month with bonuses based on the catch: five shillings for each whale and ten ore (a tenth of a Norwegian krona – about an English penny) per barrel. About fifty to seventy barrels of oil was extracted from each whale. Nothing was wasted.

I got back on the bike and retraced my route south. The bike frame and petrol tank were quite warm from the engine's hours of running. I was feeling cold and tired by the time I got to Newcastle. Not being suitably dressed for such a journey (I only had some thin waterproof legging over my trousers), I decided to call at my Mum's cousin Lily Watt and her husband Charlie who lived then in Newcastle and she kindly fed me and put me up for the night.

I had told Mum I might call at the Watt's on the way home but there was no way of confirming it (we didn't have telephones) so Mum would have only eventually realised I wouldn't be home until the next day. How good parents suffer when their chickens leave the nest!

Now I was prepared to join the whaling fleet going to the Antarctic to make my fortune. In September of 1947, I was instructed by Salvesen head office in Leith to join a whale catcher vessel *Southern Truce* at Smith's Dock. *Southern Truce* had been there for a refit. She was built in 1934. I was only aboard for transport to Leith Harbour, South Georgia. It was very convenient for me living so near.

It was unusual to service catchers at Smith's now because the catchers were serviced during the closed season winter months at the factory workshops on the island of South Georgia There was a dry dock and every facility at the whaling station. It was early after the war, whale catchers were being converted back from Submarine chasers to whale catchers, men were being released from the navy to take up civilian jobs, whaling was not popular for men who had been away for long periods during the war.

I was posted on *Southern Truce* as a supernumery (not a member of the crew) to join a more modern whaler named *Sondra* at South Georgia built in 1937. With the crew I had signed on *Southern Truce* at a shipping agent's office (Cairns Noble) in Middlesbrough.

I arrived at Smith's Dock by taxi (expenses paid – how different from the early days!). I walked to the engine erection shop and had a last word with my 'old' chargehand Tommy, and one or two other well wishers, then went over to the jetty where *Southern Truce* was lying.

I went aboard a couple of hours before she sailed, stowed my gear and was on deck as the engine room telegraph rang standby. The deck stirred as the engineer on watch answered the command.

The *Southern Truce* looked very small to be going on such a long journey. From the bridge came the command: 'Cast off forrard', then the order to 'Cast off aft'. It appeared a nice mid-September day. Finally, 'Let go the spring' (a wire rope from amid ships to a bollard forw'd on the jetty that allows the ship's bow to swing away from the jetty).

From the north-west, a squall with sleet and hail blew up for a few minutes. The few workers standing on the jetty to see us off scurried away for cover, It did nothing for the trepidation I was already experiencing. It occurred to me that I was going into the unknown for nine months! Eight thousand miles away down the Atlantic Ocean to the ice-covered island of South Georgia. What was I getting myself into? I didn't know anyone who could tell me; I was only doing what many fellows had done before. The telegraph rang again and *Southern Truce* moved ahead down river to the sea.

Before I had signed up Dorothy and I had decided to be married on my return. Communication was not going to be easy, letters took weeks as there was only two or three ships calling at the island whaling factory during the season.

Half a dozen letters arrived at once. Telegrams could be sent but it may take a few days before my catcher came in for bunkers (fuel, water and stores) every ten days or so when I would be able to read a telegram.

Now I had to put my doubts and thoughts behind me, *Southern Truce* was steaming steadily past the riverside where I had worked for eight years, going home to Mum each night. She was on her own now. I knew she was not a 'clinging' mother but I felt sad at leaving her after all we had been through. I had made her an allowance from my pay, a pound per week. I was relying on the bonus paid for the whales caught to make it all worth while.

There was work to do! Stores were still stacked on deck waiting to be stowed away, mainly engine room spares, cleaning materials, small tools and so on. The chief engineer detailed me to help stow them away so there was no time for more contemplation.

CHAPTER FOUR – *Whaling*

Before we had got half the gear stored away in the steering flat (the small after space where the steam steering engine was housed) the *Southern Truce* was out in the open sea, bucking about like a young horse!

Making matters worse, the skylight had been left open and the sea was now pouring into the flat. A whale catcher is definitely a wet ship! The door of the flat was designed with a high sill to stop the sea from getting in. The sea having found another way in, could not now escape, and had to be bailed out. The skylight was slammed shut in record time but the sea sloshed around with the roll of the boat up to our ankles at times and anything loose flew about until eventually feeling a bit sick and wishing I'd never joined, order was restored and another lesson was learnt, batten down the hatches before leaving port.

The chief engineer should have seen to securing engineering spaces for sea and was probably a bit embarrassed to ask me to help with this job. I was in my home port and as a supernumary I hadn't expected to have to 'turn to', as the crew had been aboard for days. The stores should have been stowed and all shipshape. I had only joined that afternoon. I found later that most ships depart like this, always a last-minute delivery and scramble!

Passing down the east coast was quite nostalgic. I recognised Whitby and Scarborough, as it got dark. When next I looked, the coast became just winking lights. It occurred to me that those lights would be burning every night that I was away, they looked so homely and constant. Why did my life require me to go to the end of the Atlantic Ocean? I knew the answer, of course. I couldn't ask Dorothy to marry me without the means to provide a home for her. Money!

We slipped by on the now calm sea and I went below to write to Mum and Dorothy, letters that were to be given to the coastal pilot to post, who would leave us at Dover. I handed the letters over to him, that was it! British seamen had been doing this for hundreds of years. This is what had made Britain Great!

We passed through the English Channel – it didn't seem very busy as far as I can remember, however crossing the Bay of Biscay things really got lively. *Southern Truce* bounced about like the biggest fairground ride imaginable. Topside, the lower deck, only three feet clear of the sea was impassable and to get forward it was necessary to use the upper deck, to get to the mess room amidships under the bridge.

I was berthed up forward, being aboard only for transport to South Georgia whaling station. Normally the engineer's cabins were aft on the starboard side. Here on *Southern Truce* I was up forr'ard in the top bunk in a two-berth stoker's cabin on the port side (left facing the front), there was only room to walk into the cabin and get into the bunks, lockers were fitted on the narrow forward bulkhead.

Being in the bow of the ship in heavy weather as the bow fell into the trough of a wave, about twenty feet or more, my body, laid in the bunk floated weightless. Then as the ship lifted up the next wave, which it was designed to do with its flared bow, my body weight increased several Gs, somehow I managed to sleep, but with the constant hanging on and staggering about all day on a heaving deck, it wasn't that difficult!

I had some experience of small ships at sea with trips on the wooden steam drifter *FisherQueen*, which my Uncle Arthur had arranged for me. The shallow North Sea had been the worst seas I had experienced for a small vessel. The whaler beats them all, designed for manoeuvrability, with a flared bow to lift the gunner over a heavy sea, this was to be my home for the next nine months.

Southern Truce passed through the Bay of Biscay and headed south east and after many days of more moderate sea, we arrived at Aruba, a small island off the tropical north coast of South America.

We only stayed here for four hours, to top up our fuel, water and fresh stores. A few bum boats came alongside. The ship was moored offshore. I had been warned of boarders who might steal anything they could lay their hands on. Our cabin door was locked. I made a trade with cartons of one thousand cigarettes, costing one pound and ten shillings, for a couple of bottles of brandy. I thought it might come in useful as medicine if things got a bit rough.

I wanted to buy a wristwatch, too, as the watch I had was not very reliable, a spare would be handy to have. As I lent over the side to examine a watch the seller was offering the local police guard on deck stopped me and said I should buy his watch. I looked at his mean swarthy face and the heavy revolver at his waist It seemed to be a good idea. He wanted sterling for it, not cigarettes, but at one pound and ten shillings, it didn't seem a bad deal and it hung on a nail above my bunk for the whole of the season. I never wore it during the time, I always knew what time it was. Eight bells and I was on watch.

With sixteen men aboard (maybe seventeen with me), the cabin boy, a lad of sixteen, seemed to be constantly with the skipper. Maybe he was family, a son or nephew.

The skipper (gunner) turned out to be an alcoholic. I only saw him once in the thirty-day trip, I saw him looking over the bridge, a horrible sight. His face glowing red, eyes swollen, unshaven and hardly recognisable from the chap I had seen when we set off. There were a few chaps like this in the whaling fraternity who were 'covered' by the other officers. Frantic efforts were made to sober them up before coming into contact with higher management. Misplaced loyalty, I thought, but they probably knew their families and had sympathy for them. It probably happens in most shipping companies.

Whale catchers were not designed for long voyages or hot weather, and we were sailing eight thousand miles to South Georgia.

CHAPTER FOUR – *Whaling*

We travelled at an economic speed of ten knots, the engine just turning gently. This extended the ship's range with care. Careless navigation or bad weather would have made it precarious, it takes more fuel to push through heavy seas. As we progressed south into the tropics the skies cleared and I enjoyed glorious days of sunshine on deck off watch.

At Aruba, off the coast of Venezuela, as well as fuel for the ship, fuel for the crew came aboard in the shape of a very lively small black hairy pig. The pig was berthed in the low wooden box that normally held harpoons on deck and it was fed with porridge, which we had every morning for breakfast – until we were to have pork for dinner. I fed the fish with my porridge every morning for quite a few days but I always came back for my fried smoked bacon and was delighted the first morning when the sweet, milky porridge stayed down!

I was getting used to the food, and the motion of the ship didn't bother me, as the sea was fairly calm. *Southern Truce* was built in 1934 and did not have a freezer or fridge aboard. The meat was salt beef in the port barrel or salt pork in the starboard barrel, there were tins of meat balls and corned beef but not often, probably subject to budget. Fish was of the salted variety and came dry, in wooden boxes. When the lid was broken open, it was difficult to tell which was fish and which was the lid. Salt fish of this kind looked like broken floor boards and was soaked overnight and made into fish soup, we ran out of bread after two days and it was replaced by ship's biscuits. They were okay, about three inches square, not too hard. I had good teeth in any case!

As well as the little pig, about a dozen hens came aboard in open crates. The sailors used net cord to rig up a bit of a hen coop round the after steering binnacle.

The pig was first to be sacrificed. He wasn't enjoying the trip on the fore deck anyway. The Norwegian sailors despatched him smartly and everyone not on duty or asleep helped with the ritual. A couple of empty tins were found (the best tools to scrape his hair off, in a bath of hot water) and he was prepared for the pot, the offal being thrown over the side. My Mum would have been glad of that, kidneys and heart, what a waste.

I don't remember any food being roasted. Stew was the plat du jour but it didn't last long when shared among the sixteen crew, Although berthed forrard, I ate with the officers. Sunday's main meal was smorgasbord. It being the cook's day off, he set the table with slices of, to me at that time, funny big sausage, goat's cheese and other continental things which, after the war didn't bother me, I could eat anything and enjoyed what I ate. The goat's cheese required me to have an education in the taking. I took a ship's biscuit and cut a chunk of cheese from the piece, I sensed immediately I had made a mistake! The Mate very kindly showed me how to cut a thin slice from across the top of the piece, wafer-thin. 'That way you will get the most flavour,' he said. He was right. It wasn't rationed, I could take as many slices as I wanted, but it was nice and strong, so a couple satisfied me.

A few days later the hens were dispatched. I was asked by the mate (chief officer) to give a hand and after he chopped the heads off I had to catch the headless bodies as they ran a yard or so flapping and kicking in danger of going over the side. I managed to get out of plucking them. Chicken stew was the result of our labours. It didn't have much flavour. Mum would have put an onion in it.

Fresh vegetables only lasted a day or so, after which we were on dehydrated potato and the like. The cook would make sweet soup with mixed dried fruit which was in a hundredweight bag in the store. We were encouraged to drink Rose's lime juice every day to prevent scurvy. I had no problems with the food as there was plenty of it. A fresh apple was available for desert for a while.

By this time we were passing through the doldrums, the sea undulating with gilded swirls and blinding sparkling reflections of the sun as we glided gently past a background of blues and greens in the sea.

I was put on the four-to-twelve watch (noon to four and midnight to four in the morning), not to have duties but to avoid boredom on the month-long voyage. I suppose it got me into the steady rhythm of four hours on and eight hours off, seven days a week, which was to be my lot for the next seven or eight months.

Coming off watch at four in the morning the sea being oily calm I would walk round the lower deck to pick up the flying fish, which had, in flying to avoid a predator, landed in the frying pan so to speak This bonus lasted for quite a few days. There never was more than a dozen fish and only a few crew about. I would light the galley fire and share them with the sailor on watch for breakfast.

We passed through the Sargasso Sea. Being a small ship with a low freeboard (deck level above the sea) we were more intimate with the ocean, clumps of seaweed swirled passed us, not as much as I had been led to believe from books telling tall stories of sailing ships stuck fast in acres of thick weed. Old sailors tell a lot of weird stories.

Amazingly, the weather remained fair for the whole trip down the Atlantic. After many days at sea, I hadn't bothered to count them! It turned out to be thirty. One evening the engine telegraph rang 'stop engine', in the middle of the Atlantic. I asked the Mate: 'Why we had stopped?'

'It is getting dark. We will wait for daylight because we are afraid we may miss the island of South Georgia, we are somewhere near,' he said quietly. I knew enough about geography to know that if we missed the island, we would be into the ice cap only a couple of hundred miles or so further south and fuel was low.

His navigation was very good. I have read that sailing down the meridian is not complicated, the angle of the sun being involved. I wish I knew more about it. The Norwegians seem to navigate by the seat of their pants.

In 1946, a new whale catcher left Smith's Dock and never got to South Georgia because after taking bunkers somewhere they sailed 180 degrees off course and hit rocks, causing the ship to be a total loss. An alcoholic error, it seems.

It was a quiet watch that night, gently rolling to the swell. I sat in the engine room on watch. The shiny connecting rods of the engine stood still. I thought about the morrow, and relaxed, after all 'What will be, will be'!

I came on deck at four in the morning, it was just breaking daylight. I scoured the horizon ahead and there on the starboard bow was the white saw-edge peaks of South Georgia, ten thousand feet high, glinting in the early sunlight. Only a hundred and twenty miles long, the full length of the island was visible in the clear, crisp air, eighty miles away. We could have missed it in the night!

The telegraph rang, the propellor churned the sea below our stern and the *Southern Truce* swung her bow to head to the whaling station of Leith Harbour, South Georgia.

On 17th January 1775, Captain James Cook, exploring south, arrived at the island of South Georgia. With a small party, he went ashore and found it deserted. He claimed it for his King, and spent three days sailing round to discover it was an island and used his navigation skills to mark it on his charts.

Longitude had been a problem in charting accurately places on a map. Cook had, for the past couple of years, the use of the 'chronometer' a clock accurate to a few seconds in months.

This clock was created by John Harrison, born in 1693 in Yorkshire. He was another self-educated man who, like Cook, helped to put the great into Great Britain. He spent most of a lifetime creating this super clock to solve the problem of longitude and enable man to mark a place on a map and know with certainty how to return to that same place.

Captain Cook's maps were used, until recent developments in satellite instruments, as late as the 1990s. The sailors were courageous who accompanied him to sail in those waters with no engine to run for cover when a gale blows up!

January is the Antarctic summer. Captain Cook did not stay long. As he observed, snow and ice covered the island of South Georgia the whole year and only three species of plant were found ashore, penguins and seals the only creatures. The summer was a very short period of the year.

Whaling had existed for centuries in the Arctic. Many whaling companies had gone bankrupt as the numbers of whales were reduced and hunting became uneconomical.

With the advent of the steam ship, the Antarctic seas became more viable in which to hunt whales. For sixty years the oil provided light in cottages, margarine on bread and fertilizer on the fields.

Now the work of building the ships and the men who sailed in them long ago are forgotten. The benefits whaling brought to Europe in general and Britain in particular are not appreciated now, in a time of plenty.

Thankfully, men have found ways to replace those benefits and men no longer need to endure the hardships of many months in deep and dangerous waters.

Southern Truce, with only two days' fuel left in the bunker and another eight hours steaming to go, there had been very little room for error. Eventually we entered the three-mile-long fjord at the end of which was the Leith Harbour Whaling Station. *Southern Truce* came alongside after thirty days at sea.

I have seen old photographs of catcher vessels returned to Smith's Dock for repairs, with a sail rigged from the forrard mast, evidently with a favourable wind, to reduce fuel consumption and complete the long journey.

I had my gear stowed and wasted no time leaving *Southern Truce*. I had no desire to sail with an alcoholic skipper. It was only a short walk along the rugged waterfront to find my catcher, *Sondra*.

Three catchers, each a hundred-and-fifty feet long were laid alongside each other at the short wooden jetty that stuck out fifty feet or so from the blunt end of the fjord, It was short because the depth of water made it difficult to drive piles further out.

This was the catcher's bunker jetty. Fuel, water (straight from the mountains) and stores were taken on board here, roughly every ten days. When we came in for bunkers, it was my duty to fill the fresh water tanks, it was crystal clear and free. The sailors brought the stores from the supply depot on a four-wheeled flat bogey, it was a rough two-hundred yards track of mud and scree from store and personnel buildings. Snow was everywhere but had obviously receded round the shoreline now summer was approaching.

When foul weather at sea made sighting the whales impossible, the gunner would decide not to return to sea immediately. It was to rest the crew, but he only gave us one night alongside. I was free to go ashore, there was a kino (cinema), which had hard bench seats. I went once or twice. Silent films. Continental with sub titles, not always in English! Schubert was one!

I was fortunate to see the live variety show the shore lads put on once or twice a season. The kino seated about two hundred and had a fair sized stage. It was surprising the talent among the people down there! A seventeen-year-old Norwegian lad, blond, tall and slim, dressed up as Carmen Miranda, with lipstick and Spanish skirt slashed up to the thigh. He gave a terrific mime performance to a record. Being naïve at the time, I thought it was just an act!

He was nicknamed Josephine by the shore lads. I'd never heard of a homosexual until I was about thirty years old!

Later in the season I heard that, because of some embarrassment with the chemist and photographs he'd taken of 'Josephine' in the lab, the Port Captain was going to send him back home on the next ship, but Josephine had friends in high places! He settled for a move to another factory of Salvesen in Newfoundland. I wonder if it was a promotion?

I still wasn't sure what all the fuss was about, nude photos of a young bloke didn't seem a sin. I had been skinny-dipping with my pals, what's wrong with that? I wondered.

There was no booze allowed unless issued but I was once in company where a brew was going. The fermentation took place in a cut-down forty-gallon oil drum. This was steamed clean, then filled with a few gallons of water, with dried fruit, sugar and yeast from some galley. It only took five days to ferment. Creamy with the yeast, it was sweet-tasting. Two glasses put a warm glow in one's body. I walked a bit unsteadily back to the ship but no one would notice because all catcher men walked with a rolling gait. Coming ashore, it took days to lose the rolling gait created by the constantly heaving deck.

Here ashore was a small wooden shack office for crew who had problems or wanted to send a telegram home. I was embarrassed here one day. I went in to send Mum a telegram.

A young Scottish lad about my age was crying to get off the catcher.

'Ah canna sleep, ah canna eat, get me off that boat'! He was desperate, tears streaked his anguished face, I didn't wait to hear more, I was shocked that anyone could get into such a position without knowing what he was getting himself into. The season had just begun. He didn't appear to be suffering from seasickness, that makes people helpless, he seemed more terrified than anything.

I left the office and strolled round the amenities and saw where the 'sauna' was (I used it twice during the season), then I found the 'slop chest' (general store), where I bought a zip cardigan for off duty wear. Cigarettes were one pound and ten shillings for a thousand. I bought 'ship's Woodbines', not that I was a heavy smoker. Ten a day was about my limit. No money was exchanged. All was put on account and deducted from my pay when discharged in the UK. I returned later to send the telegram – the poor lad had gone.

A painting of the Loss of the whale catcher Simbra – *by Arthur Dinsdale*

SHETLAND WHALERS REMEMBER

An excerpt, word for word, of John Leask's account of the
loss of the whalecatcher Simbra.

I joined the whale catcher *Simbra* in Smith's Dock, Middlesbrough in England, the same place as I joined the *Southern Wheeler* for the previous season. Except for a steering problem crossing the bay of Biscay, the voyage was uneventful.

After arriving at Leith harbour, South Georgia, we took on supplies, whale ropes, harpoons, stores, etc. and left in company with eleven other catchers and the new factory ship the *Southern Harvester*. After two or three days we started whaling and worked our way into the Weddell Sea area of the Southern Ocean, this would have been approximately early to mid-November.

After about two months' fishing, on the evening of the 11th of January 1947 the *Simbra* was lost. With a lot of high speed chasing, fuel was taken on every four to six days. On the morning of the 11th we delivered whales to the factory ship then went alongside for bunkers and stores but we were refused bunkers as the factory ship had a tanker alongside replenishing her tanks. It is possible that, with normal procedure, the *Simbra* might not have been lost for with full tanks the stability of the ship would have been much better but as it was, we carried on fishing with what bunkers we had left.

The crew were all Norwegian, except for the deck boy, who came from Edinburgh, and myself. I was on watch that evening of the 11th from 4pm to 8pm. We had caught and flagged two whales close up to an area of pack ice. It was my hour in the crow's nest from 6pm until 7pm. We were running before the wind chasing the rest of the pod which had taken fright so it took a long chase to catch them up. Perhaps that is why, as I was looking around, I saw the skipper on the bridge talking to my watchmate, probably telling him to turn round and go back to pick up the two whales we had caught before dark, because at that moment she started coming round to starboard into the wind and, as is normal when turning sharply, she started keeling over to port – but this time she just kept going over.

As I realised that things were not right. I got out of the crow's nest to come down the rigging, but she had keeled over so far I had to come down the rigging head-first, on my hands and knees. As I looked down the sea was starting to pour down the hatch. I got down to the ship's side and to get aft to the lifeboat I had to shuffle my way along the outside of the ship which I managed by keeping a grip on the bulwark and going down crabwise along the ship's side. When I got to lifeboat the crew were already there.

They had got the covers off and my watchmate was cutting the boat adrift from the davits as there was no chance of getting it launched. By this time the sea was coming down the engine room skylights, so we all got on the side of the ship ready to jump. That was a bad moment because with no distress signal sent out and no lifeboat launched, when we all had to jump, it was just like jumping to our deaths.

The shock of the cold water was bad but I managed to get hold of the lifeboat strongback, the wooden spar that the covers are fitted over. The skipper and my watchmate also got hold of it. The lifeboat luckily had floated free. It was quite close but upside down. We started paddling towards it but the Skipper soon lost his grip and went under. It was slow going against the wind so my watchmate let go and swam towards the boat. I could make no headway myself as I wasn't a swimmer but I struck out and made it. The fact that I was wearing a kapok-lined coat gave me the buoyancy to get me there. The wireless operator also made it and between the three of us we managed to heave her over.

After getting on board we pulled another four of the crew on. The boat, of course, was full of water. We tried bailing but it was no use – the sea just kept slapping over the side.

Three of the men died very quickly so we put them back over the side. Nobody else made it to the boat. The deck boy kept shouting my name but he, too, soon went under. We tried bailing again but it was no good. By sitting right up on the stern of the boat I managed to get out of the water, except for my legs below the knees. I had lost the mitten of my left hand but it wasn't long before my hands and legs were numb. I saw the smoke of a catcher as it was getting dark. I set off a flare but it wasn't seen.

The three men left in the boat with me didn't last long. The wireless operator, the fireman and the mate soon died. It was probably no more than an hour, hour and a half. The mate was last to go. It was a long, cold night just sitting there. Thankfully, the wind had dropped. An iceberg floated past close by and a couple of whales went past. I must have been in a semi-conscious state when the sound of a harpoon gun going off brought me to my senses. I looked round and a catcher no distance away had just shot a whale. I managed to get to the middle of the boat and although I had lost all feeling in my hands and feet, I managed to get an oar with a bucket on it and placed it where the mast went.

They saw me and it wasn't long before they had me on board – that was about 11am. I spent some time in hospital on the *Southern Harvester*. My knees were badly bruised and I think it was a week before my legs and hands came right, although it was a fair while until my left had got back to normal.

CHAPTER FIVE

My first season on *Sondra*

I stepped aboard *Sondra* and walked along the side deck to the aft accommodation. From the deck I stepped over a door sill into an L-shaped narrow passage way. The short leg of the 'L' across the ship had a door to the steering flat, opposite were two toilets. In the ninety-degree angle was the almost-vertical companionway down to four cabins across the stern of the vessel, with two engineers' cabins on the starboard side. One was the Chief's single berth. A double berth had two bunks for the second and third engineer, me! The centre cabin was for the cook and mess boy, the port cabin for the first and second mates.

The second mate appeared. There was no one else around. I introduced myself. The ship had just come from South Africa. It had been on active service during the war. Now converted back to a whaler, it was in a bit of a mess, probably as a result of the refit. The bed was infested with nasty little bedbugs.

The cupboard under the sink was alive with cockroaches. I had never seen things like this in my life! It was difficult to believe that anyone had sailed in this cabin from South Africa.

The mate disappeared and came back with a tin of DDT. He showed me what the little bugs looked like and helped me disinfect the place, the cockroaches were given the same treatment and in a few days the cabin was respectable. I was assured that the cold would soon kill off any vermin aboard. From what I'd seen it could kill off anybody.

I did get a bite or two until the DDT took effect. The little devils didn't wake me up, but left a few small red spots.

I met the chief engineer, Anker Andersen. He was well-built, with hair thin on top, a full, round face and a pursed mouth, as if he was going to whistle. He was quietly spoken. Weighing me up he said: 'You can take the watch tomorrow?'

Silly question, I thought.

'I think so,' I said modestly.

'You only think so!' he said.

'No! Of course I can,' I replied.

He hadn't understood the English understatement.

I made a mental note, to be very positive when speaking to another national, no matter how good their English was. He explained to me the engine room commands would be in Norwegian. The language isn't so difficult for an Englishman as the syntax is the same, for example: 'Jeg skal har' in English is 'I shall have'.

He instructed me in the engine room commands. When I heard the cannon go off, the harpoon being fired, I had to stop the engine dead. This was to prevent the rope going round the propellor. Perish the thought with eighty tons of whale meat dragging us down.

It was my duty during the midnight-to-four watch, when there was no chasing, to top up the boiler before daylight and also to change the boiler feed water filters and wash the removed filters in soda to remove the light deposit of oil, ready to replace the filters the next night.

I also used to do my 'dobeying' (washing my clothes) in a bucket of hot boiler water and dry them on top of the engine cylinders. This was not a duty, but it saved me a precious few minutes of free time.

When the weather was moderate, I took a 'bath' (not on my own watch) behind the boiler. It was private and nice and warm. With hot water from the boiler mixed with cold, I first put one foot in the bucket and washed that side of me, and then put the other foot in the bucket and did the other side. It became a bit hairy if a chase started as the ship swerved and the bucket slid across the steel deckplates. It was hilarious! I always managed to see the funny side of it. The washbasin wasn't much use for a good swill. Whalers had no bathrooms, fridges or freezers. Unlike the herring drifter, though, we did have toilets. The toilet floor had a drain hole to the deck for washing-out purposes. In heavy weather a couple of inches of sea managed to slop in about one's feet in there. It ran in, then, as we heeled over, it ran out, but came in faster than it went out!

I went to the cabin I shared with Malbut, the second engineer, and sat on the day bed, a couch that extended along the bulkhead opposite the bunks. The bulkheads (walls) of the cabin were all curved to the cabin floor since they were the stern plates of the ship, painted with cork chippings to reduce condensation. I didn't sit long – it's not good to be alone too much at times like this and I was a bit peckish. I left the cabin and climbed the near-vertical companionway, walked round the casement at the stairhead and went out of the port side door (at sea kept closed) on to the deck and walked along to the mess room.

It was now near six o'clock. The steward (also the cook), told me where to sit. His name was Louie. He had dark hair, parted and thin, stuck across his head and a full, round soft face that reminded me of Stan Laurel's chum, Oliver Hardy.

Louie had been in America for years and spoke with an American drawl in the same defensive manner as Hardy. He turned out to be an excellent cook with what was available. I wondered what he was doing on a ship like this.

1947 – The fuel jetty at Jericho, Leith Harbour, South Georgia.
Two catchers, Sondra alongside the jetty, Sobkra alongside Sondra.

Good cooks were always in demand especially in America. Was he a fugitive, and if so from what? That thought could apply to most of us on this rough little ship, I mused.

As the officers I had not already met came in to the small mess room, overcrowded with most of the officers off watch, I introduced myself.

The Captain (also Gunner) was Christian Christiansen, a typical blond Norwegian chap in his mid-fifties, six foot four inches tall with pale blue eyes set in a wrinkled weather-beaten but friendly face. Each of his hands as big as a shovel.

Being out of Norway when the Germans invaded his country he had joined the Royal Navy.

He had been given command of a destroyer during the war.

An authorative figure, I was sat next to him on the inside of the curved upholstered bench seat. He asked about my background and wished me a good season. I suppose he needed a ship like a catcher – a boring merchant ship would be an anathema after the thrill of a destroyer in wartime.

Louie, the permanently harassed cook-cum-steward, wore a slightly stained white apron that also served as a hand towel. He served the mess from the adjacent galley. In this small mess room we sat round the curved edge of the quadrant section three-sided table. Our backs supported by the rounded, upholstered bulkhead.

This meant that only the two end officers were able to leave the table without disturbing the others.

A brass chronometer reading Greenwich longitudinal time and a brass aneroid barometer were fastened side-by-side to the bulkhead near the seaward door. They didn't mean much to me except to tell me when to leave for my duty watch. The weather would have its way with us and it changed so rapidly around South Georgia that advanced warning was of little use to me. A single nine-inch glass porthole with brass turnbuckles gave a view of the fore deck.

This foredeck was a clutter of ropes, shackles and chains. Five pairs of bollards on the port and starboard deck were used to secure the whales with chains for towing. Amidships a door set in a steel hood, gave access to the crew's quarters in the fore peak and the hold where port and starboard boxes contained the harpoon manila ropes. These ropes, hundreds of feet long, roughly three inches in diameter were carefully coiled round the box to fly out through the deckhead as the stricken whale dived.

Above this conglomeration of tackle ran the catwalk from the bridge to the gun platform.

The harpoon gun was mounted on a platform at the bow. The narrow (catwalk) gangway with handrails each side ran from the bridge to the platform to give the Gunner quick access to do his job. A pedestal telegraph on the platform enabled him to direct the engineer below in the engine room to change speed as required for close contact and ensure a safe and quick despatch of the whale.

In the mess room, the Captain sat at one end of the curved bench seat nearest the door, the Chief Engineer at the other end with access between the table and the dividing bulkhead. The galley beyond the bulkhead and the mess room together formed an elongated semicircle.

The seating arrangement was for action stations, the Captain to the bridge or gun, the Chief to prepare the massive winch. Meals were served before and after the watch-change hour for engineers and deck officers.

The powerful steam-driven winch situated on deck, in front of the mess room/galley superstructure had twin multi-grooved drums, to which the harpoon rope was wound round many times when the time came to haul in the whale.

The thick hemp rope used was spliced to the fifty meters of lighter nylon rope that was attached to the harpoon. The heavier hemp rope came from one of two wooden boxes, fifteen feet by ten, below deck on the port and starboard side of the hold. Normally only one rope was required; the other would be needed if a bad hit created a difficult kill.

This very rarely happened because of the hazards involved.

A sailor had to stand in the box to lay the rope out round the box as it came in. He would get out smartly if it had to be run out again.

Below the harpoon gun was coiled the 'foreloper', the lighter nylon rope.

This foreloper flew out with the harpoon. Nylon was a fairly new war-time invention and improved the business.

The heavier rope came through the deck by way of a wood-lined steel 'mouth'. This prevented the sea getting into the rope locker. It then passed over a pulley high up on the mast. This pulley was suspended from a wire rope, which itself went over a pulley fastened to the mast. The wire rope went down the mast through the deck and was wound round spring-loaded pulleys in the bowels of the ship.

This configuration made the mast a big fishing rod. When the spring-loaded rope pulley came down the mast with the load near to the breaking strain the Chief would release the clutch on the winch and allow the rope to give way. As the ship moved slow ahead towards the whale, he could haul in again. The strain on the rope was enormous, with a whale of seventy or eighty tons and the bow rising and falling. Breakages were very rare. The business had been carefully calculated, as had the risks. This reduced any cruelty to the whale to a minimum.

Officers off watch sat inboard round the mess room table. Being next to the Captain, I was under the scrutiny of his eagle eyes. One day trying to chew some tough salt beef, I gave a quiet 'ouch!' Toothache. He noticed and asked what it was. I made light of it: 'Oh, nothing – just a twinge', I said.

Days later as we came in for bunkers. The Captain instructed to me go ashore and see the doctor! I protested mildly: 'Oh, my tooth's okay, now,' but my protest was ignored with a benevolent smile. He had radioed ahead.

'The doctor is waiting for you. That is an order!'

It's difficult to refuse such a kindly order but there was a steely edge behind the smile. The older Norwegians were in the habit of clicking their heels when addressed by the Captain. I was his noon-to-four 'driver' on the engine (a busy time in chasing) and was not allowed to be off-colour. I wasted no time in obeying his order.

This was the kind of man he was – attention was paid to the finest detail. I was influenced greatly by these characters I met in my journey through life, even if I was unable to reach the level they had achieved. Never leave things to chance!

I put on my sea boots and heavy coat and stepped ashore. The deck was always fairly level with the jetty. I don't think there was much tide down there. I crunched my way along the muddy scree-packed track, passing the office and personnel buildings to the small hospital. The male nurse was expecting me and motioned me to climb up into the chair. He was a man of few words from the Shetland Isles. I didn't expect to be there long but it was forty minutes later before the doctor lowered the chair and I was able to get down.

The ex-Indian British Army doctor was past middle age, with strong dark hair parted near the middle, high cheek bones and a long nose, his breath smelling strongly of whiskey. He brought out a red velvet-lined box of dental surgical tools. Next he charged a syringe from a bottle of anaesthetic and injected me in the vicinity of the offending lower left sixth tooth. This seemed to freeze my face up to my eyebrows. Just joking!

Actually it was very local and, in spite of the surgery, I felt nothing for the full forty minutes!

From the box he chose a tool that looked like a pair of side cutters used by electricians to cut cable. The rotten crown of the tooth broke off and left a short stump. He tried one or two of the instruments from the box but was unable to get a firm hold of the stump. The Doctor looked around the surgery for some time. I think he was wondering what to do next – engineers often use the same manoeuvre hoping in the meantime the problem may go away. Then he apologised that there wasn't an elevator with which to lever out the remainder of the tooth.

He told me he was now going to sever the nerve, which would prevent me having any more pain with the tooth. Taking a scalpel and pressing it hard into the bone below the tooth, he cut the nerve. Satisfied that this would prevent further toothache. I was told that on my return to the UK, I should see my dentist to have the stump removed. I thought he performed brilliantly and I felt no pain. I had no more bother with it during the season.

On returning home, my local dentist removed the stump without difficulty with the necessary elevator to lever out the root. I then had a course of dental treatment to ensure there would not be a repeat of toothache at sea. It could have been very disagreeable.

In bad weather, the cook had problems. First the table cloth would be wetted to stop the plates sliding about. In very bad weather – fifty per cent of the time– wooden dividers were clipped to the table. When it got really rough, I'm talking of the bow rising and falling twenty feet or more, Louie lashed an enormous dixie on to the galley fire and made 'storm soup' – the dixie being only half full, the soup wouldn't spill over. The mess room was kept shut off. The crew would stagger into the galley on the port side with rubber boots and oilskins, bringing in buckets of sea water with them on each occasion.

With six inches of sea water sloshing around the galley, up our sea boots, two or three men would stand in the small galley, hanging on to the ship with one hand, with the other hand dipping a pint pot into the dixie then slurped a mysterious soup of salt beef and dried veg. With a couple of ship's biscuits, this fortified us for the next few hours. Louie almost apologised for his meagre fare. He was a gem, probably the most important job on the ship and on the go all day.

The cast-iron galley stove was oil-fired with solar oil – a light oil, stored in a large tank outside the galley. A brass rail ran round three sides of the top of the stove to prevent pans from sliding off and tie the dixie down.

Coffee was the predominant brew on this ship and a huge jute sack of green beans was kept in the food store. The beans were roasted regularly in the oven and a pound or so put in a tin for daily use. I was instructed how to put a handful of beans in the grinder and crank the handle, pull the little drawer out and tip the ground coffee on to the boiling water in the steam-heated copper tank. The ground coffee landed on a muslin cloth, which draped across the tank and sagged into the boiling water for a few minutes.

The Norskies (British slang for Norwegians), would fill a mug from a brass tap in the little coil-heated boiler tank, put condensed milk into the coffee and sipped it through a sugar tablet held in the teeth.

Louie asked me if I would light the galley fire when I came off watch at four am each morning , grind the coffee and brew up for the lads. I agreed, and for this little service I was given permission to take a couple of slices of smoked bacon from a whole side of the animal hanging in the food store. This I fried for my breakfast each morning provided the weather wasn't too bad. I don't remember ever having bacon at any other time, but of course I was never at the day time breakfast.

Immediately after my bacon, I went to my bunk and slept until called at eleven-thirty. There was an enormous jute bag of dried fruit in the store, which contained dried apple rings, apricots, dates, prunes, and so on. I often took a handful and nibbled it on the way down to the engine room below. That bag would last two seasons and more. The cook used it to make what he called a sweet soup.

In bad weather, I would have a tot from one of a couple of bottles of brandy that I had bought with cigarettes from the bum boat that came alongside in our bunker stop at Aruba.

I think this 'brandy' was made from bananas but it eased the ache in the abdominal muscles that resulted from the strain of hanging on as the ship heaved and bucked. This wasn't sea sickness – just stomach muscles doing unusual exercises.

I was sorry when my supply of spirits had gone because there was no general issue of booze but a regular tot was given quite often.

The Captain would send a bottle forrard for the sailors and a bottle aft for the officers if we'd had a bad day and that happened often. It was very generous of him. The crew had a lot of confidence in him, but he was the last one to run for shelter in bad weather and would stick it out. This was why we were 'top boat', out working when others had run for cover!

The Captain's cabin and chart room was above this mess room and galley, the open bridge was above his cabin and the whole superstructure stood in front of the funnel. Behind the funnel two big ventilators (without fans) scooped air down to the engine room. The scoops faced astern normally in the Antarctic regions and could be turned with a spindle by the engineer from below when seas were breaking high over the ship.

The deck forward of the superstructure was the business end of the catcher. It held the winch, mast, harpoon box, ropes, flensing knives, bollards and fairleads to secure the chains round the tails of the whale for towing them back to the factory.

The catcher could tow five whales each side from amidships forward. It only happened once in the two seasons I was there. We had had a good day. The weather was brilliant, blue sky, flat and calm. We had caught eight good-size fin whales, each an average of seventy feet. It had been too good to be true! At the end of the day we had towed them quite a way to the island when the cry went up: *'arr sett blost'* ('I see a Blast'). We all used the Norwegian commands.

The crew were horrified that the Captain would cast off the whales we were towing to go chasing after another two. A gale can blow up in twenty minutes and all may be lost! Our bonus was paid on the catch.

The order was given. 'Cast off the starboard whales'. *Sondra* turned in a big circle, then the port side whales were cast off, all with quick-release shackles. Each whale surmounted with a bamboo pole bearing *Sondra's* red number three flag and a battery operated white lamp for night time pickup. They looked like a troop of cavalry with lances flying forming a large circle. About a week's wages in bonus to me (seven pounds)

I hoped we would be able to pick them up again before dark!

Our luck held and within the hour we were back on our way to the factory. There was some anxiety towing such a haul in case a storm blew up and the whales were torn away from the ship's side The engine, at full speed now, moved the ship at little more than four knots as we slowly towed the ten whales the last few miles.

The weather held good and we entered the fjord with ten whales, much to the delight of the shore gang too, their pay was also based on the catch.

For my first watch, I was told we would sail at midnight. I was on midnight until four o'clock in the morning, so thankfully there would be no chasing *'jager'* (in Norwegian) this first time.

I arranged for the mess boy, Jamie, a fifteen-year-old Scottish lad, to call me with a pot of tea at eleven-thirty, in case I slept over.

Jamie came with a good brew on the dot! He was a bright lad I was glad he was British. This made six of us: Malbut (Geordie); Davie (a deck hand from Arbroath); two 'North-Sea Chinamen' (sailors from the Shetlands), who normally spoke Gaelic; and me, from Teesside. The full ship's complement was eight officers, four sailors. the cook, mess boy and two firemen. Sixteen in total.

This was to be my first watch in charge of an engine room. At ten minutes to midnight I went below to take over the watch from the assistant engineer. He was lean, past sixty, I would say. He spoke fairly good English, through big yellow teeth, long white hair that had once been blond brushed straight back, with a long white bristly face to match. He taught me quite a bit of Norwegian during the season and was very helpful, and although my first impression of him was that he was a bit doddery, he kept a good watch.

He did once manage to get the rope round the propellor with an eighty-ton whale on the other end. I was on deck and noticed *Sondra* was going astern being pulled by the dying whale.

The method of freeing the propeller from the heavy hemp whale line was to turn the propeller anticlockwise. I went down to the engine room and helped to engage a worm gear into the gear wheel attached to the engine's main shaft. This enabled us to slowly turn the engine anticlockwise using a four-foot ratchet fitted on to the worm spindle, thus unwinding the rope and allowing the winch to haul in the catch.

The assistant engineer climbed out of the engine room leaving me in charge. I would be doing this for six months, four hours on watch and eight hours off, seven days a week. I decided to get on with it one day at a time. I smiled at the fireman. He gave me a quizzical look. I had to show him I was up to the job.

The telegraph rang 'standby'. The engine cylinders were already warmed with steam by the assistant. I put a bit of steam to the engine with the brass wheel of the steam control valve just enough to move the engine slowly and blow out any water through the cylinder drain valves that may have condensed in the cylinders. Water trapped in a cylinder does not compress and could do a lot of damage!

I enjoyed the smell of steam and oil, as it reminded me of the giant traction engines of the fairground, but it was even better in the confines of the engine room.

The telegraph rang again – 'slow astern'. The valve gear already astern, I opened the throttle to the 'slow' indicator on the throttle spindle. I felt the checker plates under my feet sway as *Sondra* moved away from the jetty. Now a clang of the telegraph indicated 'slow ahead', so I had to move the valve gear to the ahead position.

I opened the steam valve to the six-inch single-cylinder engine, bolted to the main engine near the main engine control valve. The little engine chugged around pretty fast driving a gear wheel that moved the three sets of Stevenson's valve gear connected by a shaft that ran along the back of the engine

The three sets of valve gear swung over to 'ahead'. Now I opened the main steam control valve to start the main engine. Slow ahead it was!

The fireman, nicknamed 'Gandhi', lit extra burners to fire up the boiler and make more steam for the expected next command.

Sondra turned at the head of the fjord, then 'half ahead' for a few minutes, I opened the control valve more.

I could visualise the action on deck. The crew stowing ropes carefully away and cleared the deck for sea.

Now we went full ahead down the three-mile fjord. The sheltered smooth water of the fjord changed to a gentle heave as the bow cut into the open sea.

The season had began. I don't believe in lucky charms but I hoped a spirit friend would be looking after me.

It was a quiet watch with moderate sea. Gandhi the fireman (stoker, or boiler attendant) already on watch was a petite, cadaverous white-haired Norwegian with a big floppy white moustache. He only wore a singlet and jeans in the engine room which exposed his pale, skinny physique. The crew had called him Gandhi! He looked very much like the Indian statesman apart from his colour! The name was only contradicted by his bright blue eyes and a magnificent American Indian chief tattooed on his left upper arm! He was a very cheerful chap in spite of his looks and good at his job.

I was pleased when he gave me an encouraging 'thumbs up' sign as he changed watch with the other fireman. As a new boy I had met his approval, and as he was an old hand, word would get round the crew.

The firemen changed their watch during my four-hour watch. They were 'watch and watch about' – six hours on and six hours off, seven days a week.

Like me, they didn't have a heavy job, the boiler being oil-fired. When chasing whales, however, the manoeuvring of the engine required the oil burners to be shut off and on at each change of speed. The burners to spray the oil into the furnace had to have the spray tips cleaned often as the residual oil contained a small amount of clinker (carbon and sand).

The other fireman (stoker) was called Johansen, a Swedish guy about twenty-eight years old. They both spoke fairly good English. Johansen, quiet but friendly, was tall, thin and gaunt and, like Gandhi, hardly any teeth. Must be years of shipboard grub, I imagined.

My first watch was a quiet watch but I was tired and ready to be relieved after the long and hectic previous day.

Johansen told me a hilarious tale of a trip ashore in South Africa. He'd had a fair bit to drink (Swedes were like this away from Sweden!) and a local girl invited him home to stay the night. When he woke up next morning he was in a mud hut. Nice and cosy, eh?

Malbut, the second engineer relieved me at four in the morning. He was a native of the Newcastle area. I think he came from South Shields in fact.

We shared a two-berth cabin above the propellor in the aft accommodation. Fortunately, we never seemed to be in the cabin together because of our watches, thank goodness. Malbut suffered very much from a gastric stomach.

He didn't check the engine room status before taking over the watch, just sat on a box and lit a cigarette. This was contrary to engine room procedure. He had no conversation of any quality. I soon realised he was a sick man who relied heavily on milk of magnesia for his stomach ulcer. I was going to have to 'carry' him somewhat. he often came down a half-hour late for his watch. I had some sympathy for him but each minute of free time was precious to me in the rough lifestyle we lived.

I spent a few minutes with Malbut, then I climbed out of the engine room (literally up a vertical steel ladder) and went up forrard to the galley to make a pot of tea. Before daybreak, there were only two sailors on deck: one on the bridge at the wheel, the other in the galley to spell him off. They did an hour each at the wheel. It seemed to be the routine on an open bridge in Antarctic waters. On bad days the sailors on deck had a bit of frostbite on their cheeks.

I came up one morning at four o'clock to find both sailors in the galley! There were no icebergs about but the Captain would not have been happy about it. I didn't say anything. As I say, we had to trust one another.

I went aft and turned in to the bottom bunk. Malbut had chosen the top one.

The propellor throbbed under the cabin, and the engine room noises told me what was going on below. The boiler feed pumps, whining as they forced water into the boiler at two hundred and fifty pounds pressure, and the rumble of the main engine and the hum of the steam-driven electric generator told me all was well!

I slept okay but woke to hear the telegraph 'double ring'. This was an emergency ring for full ahead, not full cruising speed. This meant *Sondra* was chasing. I don't remember the gun firing the harpoon, so it may have been a protected specie of whale they had seen. The Captain would look closely through binoculars to identify its status, female with young, protected specie or under-size, before approaching closer.

I must have gone over again. I'm a good sleeper. Next thing I knew, it was eleven-thirty. Jamie gave me a shake. I had a quick wash with the water swilling about in the washbasin, and then up on to the upper deck, coming down amidships to the messroom for a meal before my watch.

I paused for a few moments to see what was going on – never a dull moment on a whale catcher. There were a few icebergs in the area, but we steamed along at cruising speed, all free hands searching for a 'blow'. The man up the mast in the barrel generally saw a whale blowing first, *'Arr sett blost'* was the call! All the commands Norwegian. It seemed natural enough and it presented no problem.

After a bowl of soup, some cheese and a couple of biscuits (the ship's biscuits were fresh, so no weevils, and were not too hard on the teeth). The main meal of the day was at six o'clock. (As it got near dark business was suspended.) I went below and took over the watch from the Assistant Engineer, Harald, I think his name was. I didn't see much of him because of our watches.

The engine and boiler room aft of the fuel tanks were all one space and took up half of the ship's length and most of the beam. Some of the auxiliary machinery, pumps and generator were fitted on platforms up the curved sides of the ship's engine room.

The officers' accommodation, aft, was built over the propellor shaft above two fresh water tanks built into the tapered stern each side of the shaft. There was room to work on the gland, which the shaft ran through into the sea. At sea, this gland was eased off to allow a trickle of sea water to lubricate the shaft running in a hard oily wood (*lignum vitae*)-lined bearing. It was nipped up in port to save having to pump the bilges out.

Going down the almost vertical steel ladder into the engine room, past a steel gantry along the engine cylinder tops, down to the lower deck plates there was a narrow walkway between the side of the engine and the boiler water feed pumps.

Here at the forrard end of the engine was the desk and main engine steam control valve.

Opposite the control valve was the desk. It was never used for paperwork. In action there was no time to write anything down. It generally contained a tin of brasso and some hand rags. We took pride in the brass gauges and other fittings and give them a polish now and then.

I kept a round tin of fifty ship's Woodbines. The best cigarettes for flavour. I would light one have a few puffs then go to check a pump or other item. When I returned the cigarette had burnt away, forgotten.

The telegraph hung above the desk, a clock-like enamel face divided into 'ahead' on the left side and 'astern' on the right. A segment 'finished with engine' at the bottom had segments from slow to full, left and right. A big brass pointer and loud clanging bell indicated the desired action, this was operated by thin wires with chains to go round corners in ducting from the bridge and also the gun platform. Directly over the desk was a ventilator two feet in diameter. Above deck it was turned aft to keep the spray from drenching the engineer. At times the sea came down regardless! I had an oilskin jacket and sou'wester that I used to put on in a heavy sea.

I soon had the opportunity to practice the instructions I had been given. A double ring on the telegraph meant we were chasing. I opened the throttle, and the engine room deck throbbed and bounced as the ship sped forward at full speed of sixteen knots.

The engine was not enclosed. The crankshaft and connecting rods were a sight as they spun round at their full speed of two hundred and fifty revolutions a minute. The bearings had to be lubricated by hand with an oilcan most of the time. There was an automatic drip feed system but it was necessary to supplement it.

The automatic drip feed system dripped oil into brass cups on the crossheads. The crossheads thrashed up and down with the pistons and connected rods, turning the crankshaft.

This oil should run down thin brass pipes to the bearings, but with the ship heeling over, the drips could not be relied on to hit the cups!

Being an open engine with only a nine-inch toe plate and a handrail at waist height, it was a case of one hand for the ship and the other for yourself!

In a merchant ship's main steam engine, oil was topped up at the measure of a pint per watch on the slow (seventy revolutions per minute) triple expansion steam engines. We could not have a bearing run hot for lack of oil during a chase so there was no limit to our use of oil.

The chase often took forty minutes or so. Firstly, the ship had to draw near to the whale then the difficult job of stalking the animal to be close enough to make an efficient hit when it surfaced for the few seconds to blow.

This took good judgement between the Gunner and the sailor up the mast in the barrel who could, if the sea was smooth enough see it approaching the surface. I was involved with instructions given from the telegraph on the gun platform for the different speeds the Gunner needed, to be in the best place to make his hit.

When the harpoon cannon was fired, it was heard all over the ship, I had to stop the engine dead. I spun the steam valve shut, reversed the valve gear to astern and put a bit of steam on the engine to hold the engine in astern against the 'way' of the ship, so that the propellor was still. This was to prevent the rope winding round the prop.

The fireman only a few feet away from me shut off the burners in the boiler front.

There was a pause, the whale having surfaced had been spotted by the deck crew, slow ahead was telegraphed. This was to put *Sondra's* bow in that direction and approach the whale. After some minutes. 'Stop' indicated that the whale was under the bow coming alongside.

My next job was to start the Westinghouse air pump. This air was injected into the carcass to keep it afloat until natural gasses took over. The whale was now cast off with a four-metre bamboo mast stuck into it with a red flag bearing *Sondra's* number and a battery lamp clipped to the pole below the flag.

At the end of a day, sometimes sixty miles from the first whale we had 'flagged off', keeping a close eye on the weather whale catcher *Sondra* turned to pick up the other whales for towing back to the island factory.

It can blow up to hurricane force rapidly and when other whales were strapped to the bow bulwarks, our way through the sea is reduced considerably. It required good judgement on the part of the Captain as to when to call it a day.

Somehow the Mate retraced our course (after chasing in all directions) to pick up the whales. I am told a navigation aid was to draw the outline of a nearby iceberg and come back to work from that They all looked alike to me, flat-topped ice islands.

A radio beacon gave the course needed to return to the factory. Usually we only caught a couple of whales in any one day and sometimes many days passed before a whale was sighted.

Approaching darkness, we towed them at night for several hours to a buoy anchored near the factory and returned to sea each time until we needed fuel.

After a few weeks, I had need to see the doctor again. I had been bothered for three days with diarrhoea. It was no trouble when cruising but on two occasions when chasing Johanson had covered for me when the Gunner had rung for a change of speed and I was in the toilet (conveniently just near the top of the engine room door)

I had reported my problem to the Mate and he had produced the 'medical chest'. This was a box about eighteen inches square, the inside being divided into about twenty-four compartments. Each compartment contained a bottle. The inside of the lid had a diagram with a number for each box. A book to accompany the chest listed the ailment that each bottle was for. My ailment was listed number nine! I was given a dose each day but it had no effect.

When we came in for bunkers and stores, I went up to see the Doctor who had been radioed to expect me, The doctor took a tapered measuring glass and poured a clear liquid into it from a medicine bottle. It was castor oil! 'Hey!' I said, 'My Mum always gives me some orange after taking that stuff!'

He laughed: 'Well we ain't got any oranges here', he said.

'Well I can't take that without something,' I replied.

He was easy to talk to and asked his 'sheltie' (assistant) to bring a tin of condensed milk from the kitchen and a tablespoon. With this spoonful of condensed milk at the ready, I downed the castor oil, The sweet condensed milk was as good as the orange at taking the sickly taste of the castor oil away.

I thanked the doctor and his assistant for their kindness.

I strolled back to the *Sondra* at the bunker jetty but galloped the last twenty yards and just made it to the loo! The astringent number nine needed to be changed to castor oil! It cured me immediately in one go!

The daylight watches were always busy but sometimes we had cruised around for ten days and not seen a *blost*.

One chase lasted for four hours at sixteen knots but we were unable to close on the more speedy whales. The Chief Enginner made one of his rare visits to the engine room. I imagine the Captain had sent him to make sure we were going flat out! He checked the steam control valve was fully open and adjusted the engine valve gear. He then checked the steam pressure, grunted a couple of times (he was a man of few words) and went back on deck. Later, the Gunner abandoned the chase. Those whales must have been fit! Survival of the fittest, I suppose.

The odd time when the weather was flat and calm, and no whales were about, the Captain would look for fish for the pot. This was indicated by a mixed flock of sea birds squabbling over an area of the sea.

Some of the birds were revolting creatures and fought with each other. One species, called 'Shag', I think, a black greasy-looking thing with a big hooked yellow bill, was as big as a large goose. They would tear into anything edible: seal or whale meat, fish or a dead bird!

They tasted fishy and a bit tough! It was a savage place, the Antarctic! Killer whales ate seals, sea leopards ate penguins, penguins ate fish, the fish ate krill (a large shrimp-like creature also eaten by the baleen whale); the food chain was endless!

We took our share for a Europe devastated by a war in which millions had died and food was rationed long after the war had ended. There was some sympathy among the crew for the whale. They had other enemies in the Orca (killer whale), who hunted a balleen whale in packs. At least our way was quick.

The ship would stop engine and glide quietly towards the area where the fish were shown to be by the sea birds. This wasn't sport: it was for fresh food. I imagine Captain Cook on his voyages would have done the same and other sailors before him!

The cook issued, to any available men, fishing lines with three 'foul hooks' set into a short length of lead pipe. No bait was required! Dropping the hooks over the side three or four yucks would catch a good-size cod like fish. The fish had a centimetre of jelly-like fat under their skin, they'd need it in that icy sea: temperature minus one degree celcius!

There must have been a big school of big fish below us as the crew yucked over the side with the foul hooks, the fish were hooked in the gills, the belly and even the tails. They were all about fifteen to twenty pounds in weight.

They were immediately stunned, gutted and hung around the upper deck handrail and 'freeze dried' in the Antarctic air. This supplemented our diet with fresh food for a week or two. Sixteen hungry mouths to feed!

Strangely enough, we didn't eat a lot of whale meat and only a few times in the season did we have whale steaks. I enjoyed it – it tasted fishy as well! Perhaps Salvesen Co. didn't like us eating the profit.

Once each season, when no whales were about, the Captain would steam due east for two or three days until we reached Bouvet Island. This French possession was a massive rock rising high above the sea about eight-hundred-and-fifty miles due east from South Georgia, near to South Africa. Without any apparent vegetation, its cliffs were crowded with sea birds. Wild geese were what the Captain was after, and with a Lee Enfield rifle (ship's armament) he shot half a dozen.

The sailors picked them out of the sea with a boat hook and they were hung for a couple of weeks in the steering flat. I think this was to reduce the fishiness. I watched as the mate told the cook how to prepare them. They were skinned (not plucked) and chopped up for the stew pot. I found the stewed bird a bit tough and still a bit fishy, like everything else down there! But it was fresh meat and a change from salt beef/pork/fish.

So we lived off the sea when possible, but Yorkshire pigs were bred at the whaling station and occasionally we had fresh pork. Not very often, though, because it would take a lot of pigs to feed eight hundred men. The company was not in the business of rearing pigs and all it entailed.

We were at sea most of the time and only got the opportunity of fresh meat when we came in for fuel, every ten days or so.

Twice in the season there was venison from the herd of deer that had increased to two thousand from twenty deer that had been taken to South Georgia in 1910.

This herd in 1947 had thrived and were culled to keep the numbers down and provide us with fresh meat.

The Captain insisted that we drank the lime juice provided and was available each day!

Scurvy was a possibility. We had enough problems with cuts going quickly sceptic so we drank the Rose's lime juice and stayed healthy! There was no chance of catching a cold during this time as we were rather isolated, which was a good thing!

My mum had given me the same hair-cutting scissors, steel comb and shears to take to sea with me that she had used to cut my hair since I was a baby. These became quite an asset! I made good friends among the crew, going forrard to cut the sailors' hair, mainly in bad weather when there was no chance of chasing whales. In the crew's quarters, up in the bow of the ship, the deck rose and fell twenty feet or more in a heavy sea. To cut a man's hair we would sit together on a long stool with me behind him. It was surprising how well this method worked!

The men who worked on deck wore their hair to the shoulders, normally with beards to match. This helped to protect their faces from frost bite. Long hair was not fashionable in the 1940's.so I found this unusual. The first six weeks, because the weather was so rough, I grew a beard, but found it uncomfortable. I left the moustache, much to the amusement of Gandhi as we tried to see who could grow the longest! He won, at seven inches tip to tip!

As a hairdresser, I was in big demand at the end of the season and it had earned me a few tots from the Captain. The sailors made me a thick sailcloth sea bag, hand-stitched, to get the extra gear bought at the slop chest home. I was even cutting hair as we sailed up the Mersey to pay off in Liverpool. It would save the guys valuable drinking time, they said.

As the weeks went by, I lost count of the date or the name of the day. The early part of the season (October and November) the days were still short and the weather bad. When it snowed, the snow floated on the icy sea and made a 'white out' for about four hours.

January was the best month and some days could be considered perfect, with bright sun and blue sky. Towards mid-February the cloud cover thickened again and grey and wet became the norm.

Whales were scarce and difficult to see in a rough sea. They could move faster than the ship in the big seas. At night, about six o'clock we stopped and drifted until daylight at five the next morning.

Some nights we lay among a herd of icebergs set out like chess pieces on a giant chessboard as far as the eye could see. Occasionally the sea was free of bergs. I suppose that *Sondra* moved around a lot. We cruised at normal full speed as long as it was light. At cruising speed we would range for about one-hundred-and-twenty miles. I never knew what part of the ocean we were in, north or south of the island. There was always the danger of the small bergs (as big as houses) they were dangerous as there was not a lot showing above the surface and difficult to see in rough weather!

At intervals during the night, the sailor on watch would telegraph for slow ahead as we drifted close to a berg then stop again until our drift required another move.

A stormy night drifting, waiting for daylight, twice brought a hundred or more seabirds down to the engine room attracted by the ship's lights. These terns (I think), came down the two big engine room ventilators acting like scoops, the wind blowing them down to flutter about in all the awkward corners of the boiler and engine room machinery.

Johansen and I spent an hour with sacks bagging them up and taking them on deck to return them to the sea, The daft little things were easy to handle but their nice white feathers were a bit sooty!

I disliked going on the boiler top. It was hot, badly lit and a steam leak at two-hundred-and-fifty pounds pressure would result in a painful shriek and was invisible at the source of the leak. It was easy to receive a burn, especially on a rolling ship. The pipes were insulated with pads of lagging but the valves had to be exposed to give access for adjustment and although we wore gloves we generally had bare arms.

The boiler was a five-drum water tube, built by Yarrow.

It was constructed of two drums about three feet in diameter at the bottom, taking up about two thirds of the width of the ship. Two more similar drums were above and closer together with a third larger drum above. All five drums, about fifteen or more feet long, were connected by rows of two inch tubes and formed roughly a triangle about eighteen feet high.

A thin steel casing enclosed the boiler and was lined with two rows of firebricks insulating the casing from the burning oil sprayed into the inner triangle formed by the tubes. The temperature was near white-hot! After one long day at full speed, Johansen called me over to the boiler furnace inspection holes. The inner row of bricks were melting! I reported it to the Chief and at the next call for bunkers shore workers came aboard to replace them.

The larger top steam drum had two sight glasses showing the water level. This level was important. The boiler only held seven tons of water and if the main engine was at full throttle and the feed water pump failed it would only take a few minutes to lower the water level and create serious damage. I don't like to think of it! A boiler tube bursting!

A six-foot diameter centrifugal fan powered by a small steam engine blew air into the furnace fronts round the burners to aid the combustion. This was termed 'forced draught'. The early vessels created an improved draught with tall funnels.

In a pitching sea, too high a water level caused water to carry over with the steam. This could damage the machinery and it was difficult to gauge how much water was in the boiler. With the ship pitching and tossing, the sight glasses were full one second and empty the next. I estimated the level by counting 'one, two, three, full' and 'one, two, three, empty'. This might have indicated a half-full glass, but it seemed to work.

At the end of my watch, with daylight approaching, I would, in a moderate sea, top up the boiler water level for the second engineer. A whale may be sighted, and it gave him less to do.

One morning, with a calm sea, I spent twenty minutes topping up the water level in the boiler. It was taken in via a steam-heated 'evaporator' to the condenser. This ensured its purity. I saw with satisfaction the sight glasses were seven-eighths full.

I was anticipating the end of my watch when we ran into a heavy pitching sea! This happened so suddenly, I was taken by surprise. It was unbelievable!

The electric generator steam cylinder started slapping badly, with boiler water coming over with the steam! My dreams of an easy end to the watch evaporated. I had to blow the boiler water down a bit! I had wasted precious boiler water!

I pulled the floor plate away from the bottom of the boiler to get at the blow-down cocks (two interlocking drain cocks, double insulated with shrouded spindles).

A special socket spanner was needed to open these important cocks. I opened the first one, which allowed me to open the second one and I heard the hard earned boiler water blowing into the sea.

I had put the socket spanner on to the floor plate near me. Then, guessing the level was about right, I went to pick it up. The ship gave a heavy roll. Bilge water was running up the side of the engine room. It passed the steel decking, which was a couple of inches short of the ship's side.

On the return roll, not all the bilge water could get back down the narrow gap and the foul water swept across the deck plates where I was sitting with my feet dangling in the bilge space to my wet, smelly discomfort!

The essential spanner skidded down into the bilges. It slipped down to the keel plate and was sloshing about in the bilge water. I dived under the floor plates and grovelled about, fishing for the thing. The boiler all the time was losing its precious water. If things went too far, we were up the river without a paddle, so to speak!

Wet through in stinking bilge water, I quickly found the spanner and closed the valves. I just had time to feed a little more water to the boiler to a suitable level before my watch relief came down.

I had not taken a calendar with me, not even a diary, and lost track of the days. Perhaps it was for the best to just take one day at a time whatever it throws at you.

The constant strain of hanging on to the heaving vessel or risk being flung to the deck was beginning to tell. At times I felt nearly exhausted, not seasick! My stomach muscles ached with straining to stand upright. I saw the funny side of it, as one never knew which way they would be thrown next. It was difficult to predict and amusing when taken by surprise. No wonder ships are called 'she' We love 'em and hate 'em!

Jamie had called me one morning at eleven-thirty. He didn't bring a mug of tea, since I normally went straight for my lunch.

I woke up only just in time to go on watch! When I saw the time, I was mad. I couldn't remember Jamie calling me and I had to do without my grub!

Coming off watch at four in the afternoon, I went to the galley for a brew and gave Jamie a bollocking! He was a grand lad so I couldn't believe I would have to do such a thing.

He responded very gently and said in a hurt voice: 'But you sat up and said thanks.'

I was stunned and apologised. I realised how all on board must be feeling. The end of the season couldn't come too soon! There was still a long way to go!

We were returning to the island with a whale but didn't go back out to sea, *Sondra* came alongside another catcher, *Sobkra*, then later in the evening *Sorcera* came in.

It was Christmas Eve. Our only night off!

Shaved and cleaned up in our best gear, it was a time for social discourse. I had learnt a bit of the Norwegian language, mainly connected with the engine room, but I was surprised how close it was to a lot of English words used in the north of the country. My Gran was from Newcastle, a Geordie and she would say *'arrs gannen yem'* – this was pure Norwegian for 'I'm going home'. An old Viking lady, perhaps!

There was a catch to the night off: someone would have to mind the shop! The Chief asked me if I would be officer of the watch while we were alongside so that the sailors and stokers could have the night off. I didn't need to think about it.

Most of the crew were long-service company men and had friends on other ships and ashore. They worked six hours on watch and six off, whereas we only did four hours on watch and I had no friend to visit. I told the Chief I didn't mind. He was a nice fellow, we got on very well, he rarely came down to the engine room, unless invited to give his opinion or have some defect brought to his attention.

The Captain sent a bottle of aquavit (Norwegian spirit) for the officers and another bottle forward for the sailors. I think it was made from spruce trees, a bit like sweet turpentine but it was forty per cent proof. It was a change from the gin. I had a tot for the toast but the Chief put a couple of tots aside for me. I had a long night's watch ahead of me and needed to stay alert.

Louie put on an interesting, if not memorable, meal for Christmas Eve. A few pathetic decorations were hung in the mess room. Dorothy's mother had made me a Christmas cake (spiced loaf, as it is sometimes called) full of fruit, raisins, nuts and butter. It had travelled well in a round tin about a foot diameter and four inches deep. I gave it to Louie and told him to send one half forrard for the lads and cut the other up for our mess. It was much appreciated.

The conversation was mixed, Norwegian and English. I never felt a foreigner with the Norskies, but my Norwegian was very limited. Malbut only talked about whaling and the sea in toothless Geordie. I don't think many understood what he was saying! Including me!

CHAPTER FIVE – *My first season on Sondra*

The Norwegians seemed to be farmers as well as seamen and looked forward to going home to their fruit trees and smallholdings for the summer. The Mate showed me a photograph of his young daughter in a bikini sitting on the lap of a handsome young lad. This was in 1947. He was worried about her but I think she knew what she was doing. Bikinis had just been invented – I thought she looked stunning!

By seven o'clock the ship was deserted, except for a young Norwegian sailor who, like me, had no one to visit. He didn't speak any English at all or was too shy to try. I went to the cabin and wrote letters to Mum and Dorothy, with no idea when a ship might be going north to take them but it was a good idea to have them written.

The boiler was on light duty since there was only steam to accommodation heating, the steam electricity generator and the pump required to return the minimum amount of water back to the boiler.

I went down to the engine room about every hour. Finding the boiler steam pressure low at about a hundred pounds per square inch, I lit one furnace burner, which took about twenty minutes to bring the pressure back to two-hundred-and-fifty PSI. This gentle increase in pressure avoided too much stress on the boiler.

Thus I spent Christmas Eve 1947, in and out of the engine room every hour or so.

I walked around the deck to check the status of the ship, brewed a pot of tea and stood on deck by the galley door. This was home.

It was a beautiful night, with no wind, I gazed at the stars in the crisp clear night air. The stars forming the Southern Cross were most prominent just east of overhead and they reminded me how far away from home we were.

Naturally I thought of the folks at home but I was comfortable with it. Mum would be okay, she led a predictable life probably playing the old melodies on the piano. Dorothy was waiting for me. I had it all to play for.

The young sailor laddie must have gone ashore. Alone on the ship, I was in my cabin reading an old magazine someone had brought on board. I had already taken the opportunity to write a couple of letters home. They would be put onboard a ship going to the U.K. sometime.

I'd been down to check on the boiler, then returning to my cabin at about five in the morning. I smelt burning! I went into the small passage outside my cabin and sniffed at the Chief's door. The smell seemed to be coming from here.

The Chief's cabin was in darkness. The door was on the brass hook. This was a precaution against a door being jammed in collision. I opened it and the light from the passage showed the cause of the burning smell.

The Chief must have returned while I was down below. He was laid in his bunk out to the world. His hand was hanging over the side of the bunk and he must have been holding a cigarette. His trousers were on the floor, a big hole, the edge of which was glowing red, was eating its way into the material.

I rolled the smoking trousers up, nipped up on deck and threw them over the side. There was no one else about.

At eight o'clock I was relieved by the Assistant Engineer and slept peacefully for a full four hours. I was back on watch at noon.

The Chief never asked where his trousers had got to and I never mentioned it to anyone! I don't think it had been the booze so much that night; it wouldn't take much when he was tired.

I had my lunch and prepared the engine for sea. We had been delegated to take the Leith Harbour football team round the coast to the Argentine whaling station of Grytviken. I didn't know they had a football team!

It was only about an hour's trip. We came into the bay and alongside their jetty. When I got finished with engine I came up and went ashore to see this Argentinian whaling station. It looked like any other whaling station: rough buildings connected by rough tracks. Perhaps it was a bit more up market than Salvesen's Leith Harbour.

The match was played on probably the only bit of South Georgia flat enough to put up a couple of goal posts. The players had to dribble round pot-holes and chunks of rock. I think it was a bit of a PR exercise. The Argentinians were a bit hostile and liked to win even then!

I wasn't interested in the football. I wandered off with another chap I had got talking to, to find the grave of Ernest Shackelton. It was in a small cemetery and had a kerbstone round the plot with chippings of scree covering the rough earth. To my knowledge Leith Harbour didn't have a cemetery, or a football pitch. I found out later that it did have a cemetery with many graves.

A stone cross at the head of the grave stood with a wreath of copper laurel leaves at its base. I thought this most appropriate as the ancient Greeks gave laurel leaves to their heros and winning athletes. He was a hero who snatched a rescue from total disaster.

I had read of Shackelton, what he did after losing his ship in the ice. Pulling the ship's boats for miles over the ice, he sailed with two chosen men in a ship's lifeboat under sail six-hundred miles to South Georgia! He landed on the south side of the Island, and with his men climbing over the mountains to the north side, trekking forty miles to the Leith Harbour whaling station to get help.

Later, they admitted they each had thought there was a mysterious fourth person with them. Well, Jesus seemed to like the men of the sea, Simon Peter and his friends, for example.

Shackleton managed eventually to get help and save all his men, whom he had left on Elephant Island. I paid my respects to a brave man and returned to my ship. He died from a heart attack on a second voyage south, by the way.

I never did find out who won the football match. Being at sea we were isolated from the 'civilised' pursuits that took place ashore. We returned to Leith Harbour with the team and I turned in and slept until I was called for my night watch.

We sailed to continue the hunt just after midnight 25th December 1947 and the routine continued.

I was watching the Captain stalking a whale one day, trying to get in the right place when the whale came up to blow. An Argentine whale catcher came from behind us with their gunner ready to shoot the whale from under our bow! Christiansen swung his gun round on to the other captain and shouted across to give way. It worked: they left us to find their own whales.

A few days later, a cruiser, HMS *Glasgow*, arrived in Leith Harbour fjord and stayed to show the flag. Maybe Christiansen, being an ex-Royal Navy commander had friends at the Admiralty. I hope HMS *Glasgow* steamed past Grytviken, the Argentinian whaling station.

The days passed, one time when we came in for bunkers the Mate who had been up to the office, handed me a telegram.

It was from my mum, just a few words printed on a strip of ticker tape and stuck to the telegram to say my sister Sybil, who had contracted polio at five years old and was paralysed down her left side, had died at the age of thirty two years.

It was a tragedy of a tragedy. I don't want to write about it. I felt the deepest sympathy for my mum and knew that my thoughts would be with her. I can't remember much of my reaction to it now. There was little I could do; it was maybe a blessing in disguise. I couldn't even send a telegram. I went on watch and kept busy.

My mum's brother Uncle Arthur had given her his New Testament Bible (Royal Navy issue 1914) for her to give me to take to sea. Now and then I would open it at the book of Saint Matthew Chapter 5, the Sermon on the Mount, and read the words, which I tried hard to live by.

Down in the engine room when the ship shuddered and dug into the great seas, the stoker and I just hung on physically and mentally for hours until the lads on the bridge could find some shelter – a big iceberg would do.

I felt a bit claustrophobic down below, but it was cold and wet topside so it was a bit better below, but it could be cold and seas breaking high often came down the ventilators.

The hull of the vessel was only made up of ribs and single plates riveted together, the higher plates a bit buckled between the ribs from the pressure of the sea. Not much to have between men and the worst ocean on earth.

109

It was some comfort to see 'Cargo Fleet Middlesbrough' embossed every couple of yards along each rib!

Looking for shelter, the lee side of a big iceberg would do nicely! We very rarely saw other whale catchers but one very wild day somehow four of Salvesen's catchers were hove to on the lee side of a massive berg, perhaps half a mile long and a couple of hundred feet high (a 'flat top' as they were called for obvious reasons). It was flat calm here.

One of the boats had a whale in tow and went alongside the berg at a convenient place and made fast (don't ask me how! These were Norwegian seamen), then the other three boats tied up to him. They had been in radio communication with each other.

There was a lot of toing and froing between the boats as the crews visited friends and probably neighbours. The Norwegians with Salvesen nearly all came from the town of Tonsberg.

We had a nice quiet evening and I had a restful sleep before going on watch at midnight. I did my routine jobs then did a bit of dobeying (washing my clothes) until about three in the morning, when the weather swung round.

It's not a good place to be, alongside an iceberg in bad weather! Voices were calling to cast off and engine telegraphs were clanging as the outside boats got clear.

The weather had abated somewhat as we all went our separate ways. On two occasions in my time, caught in a storm (hurricane is a better word), on the south side of South Georgia, the Captain took us into an old deserted sealing station for shelter.

This was into a narrow steep-sided fjord. It was a time capsule from the nineteenth century. Steel doesn't rust readily with the dry cold air. Timber doesn't rot at all.

We moored alongside a wooden jetty. A narrow railway ran along the track from the deserted sheds to the jetty. Tubs sat on the rails where they had been left when the last sealer had departed. The wooden sheds seemed sound, apart for one or two corrugated sheets that had been loosened in time. They clattered in the wind a morose note like a cracked bell tolling for the lost souls that haunted the place!

I was a bit disturbed to see a few rats scuttling about on the jetty but the sailors assured me they were too crafty to come aboard a whale catcher. What did that make the men who sailed in them?

We spent a comfortable night, but the Captain was always ready to put to sea at daylight. He knew what he was doing. I was not a deck man – I had to trust these chaps. Likewise they had to trust us engineers to keep that engine going. Many times when we were drifting at night we had to work on the engine, making adjustments. The metal in the big ends was a bit soft, not the right quality! Big end knock demanded we had to adjust the bearing clearances. I won't go into details but a rolling ship at sea is not the best place to do it.

Furthermore, a look-out had to be kept for the appearance of a berg that may require the engine to move away to safety.

In due course of the season, the factory ships *Southern Venturer* and *Southern Harvester,* with their escort of catchers, returned from their excursion round the icecap. They came into Leith Harbour, South Georgia, their season ended. They were restricted to a three-month season because they had more flexibility. Their catchers had less towing distance. The shore-based factory catchers had a seven-month season.

The factory ships would depart before us, this was an opportunity to send letters home, not that there was much to write about!

Weeks after the factory ships had departed with their precious cargo of oil to make margarine for the rations of the people and guano for the farmers of Europe, another ship arrived. It was named SS *Saluta* and was to be our transport home.

I had been asked if I wanted to 'overwinter', which meant to work through the seasons, overhauling the catchers during the Antarctic winter. This meant being away from home for eighteen months. I couldn't imagine a worse job in the world! I said I had to go back to be married but would consider it after the next season.

The weather was atrocious for the last weeks. I think the whales had all gone away for their holidays!

Finally, *Sondra* came in, the season ended. I packed my bags and without sentiment stepped from *Sondra's* low deck and walked along the fore shore, past one or two bull elephant seals that thought they owned the territory. They did, I suppose! I arrived at the steep-angled gangway of SS *Saluta* and climbed aboard.

The Chief Steward allocated me to a two-berth cabin. I was to share it with an old third engineer, Jimmy Rankin. Jimmy was about sixty-five years old, a dour Scot with a 'fine' philosophy and dour sense of humour. He complained of the cold and had the cabin door air grill sealed up with brown paper and the door always firmly shut.

The cabin was a fug of steamy cigarette smoke. When visitors arrived they were told to 'shut the bloody door!' but he was always pleased to entertain them with his pessimistic view of life! He was really amusing!

After a few days assembling the lads going home, *Saluta* set sail. The first days at sea I was dubious as to how long the ship would last in these waters. I think SS *Saluta* was built about 1890-something! Or even before that.

The forty-ton Scottish boilers were not in good health and the steam pressure had been reduced to one hundred and eighty PSI. Very slowly she put on a few miles each day, hoping for a favourable wind or current, maybe doing about six knots, no more! Looking over the side, I imagined I could have walked faster.

Traversing the cold Roaring Forties, we socialised in the saloon. I think the ship had been a passenger cargo vessel, a fine ship in her day. It was quite comfortable after a whaler.

Having reached better weather in a more northern latitude, the Chief Engineer set us to work. The ammonia refrigeration plant was in a serious state with the ship's supply of meat in danger of wasting and something like a couple of hundred men to feed. The ammonia compressor automatic control was unreliable so the Chief put us on three watches to control it twenty-four hours a day. The steel freezer coils in the freezer rooms were rusted badly and leaking a bit! We managed to keep it going until we reached the tropics. I'm not sure what failed. It was an antique and clapped out! Finally the sides of beef and other meat had to be put over the side.

We had a good feed of meat for a day or two, then I think it was bully beef.

The next major problem was one of the boilers. The triple-expansion steam engine was most reliable and would run for a hundred years with little attention. Boilers were more of a problem!

We catcher engineers were now put to double up the ship's engineers' watches. We repaired one boiler by plugging up a couple of leaking tubes. This was a hot job in the tropics.

The boiler was under reduced pressure of ninety PSI while we did the job but it was still very hot. We worked as a team, staying in the boiler furnace a few minutes at a time with wet towels and sacks until we were successful in putting the plugs and tie rods in place. The boiler was back up to its pressure of one hundred and eighty PSI in a few hours. Now I thought we stood a good chance to get the old girl home if nothing more fatal happened like the propellor dropping off!

SS *Saluta* made a stop-over, but I'm not sure where, probably Teneriffe for stores. We were able to buy full stalks of bananas here with cigarettes. The Chief Steward carried a good stock of fags for business purposes that were paid for on our account.

Many days later I was told we had passed the Kreac'h lighthouse at Ushant (I think it was), heading into the Irish Sea. The engine ground on at about seventy revs a minute, pushing us up to the Mersey River.

At the mouth of the Mersey, we stopped to pick up a pilot. A swarm of ten or more customs officers came aboard, all dressed in boiler suits. They proceeded to take the ship to pieces! Panels were removed from the cabins. They searched tanks and vessels in the engine room. What did they expect to find? We'd been nowhere to get contraband. A few cigarettes or tins of tobacco was all we had.

One poor sailor who voiced an opinion had his sea bag emptied over the deck. I felt as though we were criminals. We had been warned of their arrival and told what we were allowed to bring into the country. I hadn't the cash to pay duty on a tin of tobacco so I threw it over the side. The stick of bananas I had bought with cigarettes from a bum boat on the stop-over raised no objections. Bananas had not been in the shops in England since 1939. We gave them to the youngsters of our neigbours.

This was my first visit to the mighty Mersey and Liverpool. The SS *Saluta* finally moored up in Gladstone Dock. Ship's agents came aboard, discharge papers were given out and we were free to go. One of a fleet of taxis took us to Lime Street Station. A call at Yates's Wine Lodge first. A porter then collected my luggage from the left luggage depot and put me and the luggage on the train for Middlesbrough.

Like all drunken sailors, I had tipped him well for the service. After nine months away from civilisation, I was worried I would get on the wrong train. I slept most of the way. Sadly I don't remember getting home to my dear old Mum but I'm sure it was good, as we'd been through a lot together. Finally, I slept in my own little bed again.

1947 – A Christmas message sent by telegram to my mum – it cost me half a week's wage.

CHAPTER SIX

Between seasons

It was the end of May 1948. I had returned from the sea to be married. Dorothy had agreed to be engaged before I had sailed away the previous year. Being away from home for nine months had changed my life forever. I had asked Dorothy to arrange the wedding in June, and considering the post-war rationing and shortages of things, she had made a good job of it.

Few women went out to work at this time. In fact when we were married, Dorothy had had to give up her job in the office at the Hartlepool Co-operative Store's bakery department.

I had felt some guilt leaving Mum to go to sea. It was a decision I made with the distant future in mind, but now the guilt turned to compassion.

Mum had made some difficult decisions arising from her marriage to a selfish man. He became a successful businessman, going out in the evening, then, returning home intoxicated and abusing her.

Finally, she had to leave four of her kids with her mother-in-law while she went off with me, a baby, to make a life for herself.

Now, twenty-four years later, the baby had flown the nest. I knew a woman like her would not break down. I had learnt from her how to get through hard times. She would still play the old tunes on the piano. It was something I would always miss, her happy hour.

The miss was not so great. Even now the music and words of Ivor Novellor's music 'Sweetheart' come into my mind sung by my dear mum. Then I feel that her spirit is near me. It is a great comfort.

Little did I know she wouldn't be alone for long. A couple of years later, when I was married and settled at our first house, No. 34 Newstead Road, my eldest brother was lodged with Mum by the family.

Father was alone now with a housekeeper. His parents had both died. He was having trouble with the housekeeper over Eric, my eldest brother, and had put him out. This was the bully's way of solving any problem.

The family had made a very rare visit to Mum with Eric. I happened to be at Mum's at the time. Mum agreed to take Eric and the family arranged to pay her one pound and ten shillings a week for his keep.

Eric could read and write but lacked confidence and was retarded but he was useful. It was a good move at the time as it gave Mum a bit of company and Eric was able to go messages for her.

It worked against me when Mum's health failed and it was left to me to find a place for Eric. I rang the family for help but they had nothing to say.

After six desperate weeks in 1963, with Eric sleeping on the settee in our house, social services finally found a place for him in the Roman Catholic home, Brothers of Charity at Lisieux Hall, Chorley, Lancashire.

Mum spent a happy three years in Nunthorpe Hall, then a council home, and was able to get a bus into Middlesbrough to visit her friends calling to our house often for supper after which I would take her home.

She died in her sleep in Hemlington Hospital on 13th January 1966.

To return to 1948, two weeks after paying off Salvesen's SS *Saluta* in Gladstone Dock,s Liverpool, the old ship having finally made the eight thousand-mile journey from South Georgia despite the freezer and boiler failure. Dorothy had arranged that we were to be married at Saint Luke's Church, West Hartlepool on 16th June.

Dorothy had made all the arrangements, the invitations, and so on. She was very capable. All I had to do was to be measured for a suit and be there.

I must say, Dorothy looked stunning as she came down the aisle. She was what was called in those days a strawberry-blonde.

I was told later that it was 'unusual' for the bridegroom to turn round to see his bride come up the aisle to join him. I was quite relaxed, I was eager to see her again. I'd been away nine months.

Reverend Goldie conducted the ceremony. He was not old or stuffy but when he was finished I was sure we were joined together 'until death do us part'.

I had stayed at Aunt Jennie's the night before the wedding, where I had been brought up until I was six years old.

I owe a lot to Aunt Jennie. She supported me when I was staying all the weekends I could get away from work to Hartlepool, just to go to the Borough Hall dance on a Saturday night. For three years or more, it was to do my courting with Dorothy. In retrospect, I wish I had made Aunt Jennie some token of appreciation. I now feel that I was careless and took her for granted. She had been sacrificed to taking care of her mother (my granny) too. Their generation had suffered greatly with the First World War.

The morning of the great day I had breakfast with my granny in the old house behind the cobbler's shop. We sat at the dining table in the best room, with the best china. This would probably be our last meeting. Granny, Margaret Ann Wright (nee Scott) who had also contributed to my early years, died in 1950, aged eighty-seven, an amazing long life considering the cold damp conditions she lived in, with severe bronchitis and eating lots of animal fats: fish and chips cooked in beef dripping for supper every night at seven o'clock, except Sunday, when it was a beef sandwich with lots of yellow fat and delicious salt. When did it become unhealthy to eat animal fats and put lots of

1948 – Dorothy and I on our wedding day.

salt on the food with the tip of the knife, I wonder?

Dorothy's cousin Walter, my best man, arrived at 14 Middlegate Street to escort me to Saint Luke's church, Hart Road, 'West' Hartlepool.

I decided not to shave myself on this important occasion, Walter accompanied me to Mr Kirtley, the barber, to be shaved. His shop was just a hundred yards from Granny's place across the square, where the Salvation Army had before the war stood and played every Saturday evening.

Above the shop door was the barber's pole, white with a red stripe curling round from top to bottom. It should have been a warning of what was to come!

Mr Kirtley gave me a hot towel facial, then, stropping up his open razor on a strip of soft leather hanging by the chair, he lathered my face, rubbing the soap up first with his fingers, then using the brush to give a firm lather.

I gazed in the mirror, watching as he wielded the cut-throat razor. It came down my face from the top of my ear on each side. Before me, round the washbasin were the tools of his trade, coloured bottles of hair lotions.

One I was familiar with: a brown liquid, bay rum, a very popular product – probably the only hair dressing in those days. I don't suppose there was any rum in it! I think he used lavender aftershave. I don't think there was any other!

Now the cut-throat razor was going round my chin. I obliged by pulling my face into various grimaces at the pressure of his thumb and fingers. The result was he gave me such a close shave my face was oozing blood in several places. I thought I could have done a better job of it myself, but probably not!

At Aunt Jennie's there was no bathroom, hot water came from the copper kettle on the fire. The mirror was high above the mantle shelf. During my previous years at No. 14 Middlegate Street I had no hairs on my face.

Mr Kirtley apologised, and said I had a very tender skin. In truth there were no cuts. Being a professional, he applied his skills to stop the bleeding and I walked from his shop smelling of the after shave of my choice, lavender. It stung quite a bit. My face felt smooth, tight and fresh as a daisy.

Walter got me to the church in good time. I was surprised at the number of people there. Dorothy came down the aisle on her stepfather's arm. Standing facing the altar with Walter, I turned to see her. She smiled at me, and I knew there was no doubt in her mind. The day impressed on me the responsibility I was taking on.

Reverend Goldie said marriage was a state not to be taken lightly. I understood that but realised I needed all the good fortune there was going!

Jessie, my mum, looked very smart with a new hat, brown with a wide brim that framed her heart-shaped face with the soft brown eyes. A fashionable fox fur sat around the shoulders of her brown two-piece costume.

She stood next to me in the vestry as I signed the register. This was the parting of the ways. This was the only wedding she had been invited to attend of her three married sons.

I was surprised to become quite upset signing the register. My eyes filled with tears when I thought of the change that was now taking place. Mum understood, we all have our own life to live but it was hard to think that now she was on her own.

We had gone through a lot together in the war, but even then there had been happy times. We had many a happy hour round that old piano she played nearly every night after our dinner.

Now she was composed and, if there were any emotions in her thoughts, they were for my happiness. That was the kind loving person she was. I never heard her say a wrong word about anyone. True! She never even bad-mouthed her erring husband, Fred, but she did scorn the woman and her family who had led him astray. I don't think she realised what a weak stupid fellow he was. Maybe she did but she loved him anyway!

Mum always expected Fred would one day tire of the women who had usurped her rightful place and she would return to him to end their days together.

I don't think Mrs Scrafton had seen that in her messages. One of her final messages, my mum told me was: 'Oh, the Victory!' from someone or other. The victory was her peaceful death in Hemlington Hospital on 13th January 1966 after a happy Christmas with the nurses and hospital staff.

The spiritualist church did no harm if it gave Mum some words of comfort.

In hindsight, I wish I could have done more for her but she wasn't the clinging type and had her own friends and ways.

I took a deep breath and turned to my bride. Now we had to face the world and start a new life together.

The reception over, we went to Dorothy's mother's house near the church in Weldeck Road to change and pick up our luggage.

Dorothy was in her going-away costume, a powder-blue Harris tweed skirt and jacket. Me? I remember Fred Hawks, Dorothy's brother-in-law, a tailor, had measured me for a navy suit. Walter, her cousin, my best man, ordered the taxi and accompanied us both to the railway station. He was brilliant, everything was well organised. His army training probably.

The smell of the engine as it steamed into the station with its bright coal smoke and oil, impressed me with its assertion of power. Steam engines with their moving limbs seem to be alive. I had spent months in charge of a much larger mechanical beast. I had seen big changes. More changes were needed. I didn't want to spend my life at sea, only coming home for short vacations.

As the train slowly huffed and puffed its way along the platform, Walter's responsibilities to us were over. He put our luggage on the rack above the seat. It was an old fashioned carriage with separate carriage-like rooms, with long seats facing each other. It was designed from the stagecoach of old but the horses were long gone.

We didn't know it then but Walter had only a short time to live. He died from a heart attack at forty-eight years of age.

We, the happy couple, spent two weeks in a quaint boarding house in Harrogate. It wouldn't have been my choice, I would have preferred Scarborough near the sea but it didn't matter as long as Dorothy was happy.

Mr Souter, the proprietor, was a funny little man, very keen on the race horses. Betting on them, not riding them. He seemed to make a science of it, sitting a long time after breakfast with the sports page conferring with friends that came and went. They were not boarders, it seemed.

Street betting wasn't legal then, it was a furtive business. A boarding house would be a good cover for a bookie. Just a thought!

He knew we were newlyweds because Dorothy's ration books were in her maiden name and her wedding ring was crisp and new. I was only twenty-four years old and Dorothy twenty-two.

There was a frisson of nudges and nods from Mr Souter to the other guests when we came down to breakfast that first morning. We were a happy couple so it pleased me. Dorothy looked beautiful in the dress she had bought for this occasion, I was very proud to be her husband. This was the girl I first fell in love with when I was five years old! In spite of my broken home, the difficulties arising in my education and the uncertainty in my place in the world, I had married her – what a lucky lad! I had spent a season bashing about the Antarctic seas in order to do it. What was I going to do to follow that? I did another season!

The days were spent exploring by bus the City of York, I had been interested in ancient Roman remains since I was given a slim book on the subject as a kid. I admired those ancient Romans who had arrived in this country and shown the tribal ancient Britons how to build roads and organise and do business.

There wasn't much that interested me in Harrogate. Not even the toffee! York had plenty of interesting places. It was better than Scarborough! The magnificent cathedral, I felt priviledged to walk into it and marvelled at the men who had built it.

A trip up the river in a morning, then Clifford's Tower filled in an afternoon.

This was new to me. In my past lifestyle I hadn't had opportunity or the means for holidays that cost money. Dorothy on the other hand had been used to a carriage to the station and the train to Scarborough as a child. The trunk of clothes had been sent on ahead. Maybe that's why she chose Harrogate.

There was a bus stop nearby that took us to Knaresborough. The river was neutral territory for man and wife. I wasn't very interested in shops, I took Dorothy for a boat ride on the river, me showing off my skill at rowing. Not very exciting but relaxing.

We decided to go to an afternoon tea dance in the Pump Rooms at Harrogate but the shoes I had on were unsuitable for dancing. We went into the hall and Dorothy sat down to wait for me.

I went back to the Souter's to change my shoes. It wasn't far. When I got back Dorothy was on the floor dancing with some chap. I said I was jealous. Well, I was a bit miffed. But as Dorothy said, he was a nice young man, and it would be rude to refuse. I saw the funny side of it. The first person to dance with her as a married woman was a stranger. It was flattering, I suppose. He was a good looking guy and obviously had good taste in the girls. I would have to be careful.

This building originally was the pump room where people took 'the waters'. Water could be dangerous stuff in its many forms. I tried it, a horrid sulphurous taste if I remember. I drank the occasional pint of bitter but it was not available aboard ship and spirits became my tipple. Just for medicinal purposes, you understand.

The gardens in Harrogate were very colourful, a refreshing change from the many days I had spent at sea. South Georgia had no trees or shrubs. Sometimes when returning to the ship, I would pull a few coarse grasses from along the snow's edge where it grew in sheltered north-facing places. It was nice to have a bit of green. I would put them in an old mug with a bit of water and keep them in the cabin, to remind me that there was such things growing in the world. They didn't last long, though, when it got rough.

I was paid off for that first season with a cheque for roughly eight hundred pounds. Being away for a total of nine months, working seven days a week, That was an average of twenty-two pounds per week, working eight hours a day plus any extra unpaid hours that could be designated for the 'safety of the ship'. There was no holiday pay and no pay until we were working aboard ship again.

I received a letter from Salvesen. They would employ me 'working by' the factory ship *Southern Harvester* at Middle Dock on the River Wear at South Shields from 2nd August, until the start of the next season.

This meant I was two months without pay. Now the average pay at sea worked out to eightteen pounds per week. This included a bonus working on *Sondra* the 'top boat'. It was more than I could earn at home but the conditions were very different. If the bonus had been any lower it wouldn't be so attractive. Something to be said for a good steady job ashore!

Being ashore, I wasn't eligible for unemployment benefit. It was a state of limbo, if I went to another shipping company I wouldn't be available for the next season.

It didn't bother me, as I was enjoying the time off. In any case, I didn't anticipate spending the rest of my life at sea. There was plenty of work ashore at this time.

During the war the pay of a British seaman stopped from the time his ship was sunk by enemy action. Time in a lifeboat sailing home didn't count. Wives' and dependents' allowances were stopped.

In her diary, Dorothy wrote that we were like a couple of homeless waifs, staying at her mother's for a few weeks at Hartlepool and a few weeks in Middlesbrough with my mother. This would be a happy time for Mum to remember.

The days flew by, including my twenty-fourth birthday on 29th June. I had four more weeks, during which we visited Dorothy's Aunt Amy a few times then it was time to join the factory ship *Southern Harvester*.

I packed a small case and took the train to South Shields and made my way to the docks.

Southern Harvester was in dry dock, Middle Dock. It stood alone, where the other docks were I don't know. *Harvester,* with its two side-by-side funnels painted in company colours, red with the top third white, were mounted above the accommodation. Down in the dock, the twin propellors were visible below the aft slipway that led to the flensing deck. *Harvester* was enormous, her stern close to the dock gates indicated that she had nearly filled the dock.

I stepped up the gangway and reported to the second engineer. He was a Scot. I was allocated a berth and eventually met the other engineers as they came forward to meet the new guy. They were all about my age, and spoke broad Scots. I was the only Englishman aboard. They gave me a run-down on the job and the day-to-day drill: down below to start work at eight; coffee break in the engineers' pantry at ten; lunch at twelve noon; then finish work at five. I say 'work', we were not called on to do much, it was a way to keep us on the company pay roll. Dinner was at six, it was more formal. Washed and changed, we sat at a long table in the engineer officers' mess. I came under the scrutiny of the Chief Engineer, not a comfortable experience. Two mess boys served us, they were not used to silver service. On one occasion they served the gravy as soup.

I didn't like the way a young Scottish engineer sneered as he instructed them in table etiquette. These lads were obviously from a simple fishing community in the Shetlands, they were being employed 'working by' like us until they were put to the job they had signed on for as deck hands or mess boys. Good lads to have on small ships. The guy who sneered at them was a big ship man. Had he been used to the standards of an Atlantic liner? I wondered.

Dorothy lived with her mother and father-in-law in West Hartlepool during the time I was working on the *Southern Harvester*. They had a telephone. I was able to ring up from the ship and we arranged to meet, for ease of travelling, in Sunderland, for a couple of hours during the week. I was now working 'days' only, coming to Hartlepool each weekend. It was like courting again, meeting at the railway station, a walk in the local park. Just passing the time, until it was time to say goodbye to her at the bus stop and go our separate ways.

Then I returned to the great ugly ship up a gangway put in the slipway in the stern, where the whales were dragged on to the deck to be flensed, cut up and fed to the cookers.

With a couple of hours before turning in I'd read a magazine in the mess room for an hour, have a bit of supper in the engineer's pantry and turn in to awake next morning at seven o'clock to have breakfast. This was good. Kippers, bacon and eggs, toast with lashings of real butter and marmalade. A strong cup of coffee and a cigarette.

A feast after six years of strict rationing.

The work was only desultory in the cathedral-like engine room of this big vessel. A shore gang of Geordie workmen came aboard each day to do the work of overhauling the machines.

It was bedlam! The shore gang were a noisy lot. A couple of Geordies had a way of working that seemed to require they yell at each other from one side of the engine room to the other in their high-pitched, unintelligible vernacular.

It may have been partly for our amusement. If so, I was embarrassed for the impression it made on my Scottish colleagues. I hadn't been used to this.

At Smith's Dock the men were a phlegmatic lot. The Yorkshire boundary came as far as the river. The motto was 'hear all, say nowt!'

'Working by' a ship, as it was called was tedious as there was little work to do. I pottered around the engine room. It was interesting for a while. The engine room extended from the 'double bottom' of the *Southern Harvester* to the skylights in the top deck. It was a vast space, the whole area painted white with an overhead crane capable of running from one end of the engine room to the other.

Sections of steel ladders led from the accommodation deck via gantries to the lower deck. The 'double bottom' of the ship served a dual purpose. It gave strength to the hull and formed tanks to store fuel. On these tank tops, two big triple-expansion steam engines stood, port and starboard with their controls amidships. A row of generators provided electricity for the ship and factory. The switchboard on a half deck above them, duplicating the switch gear for each generator, extended nearly the full width of the vessel. The ship was like a small town. At sea, a few hundred men worked twelve-hour shifts in this floating factory.

A half deck at the other end of the engine room was home to a large number of evaporators used to make vast quantities of fresh water from the sea. I didn't fancy working on a ship like this.

It was a tricky job managing an evaporator. There was no automatic control in those days, it was necessary to juggle the fifteen PSI steam pressure with the cold sea water coming in and the salt-laden water going out. This was to keep the level in the sight glass steady by controlling the steam valve manually. An alarm indicated if salt was carrying over in the steam to the engine room condenser if control was poor. I preferred to be my own boss in charge of the watch on my small catcher vessel!

At this time, working by in this vast engine room, we did nothing more than adjust a few valve glands and liaise with the Geordie chargehand's simple request to open or close a valve for him to drain a vessel or seal off a line to accommodate their work.

We spent a lot of time going up to the engineers' mess room for coffee and a smoke. This operational duty called 'smoko' was held in the engineers', pantry, where we only had to wash our hands and didn't have to dress up.

There were about a dozen Salvesen engineers like me, working by, but I was the only Englishman. The other lads were Scots and I was subject to a bit of leg-pulling, in spite of my maternal grandparents being Scottish. These Scots could recite reams of the poetry of Robbie Burns and I was given the full book!

Thursday was pay day – seven pounds a week. The food we got in the merchant navy was fantastic. Britain was still rationed for butter, sugar and meat. It wasn't because it was scarce. The war was over but Britain was bankrupt; the Government could only afford to buy essential food. What was brought into the country was not the best quality either. Britain, saviour of Europe, was destitute. Our war debt to the United States of America was only paid off in early 2007.

Whaling was a great help to get the country back on to its feet! The whale would feed Europe until the people could restore the normal supplies of oils and meat.

It cost millions of pounds to send a whaling expedition to the Antarctic Ocean but it gave work to thousands in the shipyards and the local economy benefited.

Whaling is a labour-intensive, high-material-cost business and many early whaling expeditions of hand-thrown harpoons went bankrupt as the reduced number of the right whales made it uneconomical to hunt.

In a way, the business was self-regulating. When the numbers of whales caught made it unprofitable to search the ocean looking for them, the whaling stopped. The food chain readjusted itself. There was then more food for the surviving whales. They would multiply again. Man would find a more economic way to replace the products lost. Certainly there were safer and much easier ways to produce oil for margarine.

Another new experience for me was being with an all-British crew. In spite of my first season, I was very naïve. On Thursday nights after the evening meal, we would all go to the Rose and Crown just outside the dock gate. I never had more than three pints of the local draught beer, it wasn't as strong as Teesside beer, so I thought.

The first week after a visit to the Rose and Crown, next morning (Friday), I came to, as if from a coma. I vaguely remember the mess boys coming in, they left without making the beds. This was a four-berth cabin I shared with a nice guy called Ian McEwan and two other engineers. The Chief Steward then made a short appearance. He said something unintelligible to me. I was not capable of receiving visitors.

I came round about ten o'clock, when my room mates arrived in an agitated state They got me down from the top bunk. 'Come on, you've got to muster', they said, while getting me into my boilersuit.

I was half carried along the corridor to the door of the engine room, still protesting: 'I can't, I'm not well!'

'You must make a show, or you'll get the sack'

This stiffened my resolve a bit but I was very confused as to what was wrong with me.

They got me down the many flights of steel steps to the engine room deck and sat me in a corner, where I was allowed to doze until it was time for lunch. 'Oh! I don't want any lunch', I wailed. My protests were ignored.

'Come on, get up, the Chief will wonder why you aren't at the table!' The dialogue was in a strong Scottish accent.)

Now I was dragged, pulled and pushed up again to the accommodation deck. It was necessary to remove our boilersuits and clean up to appear in the saloon.

By this time, I had recovered consciousness and was aware that my presence in the mess room would be under the eagle eye of the Chief Engineer. He was a dour Scot, not a man to trifle with. I could be in big trouble!

I sat, trying to appear interested in what was being said at the table. Voices seemed to come through a muffled engine room voice pipe! I picked at my food, had a strong cup of coffee then sat back in the dining chair trying to keep my head from drooping on to my chest. I accepted a cigarette from one of my keepers and took a few puffs. Sitting well away from the Chief at the other side of the long mess-room table.

I suspected he knew of my condition, as he viewed me with a suspicious glare from under heavy bushy eyebrows. We got up to return to our duties, stumbling but managing to walk out of the mess without bumping into anything I only wanted to go to my cabin and sleep but it was impressed on me that it was not a wise thing to do.

I got below and went back to my corner. My keepers kept coming over to see if I was okay. I was beginning to sense a collective guilty conscience. 'Best to say nowt!' as they say in Yorkshire. It's nice to know who your friends are.

I might have recovered quicker if I could have been sick but bouncing about on a whale catcher for many months makes the stomach sphincter muscle very strong.

I haven't been sick since my first few days at sea.

I managed to get the day over and was later catching the train to Hartlepool for a precious weekend with Dorothy.

I climbed from the engine room feeling a bit better, relieved my trial was over. I went to my cabin and freshened up. I packed my weekend case and walked down the accommodation corridor but as I passed the Second's cabin he was waiting for me and called me in.

On a big ship, the Second would have a Chief's 'ticket', or certificate – he was the executive engineer.

I was given a warning: 'drunk and unable to muster', 'serious,' and so on. He could stop my weekend leave, but would let me off this time. There was a hint of amusement in his manner. Only a hint! Another Scot! He knew I had been slipped a Micky Finn. I think he was warning me to be on my guard another time.

I thanked him for his consideration and went ashore. Dry dock was still know as going ashore. If only he knew. There was no way I wanted another day like it. I was still a bit weak that evening when I got home. I'm still not sure if I wasn't drugged or not.

The following week I discovered the reason for my discomfort: glasses of whisky slipped into my pint when I went to the loo. Hard to believe! The beer didn't taste any better at the time but I thought it was a good pint!

I never left a pint glass on the bar again unless it was empty. I don't object to anyone buying me a dram. That's a friendly thing to do. I learnt the Scottish habit of a 'half and a half' whisky and chaser, half of beer.

Dorothy's diaries show that we went to the cinema often. We seemed to like the same things, that was a promising start. I was very happy but always at the back of my mind was the thought that I had to go back to South Georgia for another season.

Well, I didn't have to, but the company expected it, engineers for catchers were in short supply. It would hurt my pride to back out now. Being newly married, a better reason was that I needed the money.

It would be almost impossible to save any money working in the shipyard. The pay just about covered my living expenses, I might have a pound left to save each week. I was prepared to go whaling again – it was a calculated risk.

There was a high element of danger on the catchers, but this was reduced by the skill and experience of the entire crew when on watch. In severe gales a small mistake could jeopardise the whole ship. It didn't even take bad weather.

In January 1947, a whale catcher named *Simbra* had overturned on a calm sea. The only survivor was a Shetland sailor named John Leaske from the book *Shetland Whalers Remember* by *Gibbey Frazer*.

Simbra was catching for the factory ship *Venturer*. They were working near the ice and returned to the *Venturer* with a couple of whales. *Simbra* asked for bunkers (fuel) but the *Venturer* had an oil tanker alongside and was refuelling herself. *Simbra* was asked to wait. Whales were spotted in the vicinity, so the Captain decided to chase after them.

After an hour chasing being low on fuel, the Captain decided to give up the chase and instructed the helmsman to return to the factory ship.

John Leaske was in the barrel (the lookout post up the mast). *Simbra* turned to starboard. Was the ship still at full speed? Not unusual when chasing.

This would naturally cause the ship to heel over to port. Being low on fuel, the ship was unstable and failed to recover from the manoeuvre. *Simbra* continued to heel over until she lay on her port beam.

John Leaske got out of the barrel and climbed along the now-horizontal mast to the side of the vessel and got to the lifeboat. The Gunner and Mate and other sailors had got the boat ready to drop into the sea. It was not possible to lower it with the davits.

They cut the ropes and the boat dropped into the sea upside down and drifted away. The sea water temperature is minus one or two degrees here and they knew it was fatal to be immersed for even a few minutes.

Unable to swim, they used a spar of wood to paddle over to the stricken lifeboat.

The Captain, an older man, succumbed to the cold and went under. Three of them got to the boat and managed to turn it right way up. The boat floated level with the sea. Efforts to bail it failed.

The sea came back in as fast as they bailed it out. Finally, only John Leaske survived by sitting on the transom of the boat (the stern) with his feet in the freezing sea for twelve hours until he was spotted next morning at about ten o'clock by a whaler chasing in the vicinity.

John had been saved by his kapok jacket and his sense in putting a galvanized bucket on an oar stuck in the mast hole. He was rushed to the factory ship and put into the ship's hospital, until well enough to be returned to South Georgia and home.

Nine months later in October, when I joined *Simbra*'s sister ship *Sondra,* we were given orders that all boats must not chase when both port and starboard fuel tanks were empty. They must return for bunkers using the centre tank.

The following year, when I returned to *Sondra* for the second season, ingots of pig iron had been put in the bilges and concreted over to improve the stability

The next entry in Dorothy's diary was that I had received a letter instructing me to go to Salvesen's office in Leith, to sign a contract for the coming season.

On 15th August we took the train from Hartlepool to Edinburgh, changing at Darlington. It was typical August weather, heavy rain.

Owing to floods on the east coast the train had to go via Carlisle. It was late in the day when we got to Edinburgh. Every hotel we called at in Edinburgh was full.

It was 1948, the beginning of the first Edinburgh festival. Just my luck! I thought. Eventually we found the last available room at the King's Commercial

Hotel in Leith, not a long walk from the top of Princess Street in Edinburgh.

The room was most unsuitable for a newly-married couple, the husband soon to be going to sea for nine months. Just my luck again!

Two single beds were situated foot to foot in a long, narrow room. We were able to sit up and wave to each other! We saw the funny side of it and stayed two nights, taking the opportunity to see the sights of Edinburgh. A last short holiday befor we parted.

CHAPTER SEVEN

My second season on *Sondra*

I had been given orders to report to the SS *Polar Chief*, berthed at Bidston Dock, Liverpool. It's at Birkenhead, actually, on the other side of the River Mersey.

On 17th August, we took the ten-fifteen train from Princess Sreet Station to Liverpool. It was only a short journey to Upton across the Mersey in the Wirral.

Walter Punch's wife, Mary, came from Upton in the Wirrel. Her sister, Millie and her husband Alf Sherlock, kindly invited us to stay with them.

Next morning, Wednesday 18th, I reported to the Chief Officer of the *Polar Chief* in Bidston Dock.

There would be a couple of hundred men aboard on the 22nd when she sailed down the River Mersey, taking men and supplies down to Leith Harbour, South Georgia.

I was to return there to the whale catcher *Sondra*. Another season: one hundred and eighty-five days on two watches twelve midnight until four in the morning and nights as third engineer. What a terrible thought!

I was able to stay with Dorothy at Upton for the few days before *Polar Chief* sailed. *Polar Chief* was a fifty-one-year-old passenger liner. Built in 1897, it had been a North Pacific Liner, the SS *Montcalm*, the sister ship to the SS *Montrose*, whose most famous passenger was Dr Crippen – who in 1910 had murdered his wife and escaped with his lover dressed as a young man.

He was the first person to be arrested by wireless! The Captain had seen through the disguise and used the new wireless to raise the alarm.

The SS *Montcalm* performed long and faithful service during three wars. She worked as a troopship in the Boer War; as a transport ship in the First World War, surviving a torpedo in 1917 and was repaired; she then survived the Second World War and, after a few journeys to South Georgia whaling, was eventually scrapped in 1952.

After service for the Pacific Company, the *Montcalm* had been converted from a passenger liner into a whale factory ship with a slipway at the stern to haul the whales on to the deck.

Made redundant again now with the slipway obsolete and roped off, the factory equipment, boilers and so forth, had been removed. The space was now used to transport fuel, stores and spare gear to South Georgia and bring back whale oil, fertiliser from the bones and guano, and men. In 1948, on the

1947 – The author, twenty-three years old. Third Engineer Arthur Dinsdale.

Polar Chief, *ex-SS Montcalm, built 1897. A charmed vessel. Note the armoured bridge.*

1947 – A fin whale about 70ft long, flagged-off with a lamp on the bamboo pole to be picked up later in the day.

Above – The ship's doctor in cap, goggles and long-johns, takes his medicine – a tot no doubt – before his shave.

1948 – Father Neptune, alias Nobby Clark, engine room greaser.

A fine pair of heels after his shave.

1948 – Captain Begg greats Father Neptune, Lady Neptune and retinue during the crossing the line ceremony.

1897– SS Montcalm, *sister ship of SS* Montrose *that Dr. Crippin took to escape justice.*

SS *Montcalm* 16,800 tons Canadian Pacific Liner.

The remarkable history of the SS *Montcalm*:

1897	May 17, launched for Elder Dempster
1897	Sept. 3, maiden voyage Avonmouth - Montreal
1898	November, chartered to ATL
1900	June, became Boer War transport
1903	Taken over by Canadian Pacific Line
1914	August, became British Expeditionary Force transport
1914	October, rebuilt as dummy battleship, HMS *Audacious*
1916	January, bought by British Admiralty
1916	October, converted to oil-tanker for Anglo Saxon Petroleum Co, renamed *Crenella*
1917	October, taken over by Shipping Controller
1917	Nov. 26, torpedoed off the Irish coast. Survived and repaired.
1919	Returned to Anglo Saxon Petroleum Co.
1920	Purchased by Runciman, London
1923	Bought by Norwegian owners, converted to a whaling depot ship and renamed *Rey Alfonso*
1927	Renamed *Anglo Norse*
1929	Renamed *Polar Chief* for Falkland Whaling Co.
1930	Laid up for lack of orders.
1941	Became the Ministry of War transport *Empire Chief*
1946	Renamed *Polar Chief* for South Georgia Co.
1952	Scrapped at Dalmuir, Scotland

Compiled by the Author from Shipping Times and other sources.

way down to South Georgia two boilers for the whale factory were fastened on the forrard deck as cargo.

Cabin accommodation had been modified to accommodate the crews of the catchers and factory workers. None of the splendour remained in the cabins. Panelling and furniture had been stripped out and sold, probably. The original dining room we used was probably a second-class room and remained in its 1897 state.

My cabin had a porthole and a small ventilator that could be turned to the wind. The bulkheads were painted with cork chippings in the paint for insulation. Metal bunks were in twos and fours. There was nothing fancy in the way of washbasins or air conditioning. Communal toilets, showers and washbasin rooms were provided. Fresh water for washing was limited to a couple of hours each day. People ask: 'But why didn't they make fresh water from the sea with the evaporators?' The answer is, it costs money!

It takes quite a lot of steam to boil the water off, which requires fuel. Fuel has to be carried a long way to South Georgia. It's a business – we were not tourists. On Sunday 22nd August 1948 *Montcalm* (alias *Polar Chief*), left Bidston Dock and sailed down the Mersey to the sea. I'm not quite sure why we two catcher engineers were asked by the Chief of this big old tub to assist the Second Engineer in the engine room.

These big-ship men didn't like to think we were passengers. There wasn't a lot to do. Unlike on the *Southern Harvester*, this second engineer, an Englishman, was friendly enough; he actually seemed to be a bit nervous. We performed small duties, such as making a note in the log of each telegraph instruction, passing through a bulkhead to the boiler room to check the boilers. These boilers were very old and very long with three furnaces at each end. They were natural draught, not fan-assisted, probably coal-fired originally.

The fire tubes were blown clean with steam each morning to remove the soot. Naturally, we were given the job when on duty. The firemen were a bit sloppy and tended to let the steam drop a few pounds. One Glaswegian chap liked to read comics and had a pile of them. Where was Rabbie Burns?

Two tugs steadied us down the river. After a while the pilot telegraphed down for slow ahead. The engine, as big as a large house, responded to the steam and turned ponderous and slow as we moved up-river. Later, as we reached the river mouth a telegraph, 'Stop', created a problem. The main steam control valve to the triple-expansion engine had seized!

Having had some work done by the shore gang, the new valve spindle brass screw thread (a nice fit when cold) probably expanded with the heat and finally seized. It refused to budge! It was impossible to stop the engine by the normal manner.

Further telegraph signals from the bridge '*STOP*' could not be answered. The engine room telephone began to ring: 'Bridge here! What the hell's the matter?' The Second was busy, the Third waited to pass the phone to him. In desperation the Second put the engine valve gear in the midway position. Being half way between ahead and astern this unorthodox operation brought the engine to a stop.

The telephone message from the bridge seemed to make the receiver red hot judging by the way the Second was holding it. The squawks it made sounded like an angry Donald Duck. The steam control valve had been a bad job! Not Salvesen's engineers' fault!

The powers that be decided *Polar Chief* had to return to Bidston Dock for further repairs. A Board of Trade inspection found other items below regulations. There was a lot of waste oil under the boilers.

We arrived back at Bidston Dock. Not a good thing, as I'd just about spent up. We didn't think we needed money where we were going! The repairs would take a few days. They didn't give us a departure date.

The Chief was too busy to need us. I imagine he got an ear-wigging too. A shore gang came aboard to do the work.

According to Dorothy's diary she had gone home to Hartlepool on the 22nd. She would be surprised when I rang on the 23rd with the news that we were back in Bidston Dock. On the 25th I rang her to send me some money! She sent me four pounds – about thirty pounds today, perhaps?

I had bought a small Philips radio. It was about the size of a shoe box, one of the first miniature valve sets, as the transistor hadn't been invented yet. It had medium wave, long wave and short wave stations. Things like this, in short supply because of selling abroad to earn currency, were now coming on to the market. Short wave was essential for where we were going.

The wartime austerity was slowly fading from our lives, as long as you could pay for it! There was none of this 'buy now, pay later'. I had to buy a converter to power the radio from the ship's one hundred and ten volts to the required two hundred and fifty volts. I was able to buy this in a city like Liverpool.

The money Dorothy sent me was to allow me to visit the Shaw family in Upton village again.

Finally on 29th August we were on our way. Again we were pressed into service, doubling up watches with the ship's engineers. It was interesting to walk around the big open space of the engine room. The main engine, bolted down on to the double bottom tank tops, rocked quite a bit. This, I was told, was because the steel plates of the ship's double bottom after nearly fifty years were rusted a bit thin. The engine cylinder tops moved back and forth about three inches.

Unlike on a whale catcher, there was very little to do on watch. At full speed of sixty-eight revolutions a minute the engine would last a thousand years! Provided it didn't drop through the bottom of the ship! The boiler pressure had been reduced from two hundred and fifty PSI to one hundred and eighty PSI, possibly for safety reasons or the boiler's old age – I know the feeling now!

The engine would obviously go faster at two hundred and fifty PSI when the boilers had been new. I imagine as a liner she would do about twelve knots. In her 1948 state, she did six, maybe a bit more with a following sea and strong wind!

The engine was hand lubricated by a greaser on each watch. A few drops of oil were dripped into the bearing brass cups every ten minutes or so.

Engineers didn't do such things on a big ship – they walked around in white boilersuits. They even had a pumpman to start and stop the pumps. In trimming the ship, ballast had to be pumped over from one tank to another, probably in a pump room amidships. The engineer's position must always be near the controls. Records were kept of events in a logbook in the desk.

It was interesting to see big-ship routines, which I had not been aware of until now. At noon exactly, the number of engine revolutions was recorded. This was to calculate longitude. There were no satellites to give a ship's position then.

Every twenty-four hours, the revolutions of the engine were used to calculate the daily distance travelled by multiplying the number of revolutions by the pitch of the propellor. The distance travelled in one revolution in feet. This would be checked against the calculations of the officers on the bridge from sightings with a sextant if conditions permitted a sighting of the sun.

The difference allowed, called the 'slip', was two-and-a-half per cent. This variable could be for sea conditions, currents or head winds. It could even be because of bad steering but we wouldn't dare mention it! The deck officers blamed the engineers and vice versa. All clever stuff!

Good captains who knew the many currents in the sea could sometimes gain a couple of knots. The charts had information from the ancient mariners like Captain James Cook and were constantly consulted and amended as time evolved.

Somewhere over the other side of the Atlantic Ocean, two days from Aruba, we ran into a hurricane. Or did it run into us? It lasted for about three days. Weather forecasts at sea in those days were unreliable. This was my first experience of very bad weather aboard a big ship. The sea appeared to be boiling.

There didn't seem to be much pitching (up and down motion). The ship was so long. It was supported by quite a few waves. It rolled a bit and yawed slowly (swung the bow port and starboard).

Most of the big-ship men were seasick. Salvesen office clerks going to the factory to work were very seasick. A lot of it is psychological. I had a friend who came out on sea trials with me on a new ship. Poor lad, he became seasick the minute the telegraph rang 'standby', the ship still tied up to the jetty. He would go to his cabin and not reappear until we returned.

We catcher men were immune to any sort of heaving about but on an old tub like *Polar Chief*, this was a bit different! The roll was scary!

The Skipper managed to turn the great long vessel head up into the weather. It didn't help much, but I suppose it prevented the seas rushing up the obsolete slipway in the stern. Then *Polar Chief* developed a roll. And what a roll!

A deck cargo of two boilers, fastened down on to the fore deck for use in the factory at Leith Harbour whaling station, made the vessel's 'trim' a bit tender.

The roll developed like the swinging of a giant pendulum, first to the port side. It rolled over slowly, I thought each roll would never stop! When it did stop, it hung there! Was it ever going to come back? No! It hung a bit more!

After what seemed time to abandon ship, she gave a wriggle and started to come back, slowly, ever so slowly, then went all the way over to the starboard side!

This went on for two days. I hated it! Give me a small ship that bounced over the sea like a cork any time. We were cabined up all this time, rain and hail rattling against the porthole. The saloon was comfortable enough, sitting on the settee-like seats that lined the room with a foot pressed against the table to stop sliding off when the roll tipped the saloon over to near thirty-odd degrees. We passed the time telling jokes and tall stories.

The view through the rain-drenched portholes was grey and wet. No horizon, grey nothing.

Only us catcher men went to the mess room. For two days, the meals were a bit 'help yourself'. One of the lads found a big tin of corned beef, opened it and, and found some bread. The crew had gone AWOL. Someone found the butter and we got stuck in!

According to big-ship routine, the cooks had already baked the bread. It was fresh, just like Mum made. The hurricane howled and blew hard outside, but we tried to ignore the roll and satisfied our hunger. The roll wasn't so bad. It was the hanging bit that created a tinge of anxiety. I didn't fancy getting a boat away with her laid on her side. especially in a sea like that.

One result of this stress on the old girl was the cast-iron main cooling water discharge pipe cracked. This pipe carried sea water, used to cool the condenser, up the ship's side and back to the sea. Quite a big piece had broken out of the pipe.

The sea was now pouring into the engine room. The suction side of the pipe was isolated and somehow the roll was now reduced. The engine had to be slowed because the steam could not be condensed without the sea water supply. Auxiliaries such as steam generators and essential pumps were running with their steam going into the atmosphere.

Both bilge pumps were opened up while the situation was brought under control. The weather had improved a bit by now.

We catcher men again were asked to help with engine room routines while the ship's engineers assisted the ship's carpenter to build a wooded box around the fourteen-inch broken pipe. Ships carry timber and cement for such emergencies.

The pipe was put together and strapped up. The box was then filled with quick-setting cement and in a few hours, the cooling sea water valve was opened and normal service was resumed!

In a couple more days we were in normal tropical weather: calm sea and blue sky. This created hot, uncomfortable conditions aboard ship and men started bringing their foam rubber mattresses on deck. Foam rubber was comfortable enough in a northern climate but in the tropics we woke up in a morning in a pool of perspiration.

We arrived at Aruba, then a Dutch colonial island off Venezuela at the top of South America.

Polar Chief lay at a 'mole', a jetty isolated from the harbour. We were here for a few days to take on stores and fuel oil. I can't remember how many days, maybe four? Yes! Confirmed. It was four.

I put on a clean white shirt and my best Duke-of-Windsor grey plaid suit. It was my first time ashore in a foreign port. I wanted to look my best. It was hot!

A foy boat hired by the company for the time we were in port, ferried us ashore.

I bought a pair of nylons for Dorothy, as they were unobtainable at home. We were only able to take an allowance of ten pounds from the Chief Steward to go ashore. Hard to believe but sterling was rationed as well as food.

It was very hot! It was my first time in the tropics. I had been quenching my thirst drinking rum and Coke, in tall straight glasses. Coke was a soft drink so, I was told! It wasn't on sale in the UK at this time. 'Didn't it occur to you that the rum was alcoholic?' No! I had not been a spirit drinker. I thought spirits were always drunk in tot glasses, like the cowboys did in the Wild West! 'Rum and Coke' was just a name to me like 'rum and butter' toffees or 'bay rum' hair oil. I didn't even know it came from this side of the Atlantic!

I was in trouble again. Too many rum and Cokes! – I ended the day on a Danish tanker called *Christian Holm* berthed alongside the harbour. The officers of this tanker had enjoyed my company and were very patient with me until I passed out! They then put my papers and the nylons into the inside pocket my mum had made secure with a button and buttonhole, then buttoned it up and called up *Polar Chief*. Before going ashore, we had been issued with a card bearing our rank, ship and mooring berth. Personnel going adrift must have happened quite frequently.

A message was sent to *Polar Chief* by Morse code with an aldis lamp. I was told the message went something like this: 'Please send two men to return Third Engineer A Dinsdale, a distressed British seaman, to his ship'.

Later I was told two Shetland sailors were sent to recover me. They had tossed me into the motorboat hired to ferry the crew from the harbour to the mole and back – amazing, I had no broken bones! Someone put me into my bunk, I presume they did. Again, I asked myself how did it happen.

I came to the next morning, still in my best grey plaid West of Windsor tailored suit, now badly stained with fuel oil, no doubt from the Danish tanker. This wasn't like me – I was becoming a danger to myself!

The suit had been for my twenty-first birthday. Mum had taken me to a big store's tailoring department. A tailor reeking of stale beer had measured me. A couple of weeks later I had a fitting. The half-made waistcoat and jacket had been put on while drunken Charlie had expertly marked the fitting requirements and then a last fit. I was very proud of that suit. Ah, well! nothing lasts for ever!

Unlike my trouble on the *Southern Harvester*, I managed to recover enough before smoko to appear in the mess but I was on record. The officer of the watch would have recorded the message from *Christian Holm*. The Chief Engineer of *Polar Chief* said I would have to appear before the Captain on a charge! I would be logged, fined and given a 'poor' discharge paper on my return to the UK.

I was mystified. What had I been drinking? I tried to revive myself with a cup of tea. It tasted of rum and made me worse. It was funny, rum and Coke didn't taste of rum, it just tasted of Coke! Now everything I drank tasted of the damned rum and had a dramatic effect on me for a couple of days.

The ship was at the mole another two days taking, on supplies for South Georgia. I behaved like a methodist minister. Fruit juice only. None of the fancy cola!

Before *Polar Chief* departed, the majority of the crew were on record for a logging! I watched them coming back aboard. Staggering up the gangway. A big rope net had thoughtfully been slung underneath this gangway, extending three feet each side. It surprised me that no one fell into the net but one or two nearly went through the handrails of the gangway.

The ship's Doctor was up half the night stitching up wounds from the sabres worn and wielded at the first sign of trouble by the armed Dutch police.

Some of the lads tried unsuccessfully to smuggle booze aboard by climbing over the chain-link fence. The harbour was a petroleum fire hazard area –no booze allowed. This was strictly applied.

In the last moments before the mooring lines were cast off, a small vessel came alongside. Sides of beef were hoisted aboard in a rope net. I took some photographs of this action. Shipping agents did last-minute business and hopefully nothing or nobody that should be aboard was left behind. It would be nine months before we passed this way again. I was glad to see the back of the place!

Once we got underway, the Chief had a word with me and said the Captain was not going to 'log' anyone. When I asked why he said that the Captain had had a party in the saloon and they'd wrecked the place! The carpenter had repaired the damage. As long as we had done no permanent damage to the ship we were okay. Moi? Do damage to this old tub? I was the only thing that got damaged, an innocent abroad!

Passing through the tropics, the cabins became hot and humid. The modern foam rubber mattresses were not suitable for a ship without air conditioning. For a week or so, we took to sleeping on deck until we moved to higher latitudes.

One or two bright lads made scoops from empty bully beef tins. These were sticking out of the portholes about eighteen inches and deflected air into the cabin. With the ship moving at six knots, it was almost as good as a fan. In a few days the ship had rows of them on each side.

It seemed a miracle to me how a big, slow ship like *Polar Chief* had escaped being sunk by U-boats during the war. Probably didn't think it worth a torpedo or that it would founder before it made port. The bridge was armour-plated. It had not been removed in its peacetime role. But it was a lucky ship! And had a good skipper.

The heart of the ship, the old steam engine, was a simple machine only twenty-five per cent economically efficient but very reliable.

I later discovered that earlier in her life as the Pacific liner SS *Montcalm*, under various aliases, with names like *Empire Chief* whilst on duty as a transport vessel in 1917, it had been torpedoed off Ireland but got to port and survived to fight again as a transport in the Second World War.

Approaching 'the Line', zero latitude, the Captain had arranged for Father Neptune to come aboard. This was a great day and full of fun. A swimming pool was constructed on the fore deck. It was made from wooden planking and lined with a big tarpaulin. Filled with sea water (fresh water was at a premium, only available at set times), the pool had a platform on one side level with the four-foot-deep pool. All crew on 'free watch' were invited to the visit of Father and Lady Neptune, accompanied by his retinue. The retinue was nine-strong!

All were appropriately dressed in the weirdest costumes, some borrowed from the bridge signal flags, the galley and ship's hospital and, in one case, a toilet! A toilet seat suitably decorated formed a ceremonial collar round Sparky's neck, the ship's electrician. Neptune's barber, a catcher Asdic able seaman with a pirate bandana on his head carried a cut-throat razor twelve inches long, made of wood!

Other assistants carried a stool for the victims to sit on, a bucket of shaving soap, a four-inch paint brush, and medicine for the victims, carried by Neptune's doctor, the ship's bosun. The medicine was probably a tot of rum.

The Captain, in full dress (tropical whites) came down from the bridge to the fore deck with his chief officer to receive our visitors.

We onlookers sat around each side of the deck. Some climbed up and sat on the deck cargo of the two boilers on the port and starboard of the ship.

From the forec'sle, the very pointy end of the ship, the paint store and rope locker, to a loud trumpet blast (the ship's steam whistle), emerged the noble figure of Father Neptune, carrying a fine trident, accompanied by his Lady Neptune and the assistant rabble! I didn't hear all the dialogue but the Captain greeted his esteemed visitor and enquired the reason we were so honoured. 'To initiate all persons not having previously crossed the equator before', was the reply! I was busy with my camera. What a pity film was still in short supply but I captured the afternoon quite well in black and white.

The entourage took up their respective positions. Father Neptune, was hardly recognisable as the cockney Nobby Clark (engine room greaser), dressed in a resplendent wig and costume made from old rope, uncoiled into curly strands of 'hair'stitched together as only these long serving sailors can.

Lady Neptune, a tall, slim young fellow, was similarly dressed but with a silver tiara on her head. The pair of them sat on a flag-covered throne (a plank between two barrels) in front of the starboard deck cargo boiler.

Neptune's barber and assistants were on the platform, level with the top of the pool. The stool was now in position, waiting for the first customer.

My photograph shows the real ship's doctor as the first victim. He had dressed for the occasion in a pair of long johns, white shirt and an old cap borrowed from some big head, three sizes too big, pulled over his ears!

Neptune's doctor administered the medicine. I don't suppose it was anything other than alcoholic, they all seemed to like it!

He then climbed the short companionway and mounted the platform, sat on the stool facing the bridge and was lathered up with the four-inch flat shaving brush!

Two bare-chested sailors in shorts with pirate bandanas (ship's signal flags) on their heads waited in the pool to ensure no harm came when our victim was not-too-gently pushed into the tank to a roar from the spectators!

This Doctor was making his first trip with Salvesens to man the 'hospital' at South Georgia whaling station. He was well liked, a good mixer and a proper sport!

About ten other first-timers followed him. It ended with the pool full of men carrying on like kids! By nightfall, all was cleared away. Morale was high; the Captain had done a good job. What surprised me was I hadn't heard a whisper about it previous to the day!

I knew Father Neptune's retinue well enough from my stint in the engine room. Nobby Clark and I often had a chat. It was a well-kept secret! A committee must have taken some time to arrange and prepare the costumes, even if the trident and razor theatrical props had been in store from other trips. I still have the photographs I took that day when we were so very happy and thankfully sober!

Whilst aboard *Sondra*, I had to visit the factory hospital during a four-hour stay for bunkers. Before I left, this doctor asked me to go into the two-bed hospital ward and have a word with Sinclair, being a catcher man he didn't have many visitors. 'Cheer him up', he said.

Sinclair was a young Scots sailor on a catcher with one of the factory ships. He was down below, passing a new rope up through the deck. This rope was put on the winch to haul it on deck. Somehow a kink in the rope got round his ankle and he was hauled up to the deckhead, where the rope went through a hawser to the deck. The Chief stopped hauling when they saw blood and flesh coming through the hawser. Sinclair lost his leg below the knee.

He told me the first aid was a tourniquet to stop the bleeding, aided by putting the stump in a bag of flour. The analgesic was a bottle of rum to drink as required.

He was then transferred to a buoy boat (a converted corvette) and taken at full speed for a couple of days to get him to the island hospital.

He looked comfortable enough. 'What will ah de wi' only one leg?' was his complaint, Would his girl still want to marry him? I made some cheerful responses, to the effect that I thought he wouldn't let it get him down. After all, he was a catcher man!

My impression was confirmed when, years later, I had read a book some chap had written that he was now a cook on one of Salvesen's vessels. A regular Long John Silver!

Passing through the tropics, the Chief Engineer gave us a few jobs to do on deck on the winches, to repair broken teeth in the gear wheels. Dentistry on a large scale! There were no power tools. Holes were drilled with a hand-operated ratchet drill and stand, clamped to any place available with which to put pressure on the drill bit by means of a screw jack. A screw thread was made in the hole and a bolt tightened into the hole. The bolt was then cut and shaped with a hacksaw, a hammer and chisel to form the tooth. The Chief was quite creative in repair work.

We took our time on this benevolent work, in the spirit of the request that we occupy our time fruitfully while the weather was fine. As *Polar Chief* moved further south, it became colder and we were left to our own devices. Sailors are great raconteurs, and we spent happy hours yarning, and listening to funny stories.

A gunner had generously given me a bottle of whisky after I had cut his hair. Now we were cabined up with the colder weather. I decided to open it. I had chosen four mates to have a tot with me. The door was locked. It was an unusual brand of Scotch, Red Hackle, that no one had heard of. With mugs at the ready, I pulled the cork and poured the golden nectar. Within two minutes a knock at the door!

It was Neptune's barber, a Scottish radio operator. He said he could smell whisky a hundred yards away. I asked him in and he joined the company. I reckon one of my mates had put him in the picture, but he was a natural comedian and entertained us. He was very welcome. With his wonderful repartee we had a pleasant evening, listening to his tales of foreign parts and characters. This was the way we passed the time at sea.

The uneventful days went by: breakfast, smoko, lunch, dinner at six o'clock. I made friends with men I would not see again. I often wonder how many are still alive today.

Polar Chief, in spite of her age and trials, came alongside at Leith Harbour, South Georgia. No one seems to say goodbye on these occasions. In dribs and drabs we drifted away to our designated posts. I carried my gear along to *Sondra*, lying at the short bunker jetty and went aboard.

I was disappointed! There'd been some changes in the crew. The Chief Engineer, Anker Andersen was replaced. This Chief was a younger man, about forty, and very cynical, making snide remarks about the British during the war. I never got to know his name.

I was astonished at his attitude and didn't feel comfortable with him. What about the Norwegian Quislings, I thought. Not a good situation to have on a small ship. However, I gave him no cause for complaint and he recognised my signals. I decided later that he was not a happy man in himself, possibly a quisling. Well, his side lost! I ignored him as much as possible.

There was another disappointment! Malbut was here, still with his ulcer and toothless grin, except when his ulcer was playing him up, which was some part of every day! I had to admire his fortitude. He was doing right by his family, painful as it was.

Other changes: no Louie, the cook! Again a younger man was his replacement, tall and strong, very blond, and not very articulate but he had a breezy attitude – a typical Norwegian sailor!

He did all right as a cook but he was not as good a cook as Louie. Louie cooked beyond the call of duty when we'd had a good day. Louie would sit with a dixie full of boiling oil and make doughnuts by the tinful with batter and a stick, spinning it round and round until the ring was shaped, then pour another and another. They were put in the tins warm with sugar sprinkled over them. These doughnuts had a professional texture and lasted us for a week. A real treat under our frugal circumstances. What a loss!

Another treat was to take a tin of condensed milk and put it in the water boiler for a few minutes. When opened it was toffee!

I was pleased Christian Christiansen had returned as Captain, I felt safe with him in command. The Assistant Engineer and firemen, Ghandi and Johansen, were still with us, which was good. We worked as a team down below.

The Second Mate told me that during the overwinter a radar had been fitted on the bridge and asked if I would like to see it. We went up on to the bridge, the holy of holies to an engineer.

A cupboard had been built at the back of the bridge to contain the radar tube. It was tiny! A three-inch tube to represent thirty miles of the ocean.

Down below in the engine room, seven tons of ballast had been laid along the bilge keel in the form of 'pigs' of cast-iron. These were then set in concrete. I was told that for one ton of material topside seven tons were required on the keel. That sounded about right to me. The more the better!

The routine was just the same: the first weeks were short days and bad weather. On one trip, with the engine at half speed, the ship was pushing into great seas. Johansen and I were at our posts, me by the steam control throttle, Johansen sitting in the deck well, in front of the boilers, both of us hanging on as *Sondra* lurched forward at each wave, up and over! Then, thump, into the trough and up and over again. To our complete surprise, the telegraph gave an emergency double ring for 'full ahead!' We glanced at each other for a split second. Full ahead in this sea? It seemed contrary to my common sense.

My Home Guard training slammed in. Don't think! Obey the last order! I had been in a Colour Guard for the Middlesbrough Victory Parade. To prepare us for this honour, the Regimental Sergeant Major of The Green Howards came from the Regimental HQ one night for six weeks to drill us in Bright Street. He was tough!

Full ahead it was! I opened the throttle full, not knowing what to expect! *Sondra* leaped forward and upward to about forty degrees, at the same time she heeled over to port until I was standing on the side of the engine. Hanging on to the throttle wheel, I looked up at the skylight above the engine cylinders, I actually saw the sea!

We were on our beam end in a trough between two giant waves. The ship reared back to an even keel, when the telegraph rang again: half ahead! Thank God! I slowed the engine and we carried on for another hour pitching and rolling until we came into the lee of South Georgia, then we were into the fjord. The telegraph now rang for full speed as we raced down the three miles of smooth water to the bunker jetty.

This was the usual approach, showing off with a big bow wave to impress the shore gang! I got 'finished with engine' and went up for a mug of tea. Passing the ship's lifeboat on the upper deck, I noticed the lifeboat was hanging on the davits. The chocks the boat had been sitting in had been bent by the sea flat to the deck!

I later learned that some ships in these waters suffered much worse damage than this. I was surprised the men on the open bridge had not been flung into the sea.

When I got to the galley, there was no one about. It wasn't mentioned, but the reason for full speed could have been for more power to push up an extra big wave or to avoid a small house-sized berg concealed behind a wave. We stayed in for the night. Next day the weather had improved and it was business as usual.

Returning for bunkers and stores, the routine was we came down the fjord at full speed. Approaching the jetty, which stuck out about fifty feet from the 'beach' at the end of the fjord, the telegraph rang half speed.

As the bow came level with the jetty – full astern – the ship's propellor churned up the sea under the stern and the vessel pulled nicely in alongside. A sailor then stepped off and threw the mooring rope over the bollard. All very tiddly: the ship was one hundred and fifty feet long, on a fifty-foot jetty, It looked good!

In the engine room it was a different story! The small single-cylinder engine that pushed the main engine valve gear over to go astern was only used infrequently and was cold. Water in the steam pipe to this reversing engine had to be drained through a small tap and the little engine warmed up to be ready for use. I'd done it scores of times, with no bother.

This single-cylinder engine had a large handwheel that was used to start it, and usually a single pull would do it! I was on duty and had prepared everything for this usual manoeuvre. When the telegraph rang down for full astern, I couldn't move the hand wheel! Steam had condensed in the cylinder and it was full of water! The few seconds it took to start it proved too long, *Sondra* lurched up on to the beach of scree. I was horrified. We had run aground!

A three-inch voice pipe over my head broadcast faint voices aloft giving orders. The telegraph returned to 'stop engine'. My common sense told me not to go astern now in case the hull was damaged! At least we were not going to sink, stuck up on the beach.

After the longest ten minutes in my life, the telegraph rang slow astern. The valve gear was already now in the astern position.

I opened the throttle: the engine turned slowly but nothing happened. We were still stuck! Half astern! More steam! I could feel the propeller throbbing through the ship but after a few minutes of this, nothing! The beach held us fast.

'Full astern!' was the order, I opened her up! The engine at two hundred and fifty revs. The aft end of the ship throbbed harder and bounced. On the bridge, they were wagging the rudder. I felt the ship stirring, slipping back from the beach, then the engine room deck plates rose and fell slightly, and I knew we were afloat! What a relief!

Now I tried again to come alongside, slow ahead – gently, *Sondra* moved forward and was made fast fore and aft to bollards on the short jetty. I shut down the engine. Thank Heaven an inspection had found no damage. An Asdic dome had been fitted, used to locate submarines during the war (we tried now and then to seek whales with little success). Fortunately it was in the raised position in its housing.

I went topside, expecting to have to give an account of my part in the fiasco but not a word was said! Well, it wasn't the Royal Navy. It wasn't any other navy way of coming alongside from half ahead to full astern!

The next time we came in, the drill was the same. I had done it many times before without incident and it never happened again. Maybe they gave me a little more time: I was certainly on my toes!

I was sorry when the boiler fireman Ghandi had to leave the ship. It happened one night in very bad weather. *Sondra* was taking a pounding from a head-on sea. Spray was hitting the ventilators and dribbling down on the engine room deck. Johansen and I were on watch, hanging on to avoid being thrown about. Johansen kept looking at the engine room clock as it got near the time for his relief. At two o'clock in the morning, Ghandi should have been down to change watch with Johansen.

Ten minutes went by and we were worried. Ghandi had to come from the fore deck and in this sea a big wave could have knocked him down or even taken him over the side!

I told Johansen to go up and see what the problem was. He eagerly climbed the vertical steel ladder out of the engine room, I waited for the cheeky grin of Ghandi to appear. He didn't – neither of them came down!

I was on my own during the pounding the ship was taking, until nearing the end of my watch, when we had made it into the factory fjord for shelter. The Chief came down to operate the boiler controls and assist me with the manoeuvres to come alongside.

Now I heard why little Ghandi was unable to be on watch. He had been flung from his top bunk and was laid behind the door, unable to move in the narrow space between bunks and bulkhead with a broken hip. No one had heard him calling for help until Johansen had arrived and the crew had had to jemmy the door off to get at him. He was taken ashore to the hospital.

We sailed the next morning at daylight with another fireman, a young Norwegian lad. I didn't have the same rapport with this lad – he worked well but was very dour.

A few weeks later when we came in for the four-hour bunker stop, I was delighted to see Ghandi standing on the jetty with his leg in plaster up to his groin and on two crutches! He was expecting to return to Norway on the next ship to come in to the factory in a week or so. He had hobbled quite a way to the jetty to say cheerio.

My delight was tinged with sadness. It reminded me how transient life is, I wouldn't see his jolly face again. I never did get used to the idea of 'ships that pass in the night'.

Half-way through the season, another Christmas went by. I tuned my little Philips radio in to the short-wave BBC overseas service, but it was only good for the news, which seemed very remote. Neither Malbut nor I were interested in the football scores on a Saturday. At least we knew what day it was, but it didn't seem to matter.

I didn't think the work could get any harder until one day, chasing hard for hours with little to show for it, a sie whale had been caught, the minimum size allowed.

While we were stopped to prepare it for towing, I saw Johansen peering through the small inspection hole of the boiler furnace. He kept a good watch on the furnace whenever the burners were turned off, as now with the engine stopped. The furnace glowed red with residual heat, the only time it was possible to see the condition of the tubes. He called me over to have a look. At first glance I didn't know what I was looking for, then my eye adjusted to the faint thread-like jets of boiler water that emanated from about half a dozen tubes. The tubes were leaking! At two hundred and fifty PSI!

How could a pinhole, because that was about the size of it, be made in the wall of a boiler tube. There were a few of them so it was serious. I went aloft and told the Chief.

We got under way. The Chief saw the leaks. I realised how serious it was when he stayed as we flashed up the boiler again, and he remained the whole time, doing the worrying for all of us.

The level of water in the sight glasses was going down. We were losing boiler water quicker than we could put it in.

We used all of our fresh water in the tanks and also had the evaporator making fresh water from the sea. Three hours later, *Sondra* came along side the jetty. There was only an inch of water showing in the sight glasses when 'finished with engine' rang down.

The boiler fires were shut down. Three rows of tubes were going to be removed and new tubes fitted. Boilermakers from the maintenance team ashore came aboard and did the actual changing of the tubes. We removed the manholes from the boiler drums and crawled inside the drums to expand a few of the ends of the new tubes while the boilermakers had a break. The job took three days and nights.

It was a cold ship, as no shore steam was available as it would be in a home dockyard. Once the tubes were changed, the boilermakers left us to replace the manholes, fill the boiler and raise steam.

We slept during the waiting time between jobs. I just laid on the cabin floor in my muck, for three days, sleeping for a couple of hours here, a couple of hours there. Raising steam took about twelve hours. The temperature has to be applied slowly, making sure the boiler water is circulating nicely. Initially a burner would be lit for ten minutes or so then turned off for five, gradually warming it through until it was sure that the boiler water was circulating and the whole boiler had gently expanded. I was able to take a break for a couple of hours as it was obvious we would be ready to steam out on my watch.

Ready for sea! Midnight, my watch! After working on and off for three days, I was like a zombie. I hadn't had my clothes off during that time. I had an easy watch, moderate sea, steady going and at four in the morning, Malbut came down and relieved me. Johansen had kept an eye on me during the watch. Without the boiler the firemen had been free of duties for the three days. He was very helpful.

I went to my bunk and slept well until Jamie brought me a cup of tea about eleven o'clock. I just had nice time to freshen up, have a meal and go below for my noon watch.

The day arrived when the Captain would try out the radar set. We'd been at sea for a few days and finally caught a good sized fin. Towing it back to the factory, as we approached the island only the tops of the snow-covered peaks were visible.

Thick white fog surrounded the whole coast. I had seen this before, I went down for my watch, so it must have been around noon.

After half an hour or so, the telegraph rang to reduce speed to slow ahead. I guessed that the boss would make use of the radar. He wanted to drop this fin whale at the factory buoy and get out again to carry on the hunt. There hadn't been much sight of the elusive whales for the past few days.

I visualised the scene on the bridge, the Captain peering into the cupboard at the three-inch screen, the dot in the middle being the ship, the sweep hand going round, leaving a fluorescent image of the mouth of Leith Harbour's entrance. Knowing him, he would have a sailor on the gun platform peering into the fog. I reduced the speed until the engine was turning very slowly, so gently that at the first impact, should it happen, I could stop. We didn't make an impact but I heard and felt the grating sound and bumps as we rubbed along the small outcrop of rock that guarded the middle of the entrance.

In a few minutes, the telegraph rang for half, then full ahead. The fjord was clear of fog and we stopped to drop the fin at the buoy.

I was pleased when the boss decided to go on to the bunker jetty and top up our fuel and 'lie in' for the night. In the morning, a breeze arose and the fog dispersed. It was business as usual. To my knowledge the radar was not used again. I think it was probably an ex-RAF job. There's more room to manoeuvre up in the air!

To illustrate the need to see ahead in fog, this story explains how a sailor can use his senses to do just that.

After the evening meal one night at about eight o'clock, the Captain had given the Chief a bottle of gin for the officers and a bottle for the crew forrard. The Chief and three of us off watch were drinking the gin with a jug of hot sugar water: a hot toddy, very nice! It eased the aching stomach muscles. *Sondra* was steaming back to the factory with a couple of whales we had caught. It had been a tough day. I would be turning in for a couple of hours sleep before my midnight to four o'clock in the morning watch. The sea was calm.

Suddenly, *Sondra* heeled hard over. Alarm! The ship continued to turn hard a'port. The Chief led the way aloft, up the first steep companionway (stairs, for those unfamiliar with nautical terms), then up the second companionway on to the upper deck. Thick fog obscured anything more than a few yards from the ship. Now, as we stood silent, we heard the splashing of the sea against the side of a towering, ghostly-white iceberg, only just visible. *Sondra* now was running alongside the iceberg. Soon the helmsman turned, less urgently after passing alongside of the towering iceberg to regain our course for home.

The sailor on the open bridge at the helm had sensed a drop in temperature of the fog that came from the giant berg, another sense to confirm the berg's presence was the sound of the sea breaking against the side of the icy walls. High up on the bridge the sound of the engine could not be heard. The sailor was alert to any change in his surroundings.

A modern radar would have 'seen' a berg but these men trusted their instinctive senses. If I remember right, the Japanese bomber planes were seen on radar that fateful Sunday morning at Pearl Harbour. They were discounted because they shouldn't have been there. Fortunately, we had finished our ration of gin. I went below to my bunk and slept peacefully until called for my midnight watch.

It was not always easy to sleep. The first and only time I had been privileged to see the Atlantic rollers, I had woken to the unusual motion of the ship. The peculiar labouring of the engine was followed by an increase of revolutions as *Sondra* almost freewheeled down by the bow.

I realised that *Sondra* must be climbing up some giant waves and sliding down the other side as it caused me to slide in my bunk also, first to the top of the bunk, then to the bottom. At the same time there was a rumbling noise coming from the lower deck above my cabin. Something had come adrift!

I didn't have long to think about it before the Mate opened the cabin door and told me to get up and give him a hand to secure a forty-gallon oil drum that was loose on aft deck.

This had been roped to the handrail around the stern. The unique motion of the ship had freed it and it was now a loose cannon, rolling up and down the deck.

I quickly dressed and pulled on my sea boots. The Mate led the way on to the upper deck to weigh up the situation.

The view amazed me! *Sondra* was steaming up giant waves that reached the top of the little ship's mast. She lowered her bow and slid down the other side before approaching the next climb.

In the few seconds before we climbed down the steel ladder (welded to the side of the deck housing) to secure the rolling oil drum, I was able to see clearly from the crest of a wave that each wave was unbroken from one horizon to the other and they were in uniform rows as far as the eye could see ahead.

The sky was jet black but where was the light coming from? It could only have been from the thousands of bright stars undimmed by the sharp clear air and assisted by the swirling phosphorous glow that emanated from the crest of each giant wave

We had to judge when to move on to the rolling drum and make a temporary lashing until the moving deck assisted us in getting the thing where we could make a proper job of it. I don't know who had roped it up in the first place, but my mum could have done a better job.

I went back to my bunk and wedged myself in to reduce the sliding effect and slept better knowing that it was a friendly sea for us. I had heard, as a boy, sailors talk about the Atlantic rollers These were feared by the big-ship men. The constant stress on the hull at bow and stern then on the crest of the big wave amidships was thought to break a ship's back. I was happy in a small ship, not too small!

Christian Christiansen, the Captain, was a proper gentleman. He was very precise in his work. I was only on the bridge once and saw how he checked with binoculars that the whale was of the permitted size, and not a protected species such as the right whale (which had been named by the sailing ship whalers, for obvious reasons: not too big to handle)

One day I went on watch at noon. The Gunner had fired the harpoon and missed twice in the previous eight-to-twelve watch. This was very unusual, as he was always careful to get near enough to make a quick kill. Ideally this would be less than sixty yards. A wounded whale meant danger and delay, meanwhile the school of whales would get too far away from us to catch up with them again.

By the time I had got settled in to my watch, the double ring on the telegraph meant we were in contact with the whales. I opened the throttle fully unil we were near enough to stalk the whale selected. The whale only comes to the surface for a few seconds to blow. The Gunner has a telegraph by the gun to signal what speed he needs to be near enough to make a kill. This operation is no more cruel than a modern abattoir. Half speed for a few minutes then full, maybe slow, this manoeuvre went on for a few more minutes, then, Bang! I rapidly stopped the engine dead! A voice from the bridge came down the copper voice pipe in Norwegian 'arr boom', which was the way of saying 'a miss'. Precious minutes wasted hauling the harpoon and line back in, then we were off at full speed ahead again.

I opened the steam valve to the engine fully, I was always concerned for the big end bearings as they were knocking a bit – we were treating them rough! Again, the harpoon was fired, again came the voice, 'arr boom!'

This was unusual. Although the whale is a big creature, the target area is fairly small. A miss goes over or under the head. The Gunner would be upset.

The Gunner's high-pitched voice came down the overhead pipe from the bridge. "Mr Dinsdale!" This was a rare event: the Gunner speaking to the engineer.

'Aye! Captain', I replied, curious as to this personal conversation.

The thin voice came again: 'Try to manoeuvre a bit quicker please, you're too f***ing slow!"

He was upset! I was upset! As well as adjusting the speed of the ship, he had to signal from the gun platform to the bridge which direction to steer to be in the correct position when the whale surfaced for the few seconds it took to blow. I was shocked and replied as before but in a contrite voice. It was all my fault?

More manoeuvres took place until finally, Bang! This resulted in the call I was glad to hear, 'arr fast fisk', which isn't difficult to interpret into English. In no more that ten minutes the whale was alongside. The ship's red flag with our number three on it, mounted on a fifteen-foot bamboo pole with a battery lamp attached was stuck in the carcase. The whale floated away to be picked up later in the day while we were off after another one.

I obeyed his request and gave the engine a bit more stick but I don't think that would improve his aim any! It was probably a difficult sea for his floating gun platform.

By the end of my watch we had a second whale. This was an average good day. Honour was restored – *Sondra* would remain top boat. After handing over the watch I went on deck to go forrard to the galley for a mug of tea, I told one of the sailors the Gunner had given me a bollocking. He said that's okay, he's bollocked everyone on deck too!

A few times we went ten days and never saw a whale. A depression took over the whole crew. *Sondra* cruised along all the daylight hours, wasting costly fuel.

I considered the lack of bonuses along with the risk factor in deciding to work another season. I decided it wasn't worth it. I am not a gambling man. I enjoyed the shipboard life. Each day was different, different sea, different sky. We sailed on day after day. The Government quota for the island catchers was six months and it could become a bad habit.

The alternative was the shipyard – not a good prospect. I had heard of work for engineers at a new chemical factory being built on the road to Redcar – Wilton Works, as it came to be known. The reports were mixed.

ICI at nearby Billingham was a terrible place, smelly and dirty, I would go back to Smith's Dock for the present.

As the season passed, I began to look forward to returning home again. Eventually, as the weather worsened, shorter days of heavy weather, sleet, snow and hail I knew that the end was in sight. I didn't volunteer to overwinter. It meant eighteen months away from home in appauling conditions. I had more to live for. However, I admired the men who did it, marvelled would be a better word, to live and work in the worst conditions imaginable.

Sondra came in on the last day of the season. It was probably early in April. I took little time to pack my gear. The little Philips radio I left with a guy who was staying to work over winter. I don't remember the 'trade'; we had no money to speak of. I was in a benevolent mood. His need was great and I didn't want the bother of getting it home. It may not have survived the journey.

As at the end of the 1947 season, I humped my gear along the shore to the *Saluta*, like the *Polar Chief* a very old lady who would hopefully take us back to Liverpool.

Nothing eventful occurred this trip. *Saluta* had been a cargo-cum-passenger ship over fifty years old and managed a stately six knots with a following sea. Passing through the tropics we spent many hours on deck. A couple of evenings two of our crew entertained us with a guitar and accordion. One song was 'Maggie May', about a girl from Liverpool who evidently was very friendly: 'they have taken you away' but I can't remember why! Then there was something about Lime Street, which ran down to the Mersey Ferry, but it was a nostalgic ballad and a bit naughty.

Coming up the middle of the Atlantic we only saw one other ship. This ship was passing across our bow about a quarter of a mile ahead of us. Even though it was dark it was visible in different shades of grey where its deck lights failed to illuminate. Merchant navy courtesies were exchanged in Morse code by aldis lamp. 'SS *Saluta* bound for Liverpool'. And the appropriate signal was returned.

Thirty days or so after leaving South Georgia we came into the Mersey and into Gladstone Dock. The customs men were gentle with us, a selective search: 'You, you and you!' I was going home to my wife this time. Dorothy was staying with Mum at No. 68 Granville Road, waiting for me.

I paid off with a cheque for about eight hundred pounds, we now had the means to buy a house.

An unexpected voyage

Afer many months at sea, it takes time to adjust to living in the 'real' world. Being on a vessel only one hundred and fifty feet long with a crew of sixteen for seven months in Antarctic waters is exceptionally unreal. A floating monastery, it's time of monotonous excitement that increases the unknown expectations of life. Not a question of what will the day bring, but one of, what may the hour bring, or even the minute!

You need to be always relaxed but ready for whatever comes. Fog, say, or a white-out from a snowstorm. Another situation I encountered being a great blow from the ice cap a couple of hundred miles south. This at times created waves as high as the top of the funnel. The sea did reach the two engine-room ventilators abaft of the funnel. One was immediately above my position at the engine controls and I got the occasional ducking.

It was difficult to estimate the height of a wave, as they look higher when the vessel is heeled over in a trough. Weather like that is very tiring. It would be a bit frightening but I became too weary to care.

The men on these vessels were never sea sick, sick of the sea perhaps but the effects of rough weather was to make the muscles of the body ache. The Captain would generally issue a bottle of spirits fore and aft to share among sailors and equal numbers of engineer and deck officers, it soothed the aches and pains.

In any tricky situation, I told myself, nothing lasts forever. The lads on deck might find shelter on the lee side of a big friendly iceberg. Some of these creatures were miles long and two hundred feet high, but like policemen there was never one about when you needed them.

If we were near the lee side of the island of South Georgia, the skipper sometimes decided to put in for a few hours. We would probably top up the fuel and water tanks and get a few hours of rest.

I felt sorry for the lads on deck on an open bridge. They probably roped themselves in to avoid being thrown about.

There were many other days when the sky was blue with little white clouds and a moderate sea. Then it was good to stand on deck in the cold dry air with *Sondra* hunting at a cruising speed of a steady twelve knots. Top speed was sixteen knots, about twenty miles per hour.

We often passed one or two small bergs as big as a football pitch, slowly and lonely drifting their way north to oblivion.

CHAPTER EIGHT – *An unexpected voyage*

I'm not sure why they only seemed to drift north. Icebergs from the Arctic North drift south. Why not east or west? There must be a reason. Centrifugal force, perhaps, as the earth spins round they climb to the equator there to melt and disappear as the sea becomes warmer.

Now back at home, life was very quiet. Dorothy and I decided to take a holiday: two weeks in London. The big city helped me to adjust. There was a lot to see, and the walking pleasantly exhausted me! I wasn't used to walking.

It's impossible to walk far on a whale catcher vessel and generally one got used to going forward as the deck heaved to suit the way you wanted to go. As the ship rose up in the sea your body weight increased immensely making movement difficult, so this governed when you stepped forward.

Up forrard as *Sondra's* bow dropped twenty feet or more the body became weightless and liable to fall over, it took practice to remain upright for a slight moment until it was possible to take a step forward.

Now back home I was out of practice with walking and talking, and there wasn't much free time at sea for a social life.

Life on the whale catcher was like being in a rolling, heaving monastery. There was nothing much to talk about with the other sailor monks and little time for chat, we had nothing much in common.

Silent prayers were probably offered up when the vast hostile sea threatened to engulf us, although if one was on duty there wasn't time to think negatively as it would likely never happen!

Faith in the vessel we sailed in, its simple engine and boiler and each other, got us through the worst days when storm soup was the *plat de jour*. The cook, unable to cook a regular meal, roped a two-foot oval dixie on to the top of the galley stove, half-full of water. He boiled salt beef, onions, probably dried fruit of which we had a big sack full, and anything one could imagine to make this soup. The crew, timing their entrance with the roll of the ship, opened the watertight door, stepped over the sill into the galley with the odd bucket of sea water from Father Neptune to join the six inches of sea water already swilling about the galley.

It was often a relief to swear in exasperation when *Sondra* like a contrary female was in a mischievous mood. It was good for the soul, I appreciated it when the days were smooth and all was well.

Deciding not to return to whaling was not an easy decision to make. I would miss the thrill of bashing through the sea, although there was no thrill in killing the whale, on the contrary; it was done professionally by the Gunner.

The cheque at the end of the season, when set against the hours at sea and worked, was only a respectable remuneration, especially when you consider there was no holiday pay.

The risk factor was probably not much higher than working in some heavy industry. I had heard stories of explosions at the new polythene plant at ICI Wilton. Men only went whaling who needed to save some money and had no better way of doing so.

The thought of being obliged to overwinter on South Georgia probably pushed me to quit. There would be no bonus working over winter and the conditions and people who would be with you were unknown.

Developments around Teesside were creating opportunities at home that I could have missed, being out of circulation, work on the ICI Wilton plant, a greenfield chemical site near Redcar, had started in 1947 while I was at sea.

The chemical works at Haverton Hill, Billingham established in 1926 on the north side of the river, was a terrible smelly place. I passed it when I was going to Hartlepool. It was not an attractive place to work.

I knew little of the chemical industry and had been happy working in the shipyard. I had no one to ask about the latest in job opportunities but I suspected the shipyards were due for a slump.

Because of the war, I had lost touch with my contemporaries at work in the shipyard. I was a bit of a contented loner and satisfied to settle down to married life.

Even at Hartlepool I had lost touch with the friends from my childhood days. They were called up to join the army. When he returned after five years of war, my childhood friend Alan Martin went to university. I went to sea, out of touch, eight thousand miles away in South Georgia.

During the war I had made some new friends in Hartlepool. I also had a more solid connection with Dorothy who was well known in the small, close-knit village atmosphere. I had made enough money with the whaling bonus to put a deposit on a house in Middlesbrough. We looked at houses at various places around Teesside at a price we could afford.

We found a small end-terrace house in a quiet street behind Albert Park. This house cost one thousand and six hundred pounds. A deposit was paid and a mortgage was arranged with some difficulty owing to repayments being twenty-five per cent of my ten pound wage. The basic pay as a third engineer had been seven pounds weekly.

Overtime was not considered by the mortgage assessment. My wage was a bit on the lean side on the repayment issue. This was overcome with more cash deposit.

Wives generally didn't work at this time. When we married, Dorothy had to give up her job at the Hartlepool Co-op Bakery. There was no such thing as hire purchase. We furnished the essentials with what cash we had and a few items our family gave us.

Dorothy now was busy creating a home for us; she bought a second-hand solid oak dining table and four chairs for twenty-five pounds. She would go to see her mother each week at Hartlepool.

After living in our own house for eighteen months Dorothy's mother had fallen and broken her leg, the hospital had put it in plaster up to her thigh. We brought her to our house in Newstead Road and put a bed downstairs for her. When she had recovered she returned home but wasn't happy and asked if she could come and live with us, the decision rested with me.

Now I had a problem. If I said no, Dorothy's mother was unhappy, so Dorothy was unhappy, which would make me unhappy. The answer seemed to be to have her come and live with us.

Dorothy was happy, her mother was happy, so I could be happy.

I was working six days a week It turned out very well. I had two women to look after me. We had sixteen happy years together.

If you want to be happy, make someone else happy! I find that philosophy works most of the time.

I went back to Smith's Dock, the same job as before, fitting engines in ships' hulls. It was always difficult to see a ship sail away and myself not to be on it. The sea can be an attractive lazy life if you are content to live it. Your meals are provided, a steward makes your bed, you don't have far to travel to work, you have set routines in the engine room, and sea views all round.

There were some very difficult times like breakdowns. All hands in the engine room! Break watches and work round the clock until the job was finished. But you forget those times! We only remember the good times, I was afraid sea going could become a habit.

I had been away from Smith's Dock for two years, in which the orders for whale catchers had eased off. A few specialist ships of ten thousand tons were built, like the SS *Lovland*, a cargo steamer built for A/S Sunde, Farsund, Norway.

Another was the SS *Arakaka*, a cargo and passenger steamer built for a Liverpool Company. This was before the days of the long-distance passenger planes.

A third was the motor vessel the MV *Borealis*, a fruit and passenger carrier, an investment by Fred Olsen of Oslo. Now in 1949 there were a few orders for small oil tankers, and still one or two catchers.

Smith's had built a couple of small oil tankers fitted with their own design of steam engines, but being only about two thousand horsepower, two engines were fitted with twin screws.

Greek entrepreneurs had foreseen the expanding market for oil. The era of the horse, which had served man for a thousand years and more was nearly over. We still had coal delivered for a year or two with a horse and cart but the milkman and his horse disappeared after the war with the advent of the electric float, which rattled along the streets in the early hours. They returned to base in the early afternoon crawling along with their batteries needing recharging. The motor car was now affordable, not only for the doctor but his patients too!

The day of the marine steam reciprocating engine was also over. To raise steam with fuel then use the steam to move the engine was only twenty-five to thirty per cent efficient. The fuel was only the residue from the crude oil after the higher octanes, such as petrol, were extracted.

A whale catcher like *Sondra* was very wasteful with fuel, especially when towing whales back to the factory. At night, the flames from the boiler were visible above the top of the funnel. This poor economy was tolerated because of other advantages. For example, it was a quiet engine, furthermore, simplicity and reliability were very important considerations. Diesel engines were reliable up to a point but noisy.

The whale catchers built after the war had twin boilers of a more efficient type made by Foster Wheeler & Co. The design of the diesel engine had improved during the war, where the fuel was injected directly into the cylinder, which was more economical. I had experienced a ship with a multi-cylinder four-stroke diesel engine and the noise of the over-head valve gear in the engine room was hurtful to the ears.

Smith's Dock got an order for an oil tanker with a Doxford diesel engine. The engine had to be bought in from a Sunderland firm Hawthorn Leslie & Co.

After the launch of the biggest vessel yet built by Smith's, a twenty-eight thousand-tonner named *Atlantic Duke*, the Doxford engine to be installed had to be delivered in pieces. The all-steel fabricated bedplate was enormous after the cast-iron steam engine bedplates.

I worked with the squad that erected this engine in the ship's hull. When erected, it stood as high as a house and as long as a pair of semi-detached houses.

There were no valves to clatter noisily in this engine. It was a two-stroke. The pistons themselves acted as valves to exhaust the waste gases into the exhaust chamber surrounding the cylinders.

What was unusual about this engine was that each cylinder had two opposed pistons. The bottom piston was connected to the crankshaft in the usual way, with a connecting rod. The opposed piston rod sticking out of the top of the engine had a bar across it, with two rods fastened at each end, passing down through the exhaust box which surrounded the cylinders into the crankcase, where they were connected to crankpins opposed to the crank of the bottom piston.

It sounds a bit complicated but if there is any advantage in such an arrangement, it is because the power stroke is driving two pistons with one ignition. In the conventional arrangement, the fuel gases pushed against one piston and the cylinder head. This meant the five-cylinder Doxford engine had fifteen connecting rods. That's a lot of moving parts in an engine where the crankshaft weighed many tons!

The seven hundred degree exhaust gases from the engine, when running at sea, passed through a bulkhead to deliver the waste heat from the engine to furnaces of one of three forty-ton fire tube boilers maintaining steam for the ship's auxiliaries, steam electric generators and other machines. When steam was required in port it was necessary to light oil burners in the boiler furnaces to drive the auxiliaries. If the ship had to discharge the cargo of oil itself when there was no facilities ashore to do it, steam would be needed for the ten thousand horsepower cargo pumps.

The electric generator was essential to steam and, when manoeuvring the main engine, steam drove the air compressors for the two giant compressed air bottles each about five feet in diameter and twenty feet high that stood upright in the engine room.

Coming into port, stopping and starting the engine, this compressed air was admitted to the engine before the fuel was put in, to turn the engine over and thus start the combustion in the cylinders.

Coming in or out of port, engine manoeuvres required two or three engineers on watch: one engineer at the controls; another to switch over the air bottles and recharge the empty one; and a junior engineer to log all the telegraph signals from the bridge. No moving parts were visible at the control platform on the lower deck of the engine room. The engine was as quiet as a mouse, so it was necessary to look at the revolution indicator to make sure it had started. The only moving parts visible were high up at the top of the engine. The upper piston connecting rods moved up and down through the engine casing driving the sixty-ton crankshaft round. The engine speed at full ahead was one hundred and thirty revolutions per minute, driving the ship along at seventeen knots (about twenty miles per hour).

Two of the three boilers were maintained on standby. If the cargo was crude oil and very thick when cold, it was necessary to fire up a boiler to supply steam to coils in the oil cargo tanks. The cargo was heated before coming to port to warm and thin the oil to enable the pumps to discharge it ashore.

Two massive ten thousand horsepower reciprocating steam pumps capable of pumping the cargo ashore within fourteen hours occupied a pumping chamber amidships the width of the ship. When the ship was empty, the bows stuck up almost out of the water due to the weight of the engine and aft superstructure. To trim the ship, sea water was pumped to the cargo tanks to ballast and level the vessel.

Experiments were made at sea by the Chief Officer to trim the ship slightly nose down one day and another day up, to see if it improved the propeller efficiency and speed. I never heard of the result.

On Friday morning, the twenty-eight-thousand-ton *Atlantic Duke* was lying at the fitting-out jetty, newly painted with a fancy modern-shaped funnel. The shipyard platers had found this difficult to fabricate. Funnels for whalers generally were round and no problem.

She was already fuelled up to leave immediately after the sea trials off the coast off Blyth. The ship would then proceed to New York on the Sunday.

At about eleven o'clock this Friday morning, when I was looking forward to having Saturday off, the shipyard manager called me over. 'Will you go and have lunch with the Superintendent of *Atlantic Duke*? Mr Somethingopolous,' (I'm afraid I cannot remember his real name), 'would like to have a word with you,' he said.

My natural curiosity and a free lunch persuaded me to go.

Mr Somethingopolous, in a strong Greek accent and demanding voice, told me he was not satisfied with the Greek engineer's knowledge of the ship. He told me they wanted me to sail with *Atlantic Duke* and would give me an American rate of pay. He had caught me at a weak moment, talking about money! Without asking my dear Dorothy, I said yes!

My dutiful wife took the news without question. Well, I couldn't tell her a lot. How long was I going to be away? I didn't know. Where were we going to? America! That's a big place! It stretches from Nova Scotia to the bottom of South America.

It was fortunate that Dorothy's mother was living with us, as I couldn't have accepted the job otherwise. I would be away for ten months.

I wrote and sent dollars home and I had made an allotted sum to be sent to her regularly from the Atlantic oil transport comapny Livanos Co.

It was to be hard work as it was a new ship with all the teething troubles usually associated with new devices. Because of losses of ships and men during the war and the increase in trade there was a shortage of marine engineers.

A young Englishman from Hartlepool, Peter Richards, had been signed on as an assistant engineer.

He was put on my twelve-to-four watch, Peter was aged about twenty-one or two, quiet and well behaved but I thought not very interested in the engine room. He didn't ask any questions! Not a dedicated company man.

After a few of our regular trips with oil from Venezuela up the Delaware River to Marcus Hook, fifteen miles from Philadelphia, he went to the Captain and paid off the ship! In America! I was astounded when I heard the news. In retrospect he may have had relatives in the States to give him some support.

He was ready with immigration papers to become a citizen of the USA. He'd never mentioned a word of his intentions to me, but he'd had his passport and worked his passage very well! It was unusual for people to have a passport in 1950 so it had been premeditated. Clever man!

Many years later, I learnt from a friend of Hartlepool that Peter had joined the American air force and had achieved the rank of colonel. Later in the seventies, when air travel made it possible, he had visited Hartlepool to see his family.

The young Greek 'engineers' had obviously had little experience of marine engines, some of them probably only with fishing boats. They were intelligent young men though, who only needed showing the routines once.

On-the-job training is the best way of learning routine work. Experience requires many years and cannot be taught. Murphy's Law requires a lot of study as what can go wrong will go wrong at the most inappropriate moment. A good engineer anticipates Murphy by regular maintenance.

For six weeks, the Greek Chief Engineer, Michael Loupis and I worked six hours on watch and six hours off until these lads could handle a four-hour watch. This was routine stuff, checking temperatures and flows of cooling water, and so on.

The following pages you may find a bit technical but they includes a few funny stories of things that can go wrong with a new ship and crew, so ignore the technical bits and get the overall picture.

The first of the teething troubles we experienced was a loss of main engine lubricating oil. Held in a five-hundred-gallon tank mounted at the top of the spacious engine room, this 'lube' oil was gravity-fed to the engine crankshaft and bearings and pumped back up to the tank. A clever design, as the height of the lube oil tank would give a pressure of a few pounds per square inch, enough to lubricate every part of the engine.

A sight glass down the side of the tank indicated the level of oil and during the first few days on the maiden voyage the level was slowly going down, indicating a loss of oil.

I phoned the Chief and informed him, He thought this could be caused by oil lying in cavities in the bedplate of the new engine not draining down to the sump where the pump returned the oil to the tank. It was okay not to worry, just top the tank up, he said.

A couple of hundred gallons of oil restored the level but, in a day or so, the loss continued. A junior engineer was detailed to search under the engine room deck plates for a suspected leak. The return pipe was checked, and no leaks were found. I had never had this problem with a steam engine: with the primitive steam engine, oil dripped into the bearings via small copper tubes from oil boxes with a battery of tiny pumps operated by a thin steel rod connected to the engine. When the engine moved, the pumps pumped. The little oil used after lubricating the engine escaped from the bearings and ran into the bilges, and was eventually pumped away with the bilge water. At high speed, some of the oil was thrown out into the engine room, not a lot, but the engineer got his share.

Everything was visible in the open steam engine. I enjoyed seeing the steel rods flashing in the yellow light given off by the oily lamp bulbs as they went up and down, speeding round to the hiss and puff of the steam whispers escaping from the piston rod glands.

In the cathedral-like engine room of *Atlantic Duke* the Michael Loupis, came down and looked into the six-inch diameter glass windows in the manhole covers of the enclosed engine. The glass on the inside was oil-covered and the lamps inside the engine revealed nothing.

It was almost possible to see Loupis's brain working with his facial expressions, and after a minute or two his eyebrows shot up! One hand was raised with a finger pointing skywards, his mouth opened in a toothy grin. He'd got it!

'We must ask the Captain for permission to stop,' he said. He went up to the bridge and returned a few minutes later. 'Okay, stop the engine'. This would have to be logged and the reason for the stop recorded.

I went to the control module and took hold of the big steel handle with its ratchet lever that lifted the 'dog', which engaged in the teeth of the fuel control quadrant, bringing the lever to zero. The engine, going one hundred and twenty revolutions per minute, shown by the pointer on the indicator came to rest.

A junior engineer removed the engine casing's centre manhole cover. It was made of cast aluminium, and was not heavy, about three feet in diameter. There, in the sump of the engine bedplate was five hundred gallons of our missing engine oil.

The pump filter, a metal top-hat shape with holes in it, was here below this pool of oil. The junior went inside the engine and fished around for the filter. A shout of glee, or surprise, or wonder arose.

It was all Greek to me, literally! The young Greek junior pulled out on to the engine room deck plates an oil-soaked dark brown floppy object. My thoughts were: what the hell! How did that get in there? It looked like a dead dog!

This brown short-haired bundle lay on the steel deck plates, as the oil drained away what appeared to be a dog's leg gradually took the shape of a jacket sleeve. It was an old brown jacket!

Now I could place it! – The Doxford diesel engine was built at Sunderland and sent in pieces to Smith's Dock. It probably weighed one hundred and fifty tons give or take a few. While we were erecting the engine in the ship's hull, a job that lasted a few weeks, Smiths employed a canny old chap to go round with a long-handled paint brush and a gallon tin of oil. With the long-handled brush he brushed oil on all the shiny steel parts of the engine to prevent them rusting while they were exposed to the weather.

I was too amused to be embarrassed, and was thankful it was nothing worse. It had not stopped the flow of oil to the pump thank goodness. The oil was recovered and the engine started up again.

I had noticed the old chap at times take his coat off on a warm day and hang it on one of the connecting rods of the engine. He must have wondered where his jacket had got to!

In any case, the engine had not been carefully inspected before it was closed up for the sea trial. Livanos Co. were impatient to get the ship into service. These things happen, sometimes with serious results. We were lucky this time.

The engine ran on diesel oil, which is almost like paraffin. Equipment had been installed in the engine room to run this Doxford engine on boiler oil, the lowest grade of oil from the refinery. At the time, boiler oil cost three pounds a ton. Diesel oil cost eight pounds a ton.

In the engine room, high up in the forrard bulkhead, five tanks, each of which could hold twenty-five tons of fuel, were built. One was filled to supply the engine with twenty tons of diesel fuel, the daily requirement at sea. Another would be filled with the next day's supply to settle and allow any ingress of water or grit to be removed with separators.

Before the black treacle-thick boiler oil could be used to fuel the engine it had to be heated to thin it and put through these separators. These machines, Laval oil separators, running at fifteen thousand revolutions a minute, had a spindle with conical discs spinning round in a chamber. This flung any water, sand and grit out to drain while the thinner oil separated to a pump to be returned to the clean tank.

When the main engine propelling the ship was switched from diesel to this hot boiler oil the engine continued to run but the speed dropped from one hundred and twenty revolutions to no more than one hundred.

After a few hours running at this speed, reducing the ship's speed pro rata, the Captain ordered us to revert back to diesel fuel in order to maintain the ship's schedule.

No doubt Livanos's head office, based in Wall Street, New York, were monitoring the experiment. It was disappointing.

When we arrived at our port of deliver,y the Sun Oil Co., fifteen miles from Philadelphia at Marcus Hook up the Delaware River, it was my job to take bunkers (fuel) on board for our next trip.

I was in the engine room, checking the fuel situation, when the Chief telephoned from his cabin on the bridge and told me to take bunkers of two hundred tons of diesel fuel and six hundred tons of boiler oil. It was normally the other way round! We used more diesel than boiler oil.

I realized he was going to run the engine all the way on the rough fuel! I reminded him of the result of our experiment. 'Don't worry,' he said kindly, 'I have made an account'.

We departed from Marcus Hook in ballast with diesel oil fuel to the engine supplied from number one tank. The pilot left the ship at the mouth of the Delaware River, there were no more movements on the telegraph for engine manoeuvres and 'full ahead' was signalled, steady going.

Chief Engineer Loupis came down to the engine room and told me of his 'account'. 'We will make a mixture,' he said. His account was to put seven tons of diesel to fourteen tons of boiler oil, enough for a daily run and run the engine on that.

There was no means of stirring the mixture in the tank but I put the boiler oil first to be thinned by heating it, then to the separator to clean it. Now the seven tons of diesel were pumped into the now thinner boiler oil. We had twenty-one tons of fuel for a daily run.

This mixture was then switched to the engine. The engine revolutions remained steady at one hundred and thirty revs per minute. We went up on deck and looked at the exhaust from the funnel. It was clean, there was complete combustion. It was a success!

This saved Livanos Co. eight pounds per ton (diesel) minus three pounds per ton (boiler oil) which made five pounds times twenty tones per day while at sea. This saved one hundred pounds sterling per day, seven hundred pounds per week – Michael Loupis was promoted to Superintendent Engineer of the company. His remit was to go round Livanos's fleet of tankers and repeat this saving,

Before he left for this promotion, I decided I had had enough. I had hoped we might do a trip over to Europe where I could make an easy journey home but the possibility was remote.

One of my routines every Sunday morning was to change over our auxiliary machinery. *Atlantic Duke* had two of everything, and three steam-driven electric generators, in fact! Only one was required for power, with one on standby and the other to work on, if it needed any work doing.

A fifth emergency diesel generator was mounted in the aft steering flat, level with the main deck. Things would be desperate if this was required! No steam or a flooded engine room, that kind of thing.

I started it up and ran it for a few minutes each week. This was to charge up the twelve-volt batteries that turned over the diesel engine and make sure it was ready for use if needed.

My cabin door being opposite the engine room door, when an alarm went off I would go down to be sure the engineer on watch could cope. Gradually I was able to leave them to it. However, things occurred from time to time that were not in the book.

At about eight o'clock one night, number one electric generator, running to supply electricity to the ship this night, failed. The light in my cabin grew very bright then went low until only the filament glowed red.

I lay in my bunk waiting for the engineer on watch to start up the number two generator. Minutes passed. In dismay, I heard the sound of spanners and a hammer. They were going to repair it!

It was obvious a spring had broken in the governor that regulated the steam engine's five hundred revs per minute speed.

The ship was travelling at seventeen knots, at night without navigation lights or instruments.

I heard a hammer and spanner being used on the generator cover nuts.

I swung out of my bunk, grabbed my torch and went down to find three of them round the machine. They were going to change the broken spring.

'Leave it,' I said, *'avrio'* ('tomorrow' in Greek) and proceeded to start up the number two machine. The cylinders on this engine were cold, I opened the steam valve slightly, the steam was saturated, water knocked in the cylinders.

I opened the steam valve a bit more, gave the generator engine a few minutes to warm up at low revs then as the rev counter rose to near four hundred revs. I went to the main electric switchboard breaker (a big two-pole switch) on the number-two panel, pushed it in and light was restored. Soon the generator was up to full speed. I returned to my cabin and rested until my watch at midnight.

Another of these extraneous duties was when I heard muffled voices from the engine room and thought I'd better have a look. I stepped across the passage to the engine room door and looked down. The place was full of steam. As I went below, I could hear live steam hissing from somewhere but it was impossible to see anything.

On the engine room deck below, Nico the Greek, second engineer, was shouting into the ear of the Greek third engineer (the noise of the steam made normal conversation impossible), another junior engineer was standing there, looking lost.

I put my head close to Nico who spoke enough English and said: 'We must shut the main steam valve off then find the problem later'. He thought that was a good idea and disappeared into the steam.

I went up on deck to the emergency valve wheels. These were on long spindles to isolate the steam from the top of the boiler just below the ship's upper deck.

As I approached, I saw the valve wheel turn. The bold Nico was on the boiler tops, closing the steam valve.

CHAPTER EIGHT – *An unexpected voyage*

With the main steam off, the problem was soon resolved, the auxiliaries generators and so on, were on another steam main and not affected.

The Chief Officer was using main steam at two hundred PSI in one of the big ten thousand-horsepower cargo pumps to move ballast and clean tanks. After the steam passed through the pump, it was returning to the condenser at one hundred and sixty pounds per square inch, This would need more cooling sea water than that for the light running of the generator and other services.

It was good engine room practice to reduce the cooling seawater to the condenser so that the condensed water returning to the boiler was warm. Now with the reduced cooling water, the steam remained at a pressure high enough to blow the water out of the condenser and the water holding tank that was open to atmosphere where it was pumped back to the boiler.

The Chief Officer should have informed the engine room of his intentions to use the amount of steam involved and the engineer on watch, if he knew his job, should have increased the speed of the seawater circulating pump, cooling the condenser to cope with the extra volume of steam. This is why I had been asked to sail with the ship, but I couldn't be on duty twenty-four hours a day.

Even an experienced crew needs time to settle down on a new ship but with these Greeks it was difficult beyond the call of duty.

Unknown to us, this 'malfunction' had damaged the brass condenser tubes that carried the sea cooling water. While we lay at the unloading jetty and the cargo was being discharged, the pump man drew my attention to the level of boiler water.

The boiler water sight glasses were near full and excess boiler water was overflowing the condensed water tank, where it should have been pumped back to the boiler.

I tested it for salt, thinking the condenser might have been leaking the cooling seawater. It was fresh! Where was all the water coming from? I rang the Chief and he suggested I test the river water. I was surprised to find it was fresh water. *Atlantic Duke*, an eighteen-thousand-ton vessel was one hundred miles up river from the sea. America has some mighty rivers and I was not aware of the possibilities.

The condenser was leaking and it had to be repaired before we went back to sea. Salt does serious damage to a high-pressure boiler. All hands turned to and we spent twenty hours down the engine room making repairs to three condenser tubes, split with the excessive hot steam. These jobs were becoming beyond the call of duty. It was bad enough on an old ship, this new ship was a hard ship!

After ten months working two watches, seven days a week my health was suffering, but I was treated well and given a gratuity each month. On pay day, at sea when I went up to the Captain's office I was paid in dollars. This would help Britain's economic crisis, it certainly helped mine!

The food was excellent. The Captain was a gourmet! Wherever we called on the American coast he stuffed the freezers with the speciality of the region. We had salmon from Canada and big green melons from the Deep South and beef from Texas.

I particularly enjoyed the *meljanis*, which is a Greek recipe: aubergines cut in half, stuffed with onion and mince and baked in the oven, delicious! But I was worn out. I took a watch in the engine room four hours on and eight off – if I was lucky!

The Chief Engineer expected me to give him a hand with problems of the freezer chambers where the ship's food was stored. The young Greek engineers on day work could have done this and improved their knowledge. Perhaps the Chief was grooming me for a Chief's job! I found out later the the boss of Livanos had designs that way for me.

Chief Loupis asked me to assist him to take indicator cards and tune the engine. This was done by fitting an instrument to the engine cylinders one at a time. A chart clipped to a drum on the instrument indicated the pressure against the stroke as the engine was running. This was a check on the horsepower of the cylinder. Fuel was then adjusted to each cylinder to balance the engine. It was a hot but not uninteresting operation.

When having a break from this job, the Chief noticed the sun was not on our port side. 'Aaaah! The sun! It's over there! It should be over this side!' he exclaimed. 'Come!' As he ran along the gangway to the bridge I dutifully followed. Now what? I thought.

The officer on watch was busy on deck, and two sailors on watch were repainting the deck with roller brushes on poles and trays of paint. This was 1951 it was the first time I had seen a roller paintbrush.

The helm (steering the ship) was on automatic pilot from the bridge amidships. This controlled a two-cylinder steam engine in the stern steering flat (room), which moved the rudder when the hydraulic oil pressure, through two small gauge copper pipes, was varied from the bridge by the automatic control gear. This was set at the compass bearing to keep the ship on the required course.

A two-gallon copper tank under the binnacle (the steering wheel mounting, which also contained a compass) held a reservoir of hydraulic oil. The Chief lifted out the dipstick. The tank was empty. *Atlantic Duke* had been going round in big circles all morning!

We called the officer of the watch: it was the Chief Officer again! He filled the tank and reset the ship on course. For a chief officer, he obviously had no idea of delegating the simple task of checking the oil level to the men on watch.

Come to think of it, it should have been checked by the shipyard's men before the ship put to sea.

Being on the maiden voyage and only a few days out, there had to be a reason for the oil to disappear and we found the leak and repaired our loss. A daily check on the tank level would have revealed the problem before the tank became empty.

Old man Georgio Livanos would have been hysterical if he'd known his new ship had been going round in big circles for hours! The figures for the daily distance travelled, calculated for each day were adjusted for the next days until the error disappeared, 'fiddled' is the word I was looking for!

I was learning a lot of things you don't learn in higher education.

Being one Englishman among a crew of Greeks, some of whom spoke little English and others who spoke better English than me, I learnt the Greek alphabet and soon picked up some important words on an oil tanker. Like – 'fire!'

This word I learnt one night when the engine room phone rang and the Third Officer shouted from the bridge: '*Fotya!*' '*Fotya!*' I asked one of my engine room workers to interpret for me.

He said 'Fire!' was the interpretation!

I asked him: 'Where is the fire?'

'From the top of the funnel', he replied. I was relieved to hear that!

The boiler room on the mezzanine floor aft of the engine room bulkhead occupied the width of the ship. I climbed the steel ladder to the boiler room door and inspected the furnaces through the peep holes, one of the three forty-ton boilers was working, heated from the engine exhaust.

The other two boilers were banked up, they had been working oil-fired, when steam was required to steam out cargo tanks.

I found what I was looking for: a furnace with a low wall of clinker (ash-like residue left over after the boiler oil had been burnt, the result of bad combustion). This was glowing red hot, bits were flaking off and obviously going up the chimney to frighten the deck officer on watch!

I took one of the fire irons a twelve- foot-long steel bar with an end like a garden hoe and broke up the clinker and raked it from the furnace. The Sudanese fireman watched me and I asked him to be sure to tell the other guys not to let the clinker get like that again. We had about a dozen of these Sudanese firemen. It could have been any one of them who had neglected to keep the furnace clean.

I often found them on watch in the boiler room with a prayer mat saying prayers to Mecca. We needed all the prayers we could get, I didn't mind as long as the furnaces were clean of clinker and there were no sparks from the funnel.

This was a ship loaded with highly volatile crude oil that gassed off in the open air. When taking the crude oil on board, canvas chutes are put in the tanks and fastened high above the superstructure to allow the gases from the oil to escape as the tanks are filled. Some gas escaping from the open hatches contacting the paintwork of the ship caused the paint to melt and strip off from the ship's side. Which the Yanks called a 'hot' ship!

One trip to the Delaware River after unloading we went round to Chesapeake Bay up to Baltimore. Here Loupis told me we were going into dry dock. I thought I would have some rest from being on watch.

Loupis and I prepared the engine room for docking, which required the exhaust steam from the electricity generator and other auxiliaries normally condensed, to be vented to atmosphere, there would be no cooling seawater for the condenser.

I could have fallen out with him when he insisted that a certain steam valve had to be shut. I told him no but he insisted. I let him get on with it. As the valve closed, the lights in the engine room darkened as the steam generator slowed down with exhaust steam unable to escape. He swiftly opened the valve again. 'Humph!' Was all he said but he never challenged me after that.

It wasn't a dry dock, in fact, but a floating dock. The ship moored up over the big sunken pontoon and this was then pumped out to float and lift the eighteen-thousand-ton ship out of the water.

The ship's hull was going to be painted. I thought this would take all night, at least from my experience with Smith's Dock. First men on ladders scraped the hull clean of barnacles, then they painted the hull with brushes on long bamboo poles. Even with a number of men it took many hours.

I had only been in my bunk for one hour when the Chief called me.

'Come on, they are floating the ship', he said. Imagine my dismay!

I crawled reluctantly from my bunk and went on deck to see how our allies during the war had painted a ship's bottom in little more than an hour. We didn't need scraping, probably because of the new anti-fouling paints that were introduced about this time.

A gantry with nozzles and hoses had moved along the ship on rails and sprayed red lead paint over the hull. Round the stern where it was not able to reach, men with hoses completed the spraying.

This would not be as good a job as the old way. Old loose paint was scraped off and brushes were used to rub the paint well into the often rough surface.

There was a lot of unemployment in Greece for the Greek lads at this time. One young sailor chap told me he was sending his money home to keep his whole family, mum, dad, brothers and a sister's dowry.

Some of these young men were five years at sea, the ship never going near Greece. They probably dare not ask for leave in case they didn't get their job back. The ship owners were multi-millionaires!

CHAPTER EIGHT – *An unexpected voyage*

We need entrepreneurs, but I wondered if they were aware of the conditions these lads worked under. The underling managers who set the rates needed to be more generous, but it was not my problem. I had had enough. Although the food was very good, I had lost weight. In fact, I was skinny. An opportunity arose for me to get off this ship.

This part of my life, with some of the crazy things that went wrong, would take a long time to tell.

After we had loaded crude at one port, a British pilot, as he was leaving the ship, told me we were overloaded and the Captain would not discharge cargo to the permitted plimsoll level.

The pilot said the danger was the cargo (crude oil) pressing on the deck could split the welded seams and advised me to leave whenever possible. I had once witnessed myself when the ship was being loaded, crude oil coming over the tank tops on deck, the smell of the gas was intoxicating and dangerous if there'd been a static spark.

I didn't think there was great danger with the overloading. Our chaps had built the ship but the British were not sailing her. When we got to sea it was apparent we were low in the water and the ship's speed was reduced with a heavy sea running, as waves broke over the long deck. I decided I had had enough.

We had a regular run to the Sun Oil Co. at the lovely small town of Marcus Hook, fifteen miles from Philadelphia. A doctor made a visit to the ship. I went to him and showed him my tongue, which was a bit black. He diagnosed stomach trouble and reported that I needed a check up ashore.

This was where I left *Atlantic Duke*. I went ashore with the Livanos Company's Scottish Superintendent. We stood on the jetty for a while as *Atlantic Duke* moved away from the jetty. A telephone rang at a box near us. The Super picked it up, it was Georgio Livanos asking what was *Atlantic Duke* doing. The Super said: 'She is just going astern'.

Georgio said: 'Why is she going astern, she should be going forwards.'

The Super laughed as he told me as we got into his car. I marvelled as he drove me over elevated roads, flyovers, common now in England. We arrived in New York and he put me in a hotel on 47th Street off Times Square for ten days.

I went to the Livanos offices. They made an appointment for a medical examination with a doctor in his consulting room that overlooked Central Park. He said I was okay, probably a bit run down.

I decided to seek a passage home and went to the Cunard shipping offices to price a passage to the UK, it would cost sixty pounds; I could just afford it if necessary.

I visited Livanos's office in Wall street and had a chat with the big man himself,

Georgio Livanos. He asked me to stay with the company. 'You will become Chief Engineer', he said. I thanked him and said I would like to go home.

I was sick of working with nice but dangerous people. I didn't tell Georgio that! A passage home was arranged on a Livanos USA-built Liberty ship, leaving in a day or so from Newport News, Virginia.

Livanos Company was good to me. They wanted me to fly to Newport News to join this vessel going to Europe. I said I had heavy luggage, I'd never flown before and preferred passage on a Greyhound bus from the impressive New York Central Station.

The bus wheels were nearly five feet high, the engine mounted underneath. It was a twelve-hour journey, with limited stops, doing ninety miles an hour on the turnpikes so I was told.

It was dark by the time we called at Washington DC for a comfort stop and exchange of passengers. Now on the open road, we passed mile after mile of flat fields, some brown soil others with what looked like corn maize. I was surprised how flat the whole country was all the way. This was where the American civil war had been fought and over a hundred thousand men killed.

We arrived at Newport News, Virginia, on a cold grey morning near some miserable docks. It was just breaking daylight, too early to look for the ship. I sat in the comfortable bus station waiting room until about nine o'clock, until the place gradually woke up. A black lady came and sat beside me, I thought no more about it.

Twice on this journey I had made a spectacle of myself by sitting in the part of the waiting area reserved for black people. The back of the bus was also taboo. I always preferred the back at home. This was 1951 in America. Gradually it dawned on me I was in the black section of the seating area again! I stayed where I was as a matter of principle but I got some funny looks from the black folks!

I found the ship ready to sail. I don't remember the ship's name. They had been expecting me and had waited a while.

The Chief Steward showed me to a comfortable cabin and I ate with the Captain and his family. He had a wife and little girl about four years old with him. She was puzzled at first because I spoke in English with my limited Greek, then she got the idea and enjoyed trying to teach me a few Greek words.

We sailed from Newport News on this Livanos ex-American Liberty ship carrying, a cargo of iron ore. This is a dreadful cargo, which can shift and give trouble in a heavy sea. When the hold was opened up by the Chief Officer for an inspection, I had a look down; the heavy iron ore appeared to be a small heap in the bottom of the hold.

In a bit of a swell, as the ship rose to the top of the wave, the bow and stern sagged and vice versa.

CHAPTER EIGHT – *An unexpected voyage*

I don't like big ships, even this one, which was only about ten thousand tons! It was an uneventful trip wallowing across the Atlantic at ten knots with the wind in the right direction.

After many days – it seemed months, we entered the Kiel canal at night.

German customs officials came on board. I heard their voices as they passed along the accommodation corridor. They were in jovial mood and one said, sotto voce '*Heil Hitler*', to muted laughter.

It was very early morning, still dark. I dressed and went to the galley and had a pot of tea and a rough breakfast. The Captain saw me and said he had arranged for me to leave the ship with the shipping agent. An agent would arrive at about nine o'clock to see me off.

I went to see what was going on in the saloon. Four or five German officials were already there, they had arranged their interrogation interviews in the ship's saloon.

They checked everything! The ship's cook, poor chap, was going through his manifest (list) of goods with a very formal customs official in green uniform: long green overcoat with black edges to the collar, shiny black belt, peaked cap with gold braid, jackboots and fancy badges.

The interview was conducted in English but the cook spoke very little English, with the bit of Greek that I had, I was able to assist as interpreter in this assessment of the cook's stores. How many bags of sugar, raisins, potatoes, flour, and so on. What a load of useless information! Why did they need to know?

The German thought I was Greek! He congratulated me on my command of English. 'Thank you, I said. 'I am English!'

This caused a bit of a flutter among the German officials sat round the ship's saloon. They looked at one another and returned to their duties in what seemed a more respectful manner. I imagine they were wondering what an Englander was doing coming from America on a Greek tramp steamer and leaving the ship in Germany. A spy, comes to mind! In the Yorkshire vernacular, I said nowt!

I left the ship, my pockets stuffed with Camel cigarettes and Havana cigars bought in New York.

I was told by the Captain that even seven years after the war no one was allowed ashore with foreign currency. I put a twenty-dollar bill and a few smaller notes in my sock.

I had been messed about by Germans a lot in my short life and they were not going to give me any more trouble.

Foreign currency and cigarettes were *verboten* (forbidden) in Germany, even seven years after the war, because of black market problems.

It probably wasn't necessary so long after the war but Germans love having regulations. All contraband had to be handed to the customs officials to be locked away until the ship departed. I had bought Dorothy some nylon stockings, and they were not going to be locked away. I was departing before the ship. The Germans had not thought of that possibility!

A shipping agent arrived, a tall, good-looking, blond-haired young German fellow in his early twenties, wearing a brown trilby hat and a long grey herringbone overcoat.

He spoke better English than I did. He saw me to the railway station at Kiel. He bought my rail ticket, I was very surprised to see it said from Kiel to Middlesbrough with instructions to change at Nieumunster. This seems strange but I do not remember buying any other ticket on the journey. Finally he gave me a ten-deutschmark note from Livanos Co. to see me home on the route.

I still felt uneasy being in 'enemy' territory. I personally hadn't signed any agreement of their surrender. It occurred to me that if we had capitulated in 1940, he might have been in England giving me a hard time. His honest face with pale blue eyes softened my angst. He could have kept the ten deutschmarks for himself and I wouldn't have known. The '*Heil Hitler*' in the passage was probably a big joke to the Germans now! It had been a joke to us English always, especially since Charlie Chaplin's film *The Great Dictator*.

I decided to be magnanimous and took a beautiful Havana cigar, plentiful and cheap in the USA at this time, from my inside pocket and gave it to him; his surprised face and pause changed to a beaming smile which gave me so much pleasure. I thought for a second he might have had me arrested for disobeying the customs orders. It may have helped him to come to terms with our past history a bit.

The enemy syndrome that bothered me was purged. Even now the stupid war still leaves a sense of sorrow, what misery a few men caused to millions of people. Why?

After the short local train journey from Kiel to Nieumunster during which a burly passenger realised I was English and proceeded to tell me of the 'bombbing', as he pronounced it, of Hamburg: the British and Americans had totally flattened the port. With arm movements to illustrate the bombs falling he interspersed his story with German sounds of explosions: Booomb! Booomb! Booomb! 'Yes.' I replied, 'We had the same: my house was damaged). They started it, did he expect me to apologise?

I hadn't long to wait for the North Express train to come steaming into the station. I looked for a porter, a heavily-built porter in a dark grey shirt, black trousers and a soft black cap with a shiny black peak came forward to carry my three cases to a carriage of the North Express, which was coming from Sweden to go to the Hook of Holland. He put a leather strap through the handles of the heavy cases and, humping them on to his shoulder, walked to the opposite platform and stowed the cases into my carriage.

I had only the ten-deutschmark note to give him for a tip. I gave it to him, not expecting any change; I would be out of German territory and wouldn't need it. I had twenty dollars in my sock. He very honestly gave me nine marks and some coins back. Not all of the Germans were nasty! I returned the loose coins to him and said '*dankeschoen*', one of the few words I knew at that time.

I wondered what life would have been like without the war. The depression may have continued – there's a thought! Money can always be found for wars – it certainly makes the money go round!

It was a corridor train, warm and comfortable. I settled down for the long journey across Germany. I had nothing to read. It was now dark and I looked out at the lights of this country we had struggled against for five long, wasted years and brooded on where we were going now.

I got into conversation with an English gentleman in my carriage. He spoke with a cultured, intelligent voice and said he was with the British diplomatic service. He asked me where I had been,

I told him of my trip with Livanos Company and my wish now to get home.

He suggested we go along to the dining car for dinner. He didn't say he would pay, but then I wasn't a distressed British seaman. I surreptitiously took the twenty-dollar bill from my sock. I decided to have a succulent steak: meat was still rationed in the UK and I had had nothing since my rough breakfast early that morning before leaving the ship with ship's cook still asleep. I sensed an air of servility from the waiter in the dining car. I probably used the last of the German marks. I would have given him a tip as there would be some German marks change, I was tired and didn't care.

The diplomat asked me what I proposed to do now I was returning home. We discussed the options open to me and he recommended if I had no commitments to the contrary to emigrate to British Columbia in Canada. He said the climate was very good. It was north of California and there were excellent opportunities for young engineers.

It was something I would have done if I had been single and free. The problem was I had commitments, a wife and mother-in-law and my own mother living on her own. I was all she had and she would one day need me. I have no regrets.

The train stopped late in the evening as we came to the German border. Police in uniforms reminiscent of the 1939 war thrillers came down the corridor, stopping at each carriage to check passports and papers. I produced my temporary passport.

My merchant navy identity card was at Liverpool. I had sailed without it. The first few trips into the USA I couldn't go ashore! The ship didn't go anywhere else. Eventually the Livanos agent took me from Marcus Hook fifteen miles to the British consulate in Philadelphia to have a passport photograph taken and get a passport paper.

After my return from whaling in the Port of Liverpool, my merchant navy identity card was confiscated to be returned to the Liverpool passport office – not a lot of use to me at Liverpool if I needed it.

Government officials like to do this to keep themselves in a job. The passport was taken from a seaman when he paid off the ship. It would have to be applied for before he could sign on to another ship. One half of the people work and the other half think up ways to make it difficult for them to do their work. It's called 'government'.

There was only time in Philadelphia to have my photograph taken and attached with my fingerprints to a yellow sheet of official British consul paper. Thus attached, with my full name, place and date of birth and any identity features, probably my big brown eyes, I could be identified.

It would have been nice to have had a look round Philadelphia but I was taken straight back to the ship. Tanker ships were only in port a few hours to discharge the cargo of oil. Sometimes there was a delay for a day or so for maintenance.

The train waited at the German border, the German police inspecting our papers with serious faces and finally alighted, probably disappointed at being unable to discover some paper irregularity. Then the train moved slowly on a few hundred yards through no man's land and stopped again. This was Holland but I hadn't a clue where I was. Dutch police in light brown uniforms this time, more serious faces looking at the same papers.

This was late 1952, the early years of the Cold War everyone was looking for Russian spies! England had quite a few upper-class misguided fools who despised their own country for the ideology of a very dubious regime. They should have concentrated on putting their political ideas to improve their own country but they were treacherous idiots and would not be capable of it.

Finally the train pulled into the port of the Hook of Holland. There I boarded the ferry to cross the channel and home. I had felt strange in Germany, which had been enemy territory a few years before.

We crossed the English Channel in a cold but dry and fairly calm night to Harwich. I stood on the aft deck thinking, this would probably be the last time I would be at sea. The lights of England blinked up ahead, then we were at Dover. I was pleased there was no great problem with customs men.

I was tired, having travelled from Kiel to Neiumunster, somewhere near Hamburg, across Germany and Holland.

CHAPTER EIGHT – *An unexpected voyage*

The train north was there to take me to Darlington. I walked along the platform with a porter to the train for Middlesbrough. I promised myself this would be my last trip to sea. I would seriously consider the new ICI Wilton chemical factory near Redcar. It would be a change from ships and engines. I would put up with the smells!

CHAPTER NINE

Life after sailing

I returned to our little house in Newstead Road. It was December and I was reluctant to find a job immediately. I thought I would sign on as unemployed, as indeed I was! There was no holiday pay.

I had paid national insurance all my working life. Time I got some back. I went into Middlesbrough Unemployment Exchange, as it was called then, and sat next to a big Jamaican chap. We waited patiently, then he was called to the person behind the little window and after some confidential conversation he came back and sat next to me.

'They asked me if I can dig', he said with a Jamaican accent. 'I can't dig, can you dig?' '

'No, I can't dig!' I said.

I would learn to dig if I was desperate I thought. It was then my turn to speak to the face at the window and put my case, a British seaman home from the sea, unemployed. No employment benefit for a British sailor. I wasn't even asked if I could dig or anything, just told to get another ship and get to sea again! The official attitude to the British seaman seemed to be 'out of sight, out of mind'!

I was at home a few weeks, then in January 1953, applied for a job in ICI Wilton. I started on the 3rd January 1953. New starters had to attend the Medical Centre and have a fairly good medical, no hernias or anything like that. A urine sample was taken and I was accepted, given a locker, a boiler suit and a pair of boots. It wasn't what I'd been used to in the family-like shipyard, very much like the Home Guard. It took a lot of getting used to; mainly because of the type of people, there was a lack of community. Workers had been drafted from ICI works from all over the country and houses provided for them. It seemed to me they were given priority in promotion.

Thirty years later, I thankfully retired, on 28th January 1983.

There is a Chinese saying, to people they wish to curse: 'May you live in interesting times' I don't know any Chinese people. It was very interesting but I was only a number. I accepted the humiliation of being told how to do a job by supervisors with much less experience than me. It amused me when their instructions went pear-shaped. I was offered and took courses in electronics and other courses that ICI provided.

First aid training was available and I thought it was something that would be useful. It was very good training. Doctors from St John's Ambulance Service who set examinations for certificate awards.

A team of 'injured' actors wore make-up to show various injuries and, from our investigations, we diagnosed their injuries and gave treatment to satisfy the doctors of our proficiency.

When the real thing happened, there was not always time for the official treatment. One day, a leak of sodium gas blew the roof off a section of the phthalic plant. Two or three men were burnt about the face, not seriously, but they suffered shock mainly. I treat them as 'walking wounded', with blankets to keep them warm until the works' ambulance arrived.

The nursing sister arrived with the ambulance and wanted the men as stretcher cases with the blankets just so!

Fires were blazing around the plant and there was danger of further explosions so I told the ambulance man it was not necessary to stretcher the men, as they were walking wounded, but to remove the casualties quickly and be ready to return for more.

When the firemen arrived, there was a problem of using water to put out the fires because sealed drums of sodium blocks in oil might have been open. Sodium, a grey putty-like substance produces hydrogen gas when wet and explodes readily.

It was a good company overall. One or two of its lower managers who came from all kinds of university backgrounds resented a man who knew the answers to some of the engineering problems. Others wanted your expertise to a problem but also wanted the credit due for it.

This attitude damaged the company they worked for, as they promoted less able men who would not expose their own weaknesses and suppressed men who were more experienced. I became tolerant towards the system as the pay was good and the demand for the product seemed certain.

Dorothy and I decided to move to a bigger house. We looked at a new house being built in the village of Marton, six miles south of Middlesbrough.

The number of the house was 66. The price was one thousand and nine hundred pounds. We had to put a deposit on it and then sell No. 34, Newstead Road.

I had no problem finding a buyer for Newstead but I made the mistake of accepting the buyer's advice to use his solicitor, he said it would save time and money (for him it did!).

His solicitor's search found that a 'Max Lock' town planning scheme involved the Longlands Road being extended to a crosstown route. Our house, No. 34, was to be demolished. The buyer wanted us to drop our price. I took advice from another solicitor, Lauriston, who put the words in my mouth.

'You're not going to drop, it are you?'

'No', I said, but property was going up at the time and with solicitors fees we made nothing on the sale. I was content to take the loss and move to a better location and house.

Marton was the village where the great navigator and seaman Captain James Cook was born.

We attend the village church where he was baptized. He only lived there for a few childhood years then moved six miles to Great Ayton. He later worked at Whitby before his exploration days.

When we first came to look at No. 66 Gypsy lane, the walls were only up to the first floor. Gypsy Lane had already had houses built before the war. The original lane was narrow with six-foot-high hedges on both sides.

Fields opposite the house ran half a mile, all the way to Marton Village. The back of the house had fields that went a mile or more to Nunthorpe village. Here houses were being built by another builder.

There was no street lighting, a butchers shop, Bruntons, was in the village next to the Rudd's Arms pub.

Dorothy had said: 'I don't want to be buried in the country'.

'Don't worry', I said, 'the town will come out to meet us!' I never imagined we would be inundated as we have been.

The builder didn't want to put in any extras, such as power sockets (only one to a room). We had to go to town to choose the fireplaces. There was no such thing as central heating. Things were still rationed to a certain extent, as this was October 1954 and materials were in short supply and there was a lot of building going on.

Marton is not a village now, just a suburban sprawl. It has some compensations, however – schools shops and street lighting, which were lacking in the early years, when a travelling shop and a butcher came round in their vans.

On New Year's Day 1955, the North Yorkshire Hunt came down Gypsy Lane. It was a colourful sight, the huntsmen in their red coats on fine horses, the dogs milling around. The horn sounded and they were off over the fields and away.

There was much to do in a new house. The walls were painted with emulsion and the floors were bare boards. In October, we moved in. Our Indian carpet from Newstead Road went into the front room and I stained the floor boards around it. The kitchen, with its concrete floor, had only a sink and draining board, gas-heated hand-washer with wringer, and a gas oven. An old chest of drawers cut down made a work top. The breakfast room where we ate was heated with a paraffin oil heater. This produced a lot of condensation and the walls ran with moisture.

The first alarm came after heavy rain caused flood water to collect in the lane. I was at home and kept looking at the situation hoping, it would not become any worse. The water also came down the back fields and eventually reached the drive of the house.

Dorothy had had a blue Wilton carpet fitted in the hall and up the stairs. It was very expensive and had been hand-sewn around the edges to fit the area. They didn't fasten carpet down in those days.

I prepared for the worst and removed the carpet and was thinking what I could I do to save the furniture.

Luckily, the flood water ran across the road and did not get any higher. The builder, Peacock, put in a bigger drain and this episode was not repeated. We are a hundred feet above sea level and the river, I had not expected floods at this level.

Eventually Marton village was slowly absorbed into suburbia. For many years we had houses being built around us. The road was very often coated with mud from lorries passing our front door. Dorothy's beautiful dark blue carpet had to be protected with newspapers. She took it all in her stride.

Expansive plans made by town planning architects were not carried out. Two adjacent district councils disagreed about the roads leading south from Middlesbrough. From 1955, traffic increased steadily until as a result, at peak times, we have the 'Marton crawl' – vehicles moving for part of the way at two miles an hour. The area is grossly over-populated and it can only get worse.

One of my axioms is, nothing lasts for ever. The little girl presenting the bouquet to the lady opening the bazaar I fell in love with when I was five years old died on 25th June 2007.

We had been happily married for fifty-nine years. We had three years to say goodbye. Dorothy was always serene, she never complained. A few weeks before she died, after many weeks in Teesside Hospice and three weeks in a local nursing home, I noticed a change in her condition. I pulled a chair up to the bed and we sat holding hands. She comforted me! When I sat back, she said: 'Arthur, will you get married again?'

'What', I joked. 'After all the trouble I've had with you, I couldn't go through this again!' We both laughed. The idea was preposterous. She died peacefully in her sleep at six o'clock on Monday morning.

On the Saturday, I had realised she needed one-to-one care and, when my son John arrived, I told him I would stay all night. He said he would go home and return at nine o'clock to sit with me. Dorothy was heavily sedated, resting quietly when he returned. She opened her eyes and seeing us both there, said: 'I'm not going tonight, you know.'

Sure enough, next morning she was still there. The carer came in to ask what she wanted for breakfast, and she asked for a cup of tea. She had a couple of sips, that's all. The carer made sandwiches for John and me. At half past twelve I realised we were in for another night's vigil. I phoned Bette, Dorothy's friend since they went into the grammar school at eleven years old. I asked Bette to get a taxi and come to stay with Dorothy for a few hours while John and I went home to freshen up. Bette had visited Dorothy every day for the last two weeks. Dorothy's room was a haven of care and love.

The funeral was in the little church where Captain Cook was baptized in 1728.

Her body, brought home for the last couple of days, was in pink taffeta. She lay in the front room, where we had often entertained so many family and friends. It was good she would leave for her last journey from the home she had cared for so well. The church was full and later we joined friends at the local hotel for lunch. The funeral took place on my eighty-third birthday. At home we had a surprise family party. My daughter-in-law, Gill, kindly produced a fancy birthday cake, suitably iced, for me to cut. Dorothy would have approved. She loved entertaining! Coming from a broken home and not having had a family, I had enjoyed Dorothy's loving family.

Now two years later, I try to keep the house as Dorothy would have liked it. She wasn't bossy at all but she would gently wish something was done and I would put it at the top of my list.

I have to close this autobiography sometime soon. I would like to close it with a bit of advice for young people who fall in love. For a happy marriage, keep it simple: just be kind to each other!

For those too busy for love with work or business, never lose your temper! Keep control of your emotions – you can then find a way to regain equilibrium. If not, wait a while, an opportunity may arise. I discovered this when I had to deal with stupid people who were my seniors, who resented being told how a job needed to be done. If it makes your job easier, let them think they thought of it!

Before closing, I would like to thank Cliff Thornton, President of the Captain Cook Society, a cousin of Dorothy. He has encouraged me with e.mails to research whaling, resulting in my giving illustrated talks to eleven men's forums and clubs in the area.

I was able to explain why whaling was necessary after the war when Britain was bankrupt. Europe was devasted and hundreds of tons of protein was needed. Sterling was unacceptable abroad. We built the whaling fleets in the starling area, here on the River Tees.

It was no more cruel than a modern abbatoir, it was a professional kill. It was counter-productive and dangerus to injure the eighty-ton whale. The gunner stalked the whale sometimes for thirty minutes until a kill was certain. A whale can rise out of the sea like a salmon, and if one had landed on our small ship, it would have meant a swim in sub-zero seawater.

CHAPTER NINE – *Life after sailing*

There is another reason some countries still cull a few whales. The whale eats fish. Yes, even the baleen whale who eats krill, small shrimp-like creatures. Fish spawn on the continental shelves, among the seaweed. When the young fish hatch and grow bigger, they move in shoals to feed on the plankton. A couple of baleen whales can vacuum up a few tons of young fish in a few minutes. There is competition in the food chain. With over-population, the human demand for food has increased. Does man want whales or fish? A bit of both, I think.